How I Met Your Mother
and Philosophy

Popular Culture and Philosophy® Series Editor: George A. Reisch

For full details of all Popular Culture and Philosophy® books, visit www.opencourtbooks.com.

Popular Culture and Philosophy®

How I Met Your Mother and Philosophy

Being and Awesomeness

Edited by

LORENZO VON MATTERHORN

OPEN COURT
Chicago

Volume 81 in the series, Popular Culture and Philosophy ®, edited by George A. Reisch

To order books from Open Court, call toll-free 1-800-815-2280, or visit our website at www.opencourtbooks.com.

Open Court Publishing Company is a division of Carus Publishing Company, dba ePals Media.

Printed and bound in the United States of America.

ISBN: 978-0-8126-9835-0

Library of Congress Control Number: 2013948987

Contents

I

Challenge Accepted

1
Why on Earth Do We Love Barney?

Bence Nanay

Kids, Barney Stinson is the devil. At least, that's what Ted says in "Belly Full of Turkey" (Season One). And in "Brunch" (Season Two), he's genuinely surprised that Barney is allowed to enter a church. But even if he's not the devil, he is a truly awful person. Truly.

But then why do we all love him so much? More precisely, why is it so tempting to identify or empathize or emotionally engage with him?

Just how awful is Barney? Unspeakably awful. A few biographical details:

- **He sold a woman** ("The Bracket").

- **He poisoned the drinking water in Lisbon** ("The Goat").

- **He has shady dealings with the most oppressive regime on Earth** ("Chain of Screaming").

But maybe it's just his line of work. We know that Tony Soprano's job isn't exactly charity-work, but we have no problem identifying and emotionally engaging with him. Yet, he is in many ways a choirboy compared to Barney Stinson. Barney can be as awful with his best friends as in his dealings at Goliath National Bank. Again, a few examples:

- **When facing the dilemma of landing a much needed job for his 'best friend' (who had just been** left at the altar) or having an office in a dinosaur-shaped building, he chooses the latter ("Woo Girls").

- He takes revenge, many years later, on the girl who once broke his heart, by sleeping with her and then never calling her back ("Game Night").

- Gives a fake apology to Robin, whom he just broke up with, merely in order to score another girl ("Playbook").

- Sells Marshall for $80,000 of credit at the casino ("The Bro Mitzvah").

- Spends years planning his revenge on Marshall for noticing that he has a bit of marinara sauce on his tie ("The Exploding Meatball Sub").

- Sets his best friend's coat on fire ("The Pineapple Incident").

- Pulls a nasty and tactless prank on Robin when he pretends to be Robin's dad on the phone, whose call he knows she is eagerly awaiting ("Disaster Averted").

- Actively puts Robin down when she meets Ted's parents for the first time ("Brunch").

- Makes his best friend Ted believe that Mary, the paralegal, is in fact a prostitute, so that he can enjoy how Ted is making a fool of himself ("Mary the Paralegal").

- Stages a one-man show that has one purpose only: to annoy Lily ("Stuff").

- Makes a fool of all his friends, who, unknowingly, help him score with a girl ("Playbook").

And we have not even gotten into the various tricks he uses in order to get girls to come home with him. His behavior is utterly immoral according to the vast majority of existing accounts in moral philosophy. Lily nicely sums it up: he is "the emotional equivalent of a scavenging sewer rat" ("Best Couple

Ever"). But then why do we like him? Why do we identify with him? Why is he one of the most popular sitcom characters of all time?

Barney is not the first bad character in the history of the genre. In *Friends*, Joey Tribbiani did some nasty stuff: he burned the prosthetic leg of a girl in the middle of the forest and then drove away. But he loved his friends and would never knowingly screw them. All four characters in *Seinfeld* did awful things throughout the series, as memorably evidenced by the finale. But Barney takes this to a completely different level of awfulness.

We have a paradox then: how can we identify with and relate to a fictional character, Barney, who is such a terrible person that if we met him in real life, we would probably slap him or leave the room. This paradox needs to be kept apart from the famous 'paradox of fiction', the most succinct exposition of which comes not from Hume but from Chandler Bing:

CHANDLER: Bambi is a cartoon.

JOEY: You didn't cry when Bambi's mother died?

CHANDLER: Yes, it was very sad when the guy stopped drawing the deer. (*Friends*, Season Six, Episode 14)

The paradox of fiction is this: why do we feel strong emotions towards fictional events and characters we know do not exist? The paradox I want to look at here—we could call it the Barney Paradox—is different. It accepts that we feel strong emotions towards fictional characters. But then the question arises which fictional character we feel strong emotions towards. Who is our identification or empathy or emotional engagement directed at? And here comes the paradox: it seems that often we identify or empathize with the least worthy of the fictional characters.

The show's creators seem to be vividly aware of this paradox—notice the many references to how Barney himself always identifies with the bad guys in any given movie—the "wrong" Karate Kid, Darth Vader, the Terminator—and not with Ralph Macchio, Luke Skywalker, Harry Potter. There are good examples in "The Stinsons," Season Four) and "The Bro Mitzvah").

Philosophers worry about paradoxes, because a paradox shows that there must be something wrong with our assumptions. So let's try to think of some possible ways we can make the Barney Paradox go away.

1. Barney's Not So Bad

Maybe I was just picking out the worst of Barney. And maybe he's more like Joey, who in some respects is not the boyfriend you may want to take home to meet your parents, but in some other respects has a heart of gold.

There are some incidents that point in this direction. In "The Scorpion and the Toad," Season Two), Barney is allegedly helping Marshall get over Lily and get back in the game. But each time Marshall actually has a chance of scoring with a girl, Barney steps in and takes the girl home himself. The title of the episode refers to the Aesop tale about the scorpion who asks the toad to carry him across the river. The toad asks: why would I do that—you'll sting me and then we'll both die. But, the scorpion responds, if I sting you, we'll both die—so why would I sting you? So the toad agrees, but halfway through the scorpion does sting the toad and they both die—that's just the scorpion's nature. It should be clear who the scorpion is supposed to stand for here.

So far, this is a pretty damning statement about Barney, but that's not the full story. This happened at the beginning of Season Two. But towards the end of this season, we learn that Barney visited Lily in San Francisco and told her to come back to Marshall because he, Barney, can't go on stealing girls from him to keep up the hopes of the two of them getting back together alive ("Bachelor Party"). While this gives a nice twist to the scorpion-and-toad story, it's not clear whether this means that Barney stole all those girls from Marshall for purely selfless reasons. At least at that point we're led to believe that Barney is, at least sometimes, a compassionate and caring friend. But then again, this comes right after an episode where Barney steals Ted's moving truck with all his belonging ("Moving Day").

The most plausible version of this way of trying to explain away the paradox of identification with Barney is that Barney's not really bad: he's just immature. He's a little like a naughty child—we shouldn't expect him to behave responsibly or in any way that's not completely selfish. His general attitude towards life is that of a preschooler towards his toys. The show plays with this idea intermittently—especially in the last couple of seasons in a bid to make Barney proper fiancé material for Robin. This cuts the other way too: the writers also make Robin more similar to Barney—for example in "Something Old" (Season Eight), where Robin and Barney are in complete agreement that they should break up a couple just because they're somewhat annoying.

The decision to ditch Ted and his job prospects for working in a dinosaur-shaped office building could be interpreted as a manifestation of this child-like attitude (see also "Little Boys," in Season Three, which puts the Barney–little boy analogy in context).

Without denying that this is part of the way Barney is portrayed, it would be difficult to frame selling a woman or the 'Scuba Diver' trick, which deliberately and with cold calculation plays with and exploits Robin's feelings, as immature and therefore forgivable and in some way adorable childish gags.

2. We're Not Meant to Identify with Barney at All

Here's an alternative interpretation which may help us to escape the Barney Paradox. Maybe Barney was not conceived of as a protagonist of the series whom the audience was supposed to (or would be encouraged to) identify with. Married male viewers should identify with Marshall, single male viewers with Ted. Barney is there to laugh at.

While this may have been the way Barney's character started at the very beginning, this angle misses out on some of the most important aspects of Barney's appeal and of his character in general. At the very beginning of the series (in the first couple of episodes only), Barney was portrayed as a loser—as the butt of every joke, quite similar to the Stiffler character in the *American Pie* franchise, which *How I Met Your Mother* has very rich ties to. Even his haircut was a bit similar to Stiffler's. And he really was just someone to laugh at.

So at least at the beginning, while Barney was depicted as an awful person, he was also depicted as a loser—not someone the audience should identify with. But this all changed very early on—maybe because the creator of the series realized the potential of the character. Barney would not have become as popular as he did if he had stayed this 'dork', as Lily addressed him in the second episode.

3. Schadenfreude

A somewhat different way to go would be to say that while we're encouraged to have some kind of emotional engagement with Barney, this is by no means a positive emotional engagement. The emotion we're supposed to feel towards Barney is that of Schadenfreude—the feeling of happiness at other people's misfortune. We are not supposed to laugh with Barney—we're supposed to laugh at him.

This would be compatible with Barney's popularity, as Schadenfreude is not an unpleasant emotion to have. There's a long history of fictional characters whom we love to hate: from Tartuffe through Osmin and Monostatos to Dr. Evil. The idea then would be that Barney fits this illustrious list: the reason we like watching him is to see how he will eventually get what he deserves.

Again, there are many bits from the show that point in this direction. There are many, many scenes where Barney's misfortunes are supposed to provide the laughs. A quick list:

- **He's thrown out on the street naked** ("Naked Man").

- **He's forced to wear the ducky tie for a full year** ("Ducky Tie").

- **His attempt to take revenge on Marshall with the exploding meatball sub fails miserably** ("The Exploding Meatball Sub").

- **He's tied to the mechanical bull for two full hours (providing a memorable scene with perfect comedic timing when getting off)** ("Woo Girls").

- **He gets repeatedly thrown out of the prom** ("Best Prom Ever").

- **He gets stung by a swarm of bees** ("Burning Beekeeper").

- **He gets beaten up by proud Canadians at a Tim Horton's** ("Duel Citizenship").

- **His legs stop working after running the marathon without any training** ("Lucky Penny").

- He gets a nickname he hates ("Swarley").

- His long-awaited two hundredth conquest is an odious muscular body builder and not a super-model as planned ("Right Place, Right Time").

- As nobody is willing to give him a high five, he's forced to hold up his right arm for hours ("I Heart NJ").

- He's left in the doctor's office for the weekend with his 'Sensory Deprivator 5000' on ("Bad News").

But the best example of our Schadenfreude towards Barney comes from the various slap bet episodes. Here we have full episodes organized around our desire to see Barney punished. So it's undeniable that some of our emotional engagement with Barney is of the Schadenfreude nature. The episodes about the mystery woman who tells all Barney's potential conquests about his shenanigans resulting in the woman slapping him fits this pattern. We just like seeing Barney getting slapped.

But this isn't the whole story. What this pattern of Barney doing something bad and then getting punished for it makes even more conspicuous is the recurrence of those situations where Barney does something *really* bad, but goes completely unpunished.

A striking example is the ending of the "Playbook" episode, where he tricked all his friends (and especially Lily), used Robin, with whom he just split, maliciously, and got the reward of going out with the girl he wanted to. If he ever deserves to be slapped, this would be the time, but there is no slap, just Barney victoriously winking at us. Schadenfreude is not the only and not even the dominant way in which we engage emotionally with Barney.

4. Imagining from the Inside

The main way that philosophers have tried to understand why we identify with or become emotionally engaged with fictional characters (in movies, plays, or novels) is with the idea of "imagining from the inside." The general idea is that when we identify with a fictional character, we imagine her from the inside. We put ourselves, in imagination, in that person's shoes. So the possibility we need to consider is that we do identify with Barney in the sense that we put ourselves in his shoes.[1]

But why would we want to do that? Why would we want to imagine "the emotional equivalent of a scavenging sewer rat," to quote Lily, from the inside. Surely there must be more attractive things to imagine . . .

What does it mean to imagine someone from the inside? What does it mean to put ourselves in someone else's shoes? Is it imagining being someone else? Is it imagining having someone else's experiences? The most plausible way of cashing out this metaphor is to say that we imagine ourselves in someone else's situation—an idea that goes back at least to Adam Smith's 1759 *Theory of Moral Sentiments*.

If identification with a fictional character is a matter of imagining this person from the inside and if imagining from the inside amounts to imagining being in this person's situation, then the proposal is that we imagine being in Barney's situation when we engage with him emotionally. And here we may have a way out of the Barney Paradox.

Here is Alfred Hitchcock, who knew a thing or two about triggering the right emotional reaction from the audience:

> Even in this case [where we know that there is a bomb concealed in a briefcase in the plot to assassinate Hitler] I don't think the public would say, "Oh, good, they're all going to be blown to bits," but rather, they'll be thinking, "Watch out. There's a bomb!" What it means is that the apprehension of the bomb is more powerful than the feelings of sympathy or dislike for the characters involved. . . . Let's take another example. A curious person goes into somebody else's room and begins to search through the drawers. Now, you show the person who lives in

---

[1] Here are some examples: Richard Wollheim, "Identification and Imagination," in Richard Wollheim, ed., *Freud: A Collection of Critical Essays* (Anchor Press, 1974); Murray Smith, "Imagining from the Inside," in Richard Allen and Murray Smith, eds., *Film Theory and Philosophy* (Oxford University Press, 1997); Murray Smith, *Engaging Characters* (Oxford University Press, 1995); Alex Neill, "Empathy and (Film) Fiction," in David Bordwell and Noël Carroll, eds., *Post-Theory: Reconstructing Film Studies* (Wisconsin University Press, 1996); Gregory Currie, *Image and Mind: Film, Philosophy, and Cognitive Science* (Cambridge University Press, 1995).

that room coming up the stairs. Then you go back to the person who is searching, and the public feels like warning him, "Be careful, watch out. Someone's coming up the stairs." Therefore, even if the snooper is not a likeable character, the audience will still feel anxiety for him. Of course, when the character is attractive, as for instance Grace Kelly in *Rear Window*, the public's emotion is greatly intensified.[2]

If Hitchcock's right, then we can identify with characters we deeply dislike or even find repugnant. We can't help identifying or engaging even with Hitler when he's about to be blown up, in spite of the fact that we find him morally despicable. If identification is imagining oneself in the fictional character's situation, then we can certainly imagine ourselves in an evil character's situation. After all, there's nothing evil about the evil character's *situation*.

And, presumably, the same goes for Barney: the reason why we don't find it difficult to identify with Barney is because this amounts to imagining being in Barney's situation and it is Barney himself and not Barney's situation that is evil. So this way of thinking about our attitude towards Barney would not rule out our identification and engagement with him. We have made some progress.

Or, have we? It is possible to put oneself in someone's shoes, even if this person is evil, provided that there is nothing evil about the shoes, that is, about the situation one imagines being in. But this does not explain the *appeal* of identifying with Barney. On the imagining from the inside account it may not work against identifying with Barney that he is awful, but it doesn't explain why we are drawn to do so either. And what is striking about the reaction Barney triggers in the audience is not only that we can, if we really want to, engage with him emotionally, but that we are drawn to do so. The imagining from the inside view fails to explain why this would be so.

5. Emotional Contagion

An alternative to the "imagining from the inside" view is the emotional contagion account: when I see a sad fictional charac-

---

[2] François Truffaut, *Hitchcock* (Simon and Schuster, 1967), p. 73. For more on the phenomenon Hitchcock draws attention to here, see Bence Nanay, *Aesthetics as Philosophy of Perception* (Oxford University Press, 2014).

ter on scene, I do not need to actively put myself in her position or imagine myself being in her situation. All that happens is that I get infected by her sadness.[3]

This is a case of emotional contagion, a phenomenon we know from 'real life', that is from our emotional engagement with real people around us. From a very early age, our own emotional state is influenced by the emotional state of the people around us. And this influence is mainly unconscious: if, for example, faces of different emotional expressions are presented to us in a way that makes it impossible for us to become conscious of this stimulus (because they are flashed very briefly or because the stimulus is masked), it still influences our emotional state.[4] So the suggestion is that something like this happens when we are engaging with Barney.

As emotional contagion is mainly unconscious, automatic and unreflective, we react this way emotionally to other people regardless of what we think of their moral character. Even if we know that Barney is the emotional equivalent of a scavenging sewer rat, we just can't help feeling sad when he's feeling sad (setting it aside that Barney, of course, never feels sad; he feels awesome instead . . .).[5] This is an automatic emotional reaction that undercuts any assessment of Barney's moral character.

While this is clearly part of the story when it comes to understanding how we engage emotionally with real people and with fictional characters, again, it's not the whole story. If this were the whole story, then Barney's evilness would have no influence on our identification or emotional engagement with him. But, and this is the crucial point, Barney's evilness does have an influence on our identification or emotional engagement with him and a positive one. We identify with Barney more strongly and more readily than we would if he were a

---

[3] A couple of examples: Tamar Szabó Gendler, *Intuition, Imagination, and Philosophical Methodology* (Oxford University Press, 2011); Fred Dretske, "Perception and Other Minds." *Noûs* 7 (1973).

[4] Boris Bornemann, Piotr Winkielman, and Elke van der Meer, "Can You Feel What You Don't See? Using Internal Feedback to Detect Briefly Presented Emotional Stimuli," *International Journal of Psychophysiology* 85 (2012).

[5] A line taken almost directly from Oscar Wilde; see *The Picture of Dorian Grey* (Barnes and Noble, 1995), p. 119.

law-abiding nice guy. And the emotional contagion account of identification does not tell us why we do so.

6. Being Bad, Vicariously

The emotional contagion account's emphasis on automatic processes may indirectly help us to explain our weird attraction towards Barney. Just as it's hard not to get sad if we see Barney being sad, it's also difficult not to feel smug when Barney is winking at us smugly after pulling off the 'Scuba Diver' in "The Playbook." Is this a nice and commendable emotion to have, feeling smug after having screwed all of one's friends, and especially one's ex-girlfriend? No. But we can't help it—it's our automatic emotional contagion reaction to the situation.

And we can go even further. Maybe some part of us does not mind experiencing, but only in an indirect and vicarious manner, what it would be like to completely fool our four best friends for the sole purpose of getting a girl. Presumably, this is not a part of us that is normally making our moral decisions. And this does not imply that we are immoral or terrible people. We would not do anything like this in real life. But fiction and real life are very different. And when engaging with fiction we may be more liberal with what we are willing to experience—given that this experience will only be a vicarious one.[6]

Most of us don't have rails under our bed in case we need to dump a no longer needed one night stand to an unknown location ("The Fortress," Season Eight). And most of us would never even contemplate using such a device. But watching Barney do the same is different. Doing it is wrong; watching Barney do it is not wrong. Having the experience of pulling the secret lever that rails the bed away is not an experience we would like to have for sure—not unless we are sociopaths. But having the same experience vicariously is something very different and it has a certain appeal—partly precisely because we would never choose to have this experience for real, that is, in a non-vicarious way.

---

[6] On a related concept of vicarious emotional engagement, see Bence Nanay, *Between Perception and Action* (Oxford University Press, 2014), Chapter 6.

So being bad has its appeal—but an indirect and vicarious one. Part of why we enjoy TV shows, movies, and other fictional works is that we can have experiences we would never have otherwise. And this doesn't merely mean that even if we never travel to Turkey, we can have a vicarious experience of being in the Istanbul bazaars by watching the latest James Bond movie. It also means that we could have experiences vicariously the real equivalent of which we would never choose to have—and the vicarious experience of being Barney is a perfect example for this.

The creators of *How I Met Your Mother* gave us a character who is a terrible person, but we still love him. This is quite a feat to begin with and it also highlights a not immediately obvious aspect of our identification with fictional characters—that identification is mainly devoid of any moral overtones. Further, identifying with an evil character, like Barney, has an appeal that is difficult to resist. Does this mean that if we identify with Barney, we are bad or irresponsible or immoral people? It most certainly doesn't. It means that we like to do some virtual tourism into the realm of immorality. As Robert Musil says, "art ought to be permitted not only to depict the immoral and the completely reprehensible, but also to love them."[7]

---

[7] Robert Musil, *Precision and Soul* (University of Chicago Press, 1990), p. 5.

2
You Too Can Awesomize Yourself

KRIS GOFFIN

Kids, Barney Stinson is awesome. Not even the most erudite philosopher would refute this claim. But Barney wasn't born awesome. He became that way. On top of that, he awesomizes his existence every day. Being awesome is not something that overcomes you, it is something you have to do yourself. And Barney knows how to do it. He has shared this knowledge in various ways, most importantly through his blog and his book *The Bro Code*.

Barney's skills are so strong that his awesomeness can even overcome the little misfortunes of life. He calls this overcoming "mind over Barney," which is best illustrated with his quote: "When I get sad, I stop being sad and be awesome instead. . . . True story." Barney can even control his emotions and turn a negative emotion into a positive one. He can awesomize his sadness.

Is "When I get sad, I stop being sad and be awesome instead" really a "true story," or is Barney deceiving himself and others? Can you have full control over your emotions? Can you simply stop feeling what you feel and be awesome instead? Or is Barney disguising his true feelings by stating his awesomeness? Is saying, "I'm awesome!" maybe a masquerade for a deeply hidden sadness?

We are likely to think that emotions overcome us and affect us beyond our control. As a Stinsonian philosopher, I refuse to believe this. I think that we can partly transform emotions or at least, in Barney's words, awesomize them. Barney's attitude can teach us how to stop being sad and start being awesome instead.

How to Stop Being Sad and Be Awesome Instead

After analyzing Barney's attitude towards everyday life, we can extract the following guidelines to stop being sad and be awesome instead.

1. Discover yourself.
Learn to recognize a negative emotion. It is a great achievement to acknowledge the fact that you have a problem that needs to be solved. You must have a grasp on the emotion you want to change.

2. Avoid the path of self-reflection.
Once recognized, you don't need to reflect on the negative any further. Don't reflect on how your childhood made you the way you are. Don't bring in your daddy or mommy issues. Self-reflection may elucidate why you have this emotion, but it will not help you to change it. On the contrary, self-reflection makes you drown in your emotions. And drowning isn't awesome.

3. Choose the path of awesomeness.
This is a crucial part. Say "STOP!" to your negative emotion and the train of thought that it brings about. Feel the power you have. You have the power and the potentiality to be awesome. It's your decision. Don't let the emotion take over. You are not the slave of your emotions. You're in control.

4. Express your awesomeness.
Say: "I was feeling sad, but now I choose to be awesome instead." Now you have made the choice to be awesome and you are proud of it. It's *you* who did it. You need to show off your awesomeness. It's important to realize that you have the full responsibility to be who you want to be. It is not something that happens to you, but something you do. It is *you* who is upgrading yourself.

5. Be awesome all over the place.
When you have said you're awesome, act accordingly. Don't let your statement become a lie. Lying about your emotional state is not awesome, it is a weak sham. You have to actively be awesome, which can be best described as: be like Barney.

"When I get sad I just stop being sad and be awesome instead!" Barney reveals himself as an extremely optimistic person who actually believes that he can control his emotions, and choose to stop being sad. When you feel sad, just choose to be happy and your emotions will follow!

But is it really possible to choose how you feel? Can you just pick an emotion and start feeling it? Intuitively we wouldn't believe that we have this much control over our emotions.

However silly this may sound, the most prominent philosophers who discuss emotion seem to agree with Barney in saying that we can actually control our emotions. During the past century there has been a dispute between philosophers arguing for two different ideas about what emotions really are.

Some philosophers argue that emotions are essentially bodily. They are physiological responses, perhaps caused by your glands. Other philosophers claim that emotions are really about the way we think, since we don't seem to have emotions unless we judge things to be a certain way. I'm going to call the first group of philosophers *somaticists* and the other group *cognitivists*. Despite their difference of opinion, both of these two schools of thought seem to agree with Barney's theory that we can choose how we feel.

Are Emotions Bodily Feelings?

Somaticists claim that emotions are nothing but bodily feelings caused by physiological changes. For instance, being angry is nothing but the feeling of your heart beating faster combined with an adrenaline rush. The famous pioneer of psychology, William James, defended this theory. Up till the 1960s and 1970s most psychologists agreed with his idea that emotions are nothing but physiological changes.

Reducing emotions to bodily changes has some radical implications. According to this theory, you must be able to manipulate your own emotions (to some extent) by acting as if you experience a certain emotion. The logic behind it is:

1. **Emotions are bodily feelings caused by physiological changes.**

2. **We can control our body to some extent.**

3. Therefore we can control our emotions to some extent.

This theory implies the 'fake it till you make it' idea. Forcing a smile when you feel sad, for instance, can help you feel happy. We can control our bodily changes that give rise to our emotions. Therefore we're able to control our emotions. So Barney was right. We can just stop being sad and be awesome instead. In moments when Barney is in pain, he takes control over his body in order to look cool. Then he mostly screams a high pitched catchphrase. He forces his body in such a way so that he can change his emotions.

Nowadays, most of the cognitive scientists who still agree with James defend a theory that is far more nuanced than James's original claim. Most contemporary emotion theorists, however, think that James's theory is not useful anymore. They think it is rather naive to reduce your emotions to the body alone. Emotions aren't things of the body. An emotion isn't something like hunger. It is more than a bodily sensation. We feel things for a reason.

Are Emotions Judgments?

The thinkers I'm calling cognitivists say that emotions are not something of the body, but of the mind. Emotions are not bodily; they are aspects of thinking. The famous philosopher Jean-Paul Sartre argued against the psychologists of his time that emotions are some kind of judgment. Robert Solomon systematized this idea into the so-called 'judgment theory of emotion'.

According to philosophers like Solomon, emotions are judgments. If you're angry, you're angry for a reason. At the end of the third season, Ted finds out that Barney has slept with his ex-girlfriend, Robin. Ted becomes so angry with Barney that he doesn't want to be friends with him anymore. His anger is not just a bodily sensation, but a cognitive judgment. Ted's anger proves that he doesn't approve of Barney's actions. Barney fails to respect one of the most important rules of the Bro Code: no sex with a bro's ex. And even more than that, Ted is disappointed in Barney. He wants to believe that although Barney is known for his disrespectful way of treating women, he would never be disrespectful to Ted. But apparently, Ted has misjudged his friend; he was wrong, and that's why Ted becomes angry with Barney. He becomes angry because of how he judges the situation. According to cognitivists, every emotion functions in this way.

However, some cognitivists also agree with Barney's optimism. Solomon argues that we choose our own emotions. The logic behind this is:

1. **Emotions are judgments.**

2. **We 'make' judgments.**

3. **Thus emotions are activities or things we do.**

4. **Things we do are voluntary.**

5. **What is voluntary is chosen.**

6. **Therefore, emotions are chosen.**

If emotions are judgments and that we make judgments, then an emotion is voluntarily chosen. We can choose to stop feeling sad and just be awesome instead.

But is it really true that every emotion is a judgment? Ted's anger with Barney can easily be explained with the judgment theory. But is every emotion a judgment? We do sometimes seem to have emotions that don't fall in line with our conscious judgments. You could be afraid of flying although you're perfectly well aware that it's far less dangerous than traveling by car. Or you could be afraid of a poisonous snake although you know that it's safely behind glass.

Not every emotion seems to be a judgment, although most of them are. Everybody has had the experience of being melancholic all day long without actually knowing why. It is in these experiences that we realize that emotions and cognition are two different things. Some emotions seem to be rational and appropriate reactions to a situation, but we should not reduce emotion to cognition because a lot of our emotions are just stupid.

However, cognitivists have a strong point when they argue against somaticists that emotions have something of the mind and are not just bodily feelings. But is that completely true? Don't cognitivists deny the fact that our emotions also have a bodily aspect?

Body or Mind?

After half a century of discussion about whether an emotion is a bodily or a mental thing, emotion theorists got the idea that maybe it's both. Contemporary philosopher Jesse Prinz, for instance, calls an emotion an "embodied appraisal," meaning that an emotion is an appraisal, a mental act, but it's embedded in the body.

To understand the very nature of emotion, we must include both body and mind. Emotions are both bodily and cognitive. When we're angry, we're angry at someone for a reason, but at the same time, our heartbeat increases and our adrenaline production skyrockets. Some emotions we can understand cognitively, while others seem to overcome us beyond our control, in the way that feeling ravenous can preclude a feeding frenzy. An emotion is a complex episode which includes both mind and body.

If we agree on this concept of emotion, is Barney still right when he says that he can simply stop being sad, or is he just deceiving himself? If we see emotion as something both bodily and cognitive, it becomes hard to just "be awesome instead." If we want to be happy, do we have to *act* as if we're happy and at the same time choose to *judge* reality as fun? Or is this a naive idea?

I say that we can influence our emotions more than we're often inclined to think. Understanding an emotion as an embodied appraisal leaves open the possibility that we may be able to control our emotions. We have to understand an emotion as something we do, rather than something that overcomes us. We have the creative power to transform our emotions. This contemporary understanding of emotion can also give us a philosophical explanation of how to stop being sad and start being awesome instead.

Emotions Are Processes

Emotions are not mere bodily sensations. But they are not mere judgments either. They are complex processes which can include both. An emotion is not a singular thing. In experiencing an emotion we do a lot of stuff: we perceive a situation in a certain way, our body reacts to the situation, we judge the situation, we remember things, we try to make sense of what we feel, we feel the urge to act in some way, and we express our emotions. And in doing all this, we evoke even more emotions.

We have to think of emotions as processes. They are not entities that just sit there in our brain without changing our movements. Emotions consist of different actions we take. That's right, emotions are things we *do*. They don't overcome us, but we do them or make them. It is not a 'doing' like playing baseball is a doing because you don't start from nothing. An emotion is a reaction to a situation, and this reaction is something we do.

Let's take the emotion of jealousy for example and try to determine its process. When someone catches his girlfriend cheating on him with another guy, he immediately feels a bodily arousal. He feels angry, disappointed, and sad. Then he'll start to think things like: "Who is this guy?" and "Why is he better than me?" and "What have I done wrong?"

These thoughts will make him feel dizzy and unsettled. He'll get angry with his girlfriend or with himself, and he'll try to find out who is responsible or guilty. Memories will pop up in his head. The story of their relationship will flash before his eyes, while the relationship is breaking apart. The situation doesn't seem to fit in the relationship story. He'll try to place the fact that he was betrayed within the story, but it doesn't seem to fit, and that makes him angry. Has she cheated on him before? Did she ever love him? He recalls his intense feelings of love for her. Then he feels that she destroyed his trust in this bond and replaced him with someone else.

The intimacy that they have shared is now shared with the other person. A strong pain in the chest may occur—the physical equivalent of a broken heart. He might start to yell at his girlfriend, he might cry or feel a complete inability to react. For a long time, he'll keep thinking about it, replaying the scenario in his mind. All these thoughts and feelings will pop up every now and then like ghosts haunting him. He'll try to cope with it by finding a reason for it. He'll look for what he has done wrong and try to justify why she did it. And he'll probably tell his story to his friends quite often.

Certainly Ted is good at this. Every time he has a date he over-analyzes everything the girl says, and he tries to understand what he feels for her. And in doing so, he talks a lot. Both Ted's way of dealing with his dates and the example I gave about jealousy are extreme cases. Most emotions don't have this intensity, but every emotion works in a similar way.

Let's see if we can find a pattern that defines this emotional process. Psychological research has proved that the emotional process consists of two episodes: direct appraisal and cognitive monitoring.

An emotion starts off with a direct appraisal. That's the first part of the process: a direct sensation of arousal. In the jealousy example, the person directly feels something when he is confronted with his girlfriend cheating on him. This feeling is also an appraisal because it is a reaction to a situation. We feel something, and we also feel it in our body, that is why we call it a gut feeling. It is a *direct* appraisal since it is not the result of a thinking process. The starting point of an emotion is not a thought or something like that. It is a primal reaction to a situation, which is to be found much deeper than in our abilities to reason. Psychologists have shown that this initial emotional state is enabled by the most primal functions of our brain. Our more advanced cognitive functions of the brain are triggered in the second stage of the emotional process.[1]

The second part of the emotional process is the cognitive monitoring of the direct appraisal. Immediately after we have experienced a direct reaction to the situation, we use our high-tech cognition to shape this emotion. This is the sequence of thoughts and events described in my example of jealousy. We over-think the direct appraisal and try to make sense of what we feel. This cognitive monitoring can take the shape of putting the appraisal into a *narrative*.

We're constantly creating narratives in order to understand ourselves and our emotions. We are constantly writing our autobiography. Current events are related to past events. We give emotions meaning by relating them to our life story. This is what Ted is doing when he talks about his dates. He does the same thing when tells his children how he met their mother.

It's this cognitive monitoring that we can partly control. Still, most of our emotions feel like they happen to us, even the

---

[1] I feel obliged to give you some references so that you don't think I'm making this stuff up. In *Deeper than Reason*, Jenefer Robinson summarizes a lot of contemporary science of emotion in order to understand emotions as processes. Most prominent figures in the science of emotion are: Joseph LeDoux, Robert Zajonc, Richard Lazarus, and Antonio Damasio. A good book on emotion and narrative is Peter Goldie's *The Emotions*.

cognitive monitoring seems to come out of nothing. Well, it doesn't really come out of nothing, since the narratives that we create around it are based on narratives we have already heard. It is our past, our memories, and the people who are important to us who made us who we are. They did this by teaching us the paradigms by which we create our narratives.

Yet, we have some control over this cognitive part of the emotion process. Expression, for instance, is also part of this cognitive monitoring. In the way we give expression to our bodily sensations, we can slightly influence which directions our emotions go in. That is what Barney is doing when he says, "When I feel sad, I just stop being sad and be awesome instead." He is using his creative power to control his emotions. He tries to take grasp of his emotions by turning the narrative of his emotions into a narrative of awesomeness.

Self-Deception

Isn't awesomizing yourself a form of self-deception? Isn't telling yourself that you're awesome in order to have the illusion of being awesome, just a self-fulfilling prophecy?

Emotions consist of narratives, and if we're able to change our narratives, we can change our emotions. So if the fact that we can control our emotions implies that those manipulated emotions are illusions, then every emotion would be an illusion. Since we partly create every emotion that we have by making a narrative, we create every emotion.

However, this argument does not hold since we could still make a distinction between the emotions we unconsciously create and those we have consciously manipulated. The creation of a narrative is not fully dependent on our free will. Narratives are influenced by a number of factors, such as interaction with significant others, childhood experiences, and other values inherent in our culture and the narratives we have encountered during our lives. So a large part of the origin of our narratives, and therefore of our emotions, finds inspiration in the environment we live in. The narratives we create are mostly based on other stories we've heard.

But true creative people like Barney create their own narratives. They're like artistic geniuses who don't imitate other paintings, models, and stories. They shape their own stories.

That's why Barney changes from being a loser into being awesome. He used to be a soft-hearted hippie and wanted to join the Peace Corps with his long-time girlfriend, Shannon. When she dumps him for a womanizer, Barney becomes another person. He chooses to be awesome instead of sad. Was this action one of self-manipulation? Yes. Do his feelings have the negative connotation of being illusions? Probably. But isn't it more important to be awesome than to be sincere? Why not manipulate your own emotions?

A good, but also slightly controversial, example is love. Can we decide to fall in love? The emotion of love is based on a narrative, which is heavily influenced by the narratives we have encountered during our lives. Some examples of these paradigmatic narratives are our parents' relationship, our own experiences; cultural values, and most importantly, Disney movies. Our high and unreachable ideals of love are mostly based on Disney movies. Disney is the direct cause of many unhappy people who have realized that their spouse is not quite like the prince or princess they had imagined.

So much about general narratives of love. But what about specific episodes of love? Can you just choose to fall in love with somebody? One thing for sure is that falling in love is something you do. Yet this is not the same as saying that it is a matter of choice. You fall in love based on who you are and based on the narratives you consist of. They don't only originate from your narratives of love, but also from the narratives of your personality and your life goals.

Falling in love with someone is putting a person into your own love narrative. So love is something we do. I have made the distinction between an 'unconsciously done action' type of emotion and a 'conscious action' emotion. I have argued that the conscious sort is a manipulation. But this isn't a bad thing—on the contrary, it's far more creative and courageous to manipulate your emotions.

If we apply this reasoning to love, though, this claim seems rather weird. If you consciously manipulate yourself to fall in love with someone, you will never manage to convince yourself that you actually love this person. You 'fall' in love, you don't choose your love. So no matter how hard you try, manipulating yourself won't get you to love someone. The best you can do is to create an illusion instead of feeling a genuine emotion.

When I said that controlling your emotions is a courageous and creative thing to do, I didn't mean that you can choose to feel whatever you want. We cannot control our judgments or appraisals, as I have said. Falling in love is not a matter of choice. Yet, we can place our appraisals in a different kind of narrative. For instance, at the end of Ted's first date with Robin, he tells her that he loves her. He shows that he places his positive feelings in a totally different narrative than Robin does. She shares the same positive feelings (appraisals) about their date, yet she doesn't place them in an 'I love you' narrative.

In the same way, we can experience a negative appraisal. We can give different expressions to this appraisal. You can say, "I have a cold, ugh, my life is worthless. I'm a complete loser. Now I have a cold and nothing is going to make me feel better." Or you can say, as Barney would, "When I feel sick, I stop being sick and be awesome instead."

It takes a lot of courage to awesomize yourself, because you need to fight against your routine narratives. But it is possible. Everybody can be awesome.

Awesome People and Not-So-Awesome People

We could divide humanity into two groups of people: those who are awesome, and those who are not. Not-so-awesome people block themselves. They find all kinds of excuses for not being awesome. "I don't look good," or "I simply don't have the right social capabilities," or—and this one is extreme—"Because of my traumatizing childhood, I will always have this low self-esteem." These people are skilled with the abominable talent of finding reasons for why they shouldn't put energy into self-enhancement.

Still, we all carry the burden of the past with us. Some of us are less fortunate and have bad experiences which have lowered our self-esteem. Sometimes it is really difficult to overcome these issues.

However, the problem of not being awesome doesn't lie in bad experiences, but in how you deal with them. Not-so-awesome people tend to hold external factors responsible for their own misery. "I didn't get my book published because the book market is too focused on making easy money nowadays!" or "I will always be insecure because my parents mistreated me!" or "She doesn't want a relationship with me because she has a fear of commitment!"

These not-so-awesome people cease to feel responsible for their actions. The world just isn't fair. That is why they are miserable. Because 'fate' has a different role in mind for them. Their past has determined the way they are now. They can't help it, they just have become the way they are.

These not-so-awesome people seem to think that they are not responsible for who they are. And that's where they're wrong. You are responsible for yourself, and you have to take responsibility for your actions.

Most events in your life are indeed beyond your control. But it's wrong to blame everything on the events that have had a bad influence on you. For instance, maybe the reason why you didn't get your book published is not that publishers are only concerned with selling commercial books, as you'd like to think. Maybe you just don't know how to write. It takes a step to acknowledge that. The second step is to either become a better writer and work for it like hell, or to realize that you are not that much of a writer. Maybe your authentic way of living does not include writing.

How I Met Your Mother gives us another example. Lily has always wanted to be a painter. Marshall compliments Lily on every painting she makes, which makes her believe that her paintings are actually good. Which they obviously aren't. After numerous failed attempts to sell her best painting, she realizes that maybe she isn't a good painter after all. She becomes sad, but she doesn't blame anyone for that. She feels responsible for her own failure, which is a very brave thing to do. Later on, Marshall discovers that Lily's paintings have a relaxing effect on dogs. Because Lily really enjoys painting, she decides to continue to make art—for animals. She has encountered the unpleasant realization that maybe she is not an artistic genius, but she handles that realization responsibly. She takes responsibility and finds another way to validate what she loves doing. That's why Lily is so awesome.

I don't want to suggest that we're completely responsible for every emotion, as cognitivists tend to say, but I do think we're responsible to some extent. We can't control the things that happen to us. We cannot even control our direct affective responses towards them. But we can control how we deal with our emotions, just like Barney does.

On the other hand, I also don't want to argue that Barney's entire character should be an example for everyone. He has some serious flaws too. Barney treats women with disrespect, he is sometimes very egotistical, and he can act really childish.

Yet, from Barney, we can all learn the importance of taking control over our emotions. How little or how great the control over our emotions may be, we have the power to awesomize them. Instead of losing out to self-pity and complaining, we have to take responsibility for how we deal with our emotions. We can shape our expressions in such a way that emotions aren't drawn into negativity, but awesomized into positivity. By being creative with our narratives, we can turn our existence into a story of awesomeness. Responsibility and power lie in our hands. So, the next time you feel sad, just stop being sad and be awesome instead.[2]

[2] I am grateful to Annelies Monseré, Violi Sahaj, and Alex Schuurbiers for their useful remarks.

3
Me! Me! Me!

Thomas Ainsworth

Charity? You're seriously talking to me about charity? Dude, I am Mr. Charity. I frequently sleep with sixes, chubsters, over-thirties. . . . I am the Bill and Melinda Gates of the sympathy bang.

—Barney Stinson in "False Positive"

The good person must be a self-lover.

—Aristotle, *Nicomachean Ethics*, Book IX, Chapter 8

Kids, in "The Playbook," Barney has just broken up with Robin, and is determined to resume his philandering ways. He does so with the help of the Playbook, a black leathery tome full of scams, cons, hustles, hoodwinks, gambits, flim-flams, stratagems, and bamboozles that he has devised to pick up chicks and give 'em the business.

Barney's series of seductions culminates in the grandiose meta-play, the Scuba Diver. Lily has discovered the existence of the Playbook, and her disgust is exacerbated when Barney uses it on a work colleague whom she had intended for Ted. In retaliation, she has stolen it and is threatening (Bond-villain style) to post the contents on the internet. Defiantly, Barney announces he is going to perform one final play, the Scuba Diver. Lily tells Marshall to post the Playbook online, but is surprised to discover that it includes no mention of a play called "The Scuba Diver." Down in MacLaren's bar, the whole *How I Met Your Mother* gang finds Barney in a booth, dressed in full scuba gear.

He reveals that he plans to seduce the blonde at the bar, but, when questioned about the Scuba Diver, he breaks down and confesses that he has taken his break-up with Robin worse than they had realized. His recent behavior has been his way of coping. Lily and the others persuade the blonde that Barney is a good guy, and that she should give him a chance and go for coffee with him. Only after they have left does Lily receive a text from Barney, telling her to look under the table, where they discover the missing page of the Playbook, which contains the Scuba Diver. The page reveals that all the preceding events in the episode—the revelation of the Playbook to Lily, the seducing of the work colleague so that she would steal it, the faked break-down over Robin—were designed for the sole purpose of getting Lily and the others to tell the blonde at the bar what a great guy Barney is, and thus to make them complicit in her seduction.

"How could anyone behave in such a dastardly manner?" (I hear the more prim, or Ted-like, among you cry.) Nor is this particular example a one-off. The manipulative lows to which Barney is willing to stoop with a view to duping attractive women into sleeping with him are legen . . . wait for it . . . dary. If that weren't bad enough, he has been known to indulge in outrageous displays of conspicuous consumption, buying diamond-encrusted suits, thousands of dollars of postage stamps, or multiple televisions just for the purpose of smashing them, when there are children in Africa dying for lack of oral rehydration salts.

It's not just in his personal life that Barney exhibits an unusually lax moral sense. He does, after all, work for the shady organization Goliath National Bank and is remarkably evasive when asked what precisely he does for them. Everyone would love to have near limitless funds and an endless supply of hot chicks. Practically everyone anyway. However, Barney persistently ignores the feelings and wishes of others in his relentless pursuit of a good time. His selfishness is so extreme that some philosophically ignorant viewers have questioned whether he isn't becoming a poorly drawn caricature of an investment banker, or at least not a character with whom we can feel much sympathy. Philosophically educated members of the audience know better. Barney's selfish behavior is best explained by one simple hypothesis: Barney Stinson is a committed egoist, the most important egoist in recent TV history. (Sorry, Chuck Bass!)

What Egoism Is and What It Isn't

An egoist is not to be confused with his superficially similar cousin (dyslexics, pay particular attention!) the egotist. According to my dictionary, an egotist is "a conceited boastful person; one who thinks or talks too much of himself." Calling someone an egotist is probably an insult. An egoist, on the other hand, is just someone who holds a certain philosophical position, and you should try not to take philosophical disagreements personally.

What philosophical position is egoism? An egoist is typically defined as someone who believes either that everyone always aims to maximise their own self-interest, or that everyone should do so.

An egoist may not always in fact *act* in a way which maximizes his own self-interest: sometimes he may accidentally do something which fails to achieve this through miscalculation, or clumsiness; and sometimes even the most committed egoists are affected by peer pressure, and, through weakness of will, end up acting in an unselfish way. To qualify as an egoist you merely have to *intend* to act so as to maximize your own self-interest. The point is sometimes put, equivalently, by saying that the egoist seeks his own good, or happiness, at the expense of others.

What does it mean to maximize your own self-interest? Now there are manifold different views about what self-interest, or happiness, or the human good, consists in. Some philosophers (subjectivists) think it is having your desires satisfied, whatever your desires happen to be. (That's something Barney achieves on a regular basis . . .) Others (objectivists) think it is acquiring certain things, such as virtue, knowledge, a wife and children, or plenty of bimbos and a hot-dog toaster, whether or not you happen to desire these things.

Quite a lot of philosophers have (somewhat suspiciously) thought that a key component of happiness is being a philosopher. The egoist does not need to take any position on what the human good is, or whether it is the same for everyone. Indeed he is best advised to remain neutral on this point, saying that, whatever the human good turns out to be, that's what everyone does or should aim at. The point of saying that the egoist aims to *maximize* his own good is so that he is not constrained to pursue actions that are good for him in the short term but that end up costing him in the long run. Eating that last iced bun might contribute to your self-interest over the next five minutes, but you're going to be carrying it around with you on your thighs for a lot longer than that.

There are a couple of other unconventional moral views, that your mother would disapprove of, but which it is important not to confuse with egoism. Immoralism is the rather perverse position that one ought to do the opposite of whatever conventional morality enjoins. "Evil, be thou my Good," Milton's Satan declares,[1] and thereby admits to being an immoralist. As with most of these unconventional moral positions, it would be unwise for him to admit it, except among fellow-travelers.

Apart from Satan, and his followers, immoralists are a pretty rare breed. A more popular position that is often confused with egoism is moral skepticism, together with its closely related variant, moral nihilism (or amoralism). The moral skeptic believes that no one has (or can have) any moral knowledge. The moral nihilist adds that this is because all moral claims are false. Morality is bunk. It is an invention of the weak to fool the strong into being nice to them. The skeptic and the nihilist agree with the immoralist and the egoist that conventional morality is either unknowable or outright false. It's simply not true, for example, that you ought to give all your worldly goods to the poor. All of these unconventional moralists may even agree about the origins of conventional morality in a conspiracy of the weak to constrain the strong. However, while the immoralist and egoist go along with the skeptic and nihilist in their contempt for conventional morality, they don't concede that all morality is bunk. To the immoralist and the egoist, there are moral facts; they are just not what people ordinarily think.

Of these unconventional moral views, egoism seems to fit Barney the best. However, you may already have spotted a significant stumbling block for this interpretative claim. 'But wait!' I hear you cry. 'What about the time when Barney flew to California to try and get Lily back with Marshall, and kept heroically stealing his dates so that he wouldn't cheat on her

---

[1] *Paradise Lost*, Book IV, line 110.

("Bachelor Party")? Or how about when, on hearing that Ted was in a car accident, he rushed out of an important business meeting, ran all the way to the hospital, and was run over by a bus, breaking every bone in his body ("Miracles")? Admittedly on the face of it these don't look like the actions of an egoist.

There's no denying that Barney displays unusual generosity towards his friends, even buying them lavish gifts such as lap dances at the Lusty Leopard. It's possible that his kindness is purely selfish. No man is an island, and it is perfectly compatible with egoism that the egoist help others, provided that he does so only as a means to his own happiness. Barney needs friends, and you can't expect to have friends, at least not ones worth having, unless you're nice to them occasionally. One may feel, however, that in his behavior towards his friends Barney goes beyond what one would expect from a true egoist, who is only interested in friends in so far as they contribute to his own good. He certainly seems to care about their interests as well, even when they are irrelevant to, or (mildly) in conflict with, his own. If he didn't, he would hardly be such a sympathetic and popular character. He even elevates his attitude towards friends into a sort of personal moral system, in the form of the Bro Code, and then feels guilty when he breaches it to sleep with Robin, Ted's ex. ("Article 150: No sex with your Bro's ex. It is never ever permissible for a Bro to sleep with his Bro's ex. Violating this code is worse than killing a Bro"—"The Goat").

If we treat friends as other people, helping friends will imply at best an imperfect dedication to egoism. However, if we adopt Aristotle's view about friends, no such conclusion will be necessary. Aristotle tells us that "a friend is another self."[2] What he means by this is that you should treat what's good for your friend as you treat what's good for you, as an end in itself. If we expand the ego to include friends, then being nice to friends still counts as selfish behavior. Of course, if everyone were your friend, egoism would then collapse into altruism, but Aristotle is adamant that no one could possibly sustain that many true friends. How many could they sustain? Don't think of Facebook friends, but of the number of main cast members in a successful sitcom.

---

[2] *Nicomachean Ethics*, Book IX, Chapter 4, lines 1166a31–2; Chapter 9, lines 1170b6–7.

Psychological versus Ethical Egoists

There are really two main schools of egoism. Psychological egoists are those who deny that there's such a thing as an
unselfish act. However altruistic and noble someone appears,
they're really just as self-centered as everyone else. That's
because everyone naturally seeks their own good or happiness. It's just that for some people happiness is achieved by
helping the poor and needy or dying gloriously in battle, while
for others it's enough to enjoy an ample supply of fine wines
and strippers.

The psychological egoists' bitter rivals are the ethical egoists. Ethical egoists maintain that it is *not* an inevitable fact
about human psychology that everyone's ultimate goal is their
own happiness. Some people do indeed pursue the interests of
others as an end in itself—the poor fools! Only the elite few
recognise that pursuing one's own good at the expense of others is the only rational and ethically correct path. It is what we
ought to do.

Given these two sorts of egoism, a pressing question naturally arises: which sort of egoist is Barney? We will begin by
examining the hypothesis that he is a psychological egoist, and
then look at the other possibility, that he is an ethical egoist.
Apart from the friendship objection, which we have discussed,
there are a couple of obstacles to attributing a doctrine of psychological egoism to Barney. A major difference between psychological and ethical egoism is that the former says that
everyone in fact behaves in a selfish way, whereas the latter
denies this: everyone should be selfish, but only a select few
arc. Ethical egoism is more elitist and thus perhaps more likely
to appeal to someone of Barney's competitive sensibilities. This
may not seem like a particularly strong reason to discount psychological egoism, since psychological egoism is also elitist in a
second-order way: everyone is selfish, but only the select few
realise the truth of psychological egoism. However, psychological egoism is not really such an elite view. After all, it's advo-
cated by none other than Joey in *Friends*, who hardly numbers
among pop culture's more brilliant philosophical minds ("The
One Where Phoebe Hates PBS" from *Friends*, Season Five).

A more serious objection to attributing such a position to
Barney is that psychological egoism is probably false. Now

there is nothing wrong with ascribing false philosophical views to people like Joey, but Barney is evidently a few steps above a Joey on the intellectual food chain. But why do I say that psychological egoism is false?

One reason to doubt that everyone is always ultimately selfish is the theory of evolution. If you don't believe in evolution, go read some Richard Dawkins, then return. You might initially think that evolution provides support for egoism (the selfish gene, and all that . . .) However it's the survival of the genotype, not the individual organism, that nature prioritizes. Sometimes the best way to preserve a particular genetic make-up is for parents to sacrifice themselves for their offspring, and this sort of thing happens not just among humans but also in the animal kingdom. (I'm not sure about plants . . .)

On the face of it, self-sacrificing looks like the sort of behavior that offers a counter-example to psychological egoism (as long as the beneficiaries are not friends). However, the psychological egoist will undoubtedly argue that, despite appearances, these sorts of actions are in fact selfish. Perhaps, if the parent did not sacrifice itself, it would be so wracked with guilt that life would be unbearable, or perhaps it would be ostracized by the rest of the community. The psychological egoist must maintain that these sorts of selfish reasons are the only ones motivating its action. There are three possible sorts of explanation for any instance of self-sacrificial behaviour: it could, as the psychological egoist insists, be purely selfish; it could be purely altruistic; or it could be motivated by a mixture of selfish and selfless reasons. Since a willingness to sacrifice oneself under extreme circumstances is liable to preserve the species or genotype (though not the individual), we would expect that we would have evolved to have the most reliable mechanism to ensure that we act in the requisite suicidal way. And presumably the most reliable mechanism will be the one which makes us amenable to both selfish and selfless reasons for sacrificing ourselves.

The argument from evolution may not seem totally conclusive. For it may be pointed out that nature does not always supply a back-up mechanism. For example, I have only one liver (alas!) Perhaps self-sacrificing is less important to the survival of the species than other sorts of action that would be impaired if we had these selfless instincts. However, the example of self-sacrifice brings out another line of argument which I think is decisive against psychological egoism.

The psychological egoist is claiming that all human action is fundamentally selfish. This isn't merely the view that people are more selfish than we usually suppose. Since it is a universal claim, psychological egoism is vulnerable to a single counter-example: if any instance of unselfish motivation exists, psychological egoism is false. As we've seen, the psychological egoist will say of any purported counter-example that it's really a case of disguised selfishness. This may be plausible in some cases, but in others it does seem very hard to swallow.

Take the time when Marshall spends his Christmas Eve helping the delivery man deliver all the strangers' Christmas presents, because otherwise they won't get there in time ("How Lily Stole Christmas"). The psychological egoist claims that Marshall does this for selfish reasons. He's right that we can't prove otherwise. Maybe you can never know for sure what motivated someone else, for they might be lying. It seems harder to deny that we have reliable access to our own motivations. So those of us who think that we have acted selflessly in the past will be able to refute the psychological egoist. But even if we can't point to a counter-example that will satisfy a psychological egoist, that doesn't mean that we should accept his conclusion. Perhaps we should accept that it is *possible* that everyone is always fundamentally selfish, but plenty of things are possible. Just because a philosophical theory is consistent does not mean it is true, and we have not been given any reason to think that we are in fact mistaken in any of the apparent counter-examples, let alone in all of them.

One Ring to Rule Them All

If psychological egoism is false, then the charitable interpretation is that Barney is an ethical egoist. The contrast between psychological and ethical egoism is best drawn, as so often in philosophy, with the help of an Ancient Greek example. In Plato's most famous dialogue, *The Republic*, Plato's brother Glaucon, stressing that he is merely playing devil's advocate (always deny your egoism), takes it upon himself to argue that justice is in fact a necessary evil. It's like disgusting medicine or a ten-mile run. Committing injustice is often a lot of fun, but being on the receiving end can be a drag (unless you're into that sort of thing . . .).

To make his point more vivid, Glaucon tells the story of the ring of Gyges.[3] You may recognize it as having been ripped off by Tolkien, or Wagner, depending on how high-brow you are. Actually the main character in the story is an ancestor of Gyges, but, following general practice, we will conveniently forget this annoying detail and call him 'Gyges'.

Gyges was a Lydian shepherd (Lydia was a kingdom in Asia Minor, or modern Turkey.) One day, while he was tending his sheep, there was a massive deluge and an earthquake, and a gaping chasm opened at his feet. Exploring this chasm, he found, amongst other curios, a hollow bronze horse. Inside the horse was a corpse of more than mortal stature, which had a gold ring on its finger. As you would, Gyges pocketed the ring and made a swift exit. Later, at a shepherd meeting, Gyges was wearing his new ring. During a particularly dull part of the meeting, he was fiddling with it. He happened to twist the knob on it in towards his hand, and when he did so he became invisible. On turning the knob outwards again he rematerialized. Realizing what an opportunity this presented, he arranged to be sent to the Lydian king's palace as a messenger. He used the ring to insinuate his way into the presence of the king's wife, whom he quickly seduced. Plato doesn't go into details about the seduction, but no doubt he made judicious use of "The Naked Man" (this was one of the two out of three times where it worked). With the help of his wife, Gyges killed the king, and usurped the throne.

Glaucon claims that anyone in Gyges's situation, presented with the opportunity of committing injustice with guaranteed impunity, would inevitably succumb, no matter how noble and pious they might previously have appeared. If he were right, this would provide compelling support for psychological egoism. However, we have seen that there are good reasons to think that psychological egoism is probably false, and therefore to suspect that not everyone would do as Gyges does. This suspicion is amplified if we consider that Gyges's situation is not as far-fetched as it might at first appear. Certainly few of us are ever lucky enough to stumble across magic invisibility

---

[3] *Republic*, Book II, lines 359c7–360d9.

rings, but, in a more mundane way, we are often put in a position where we could commit some minor injustice, and be almost as certain of escaping detection as if we were invisible, even in New York, where CCTV cameras are ubiquitous. Practically every day you have a chance to, for example, steal something that you would like to own, with an almost vanishingly tiny chance of being caught. It is interesting that most people do not avail themselves of most of these opportunities for apparently risk-free reward. Perhaps often it is because they believe that even if the risk seems small, the consequences of being caught far outweigh the gains to be had. But it seems unlikely that this is always the case. Our rejection of psychological egoism suggests that we should draw a different moral from the ring of Gyges story. In Gyges's situation many people would not act as he does. They would do the conventionally right thing, and hand the ring in to the proper authorities. And they would be fools. For the only reason they act in such a way is because of some vague feeling that they ought to. Once you realize that this feeling is the product of a pervasive societal fiction, you are free to pursue the correct course of action—that of the ethical egoist.

Is Ethical Egoism a Contradiction in Terms?

Unlike psychological egoism, ethical egoism cannot be refuted by pointing to counter-examples of people acting selflessly. It is not a claim about how people in fact behave but rather about how they should behave. Even if nobody is ever totally selfish, it could still be the case that they all should be.

One complaint that is sometimes brought against ethical egoism is that it is not really an ethical theory at all. In some ways it does resemble other ethical theories: it issues prescriptions about what we ought to do; and it issues the same prescriptions for people in relevantly similar situations. However, the argument goes that in other ways it diverges from what is generally thought of as an ethical theory in too radical a way: for example, it does not require that people sometimes make sacrifices without any compensation. It does not provide a single neutral ranking of scenarios that are better or worse: it is better for Smith if he gets the job, better for Jones if he gets it, but egoism says nothing about which scenario is simply better or worse.

For this reason many philosophers, who are cautious by nature, and keen on introducing new 'isms' wherever possible, revert to rational egoism, the view that it is rational (but perhaps not ethically right) to maximize one's own good. Anyone who is an ethical egoist is very likely to be a rational egoist too: if you think it's right to act in a certain way, you presumably also think that this provides you with a reason to act that way. However not all rational egoists are ethical egoists: a rational egoist might, for example, be a moral skeptic or nihilist, who believes that morality is bunk. Such a person can still maintain that, in the absence of moral prescriptions, you should act to maximize your own self-interest, but their 'should' does not mean what the ethical egoist's 'should' means. It signifies a rational obligation, not a moral one. Ethical egoism is a more committal theory, but the retreat to rational egoism strikes me as too cowardly for someone like Barney. Why should the ethical egoist accept that his egoism is not an ethical theory, just because it differs from other ethical theories in some important ways? Altruists do not have a monopoly on what counts as ethical, and their stipulating that anything which fails to meet their preferred criteria falls short seems just to be unfairly begging the question against the egoist, or assuming what they are supposed to be proving.

If ethical egoism is more difficult to refute than psychological egoism, that does not mean that we should necessarily accept it. For, as we noticed earlier, it is not enough for a philosophical theory to be consistent. We must have some reason to believe it's true. This raises the thorny question of how in general we should argue for an ethical theory. Since ethical theories make claims about what should be the case, not what is the case, scientific methods that involve just looking at how the world actually is seem to be inadequate. Any argument for an ethical theory will have to begin with common-sense views about what's right and wrong. There is significant disagreement about the extent to which ethical egoism is compatible with common sense.

It may surprise you to learn that Plato was an egoist. Indeed a reasonable argument can be made that all the Ancient Greeks were. This doesn't mean that Plato approved of Gyges-like behavior. In fact he did not. He thought that virtuous action was always in the agent's interest. One reason for this was that he believed that divine providence ensured that virtuous action was always rewarded, if not in this life then in the next, a view that is shared by adherents of most religions.

In these less religious times, divine reward has less universal appeal. We may feel, then, that ethical egoism diverges from common-sense morality more than the Ancient Greeks supposed. Consider an example dear to the hearts of all philosophers—saving a drowning ex-girlfriend from a lake. From an egoist standpoint, why should you dive in and get your best suit muddy? After all, ex-girlfriends are certainly not friends. If you just stand there on the bank and watch, some philosophers will hold you morally responsible for your ex's death, since they regard acts of omission as morally equivalent to acts of commission: failing to jump in the lake to save her is just the same as shooting her in the face.

In any case, if ethical egoism requires that you refuse to help, then it does go against common-sense views about what you ought to do. This might provide some ammunition for those who think it is not well-motivated. Also, you may feel that Barney is not really so hard-hearted as to stand by and watch anyone drown.

Fortunately, the egoist has a rejoinder. If he amends his egoism slightly, he can maintain that you ought to help the drowning ex. It may be that there are certain moral rules that the egoist is constrained to abide by in pursuing his egoism, for example that you should not kill the innocent (or even allow them to die). The existence of these rules need not threaten your egoism, for it is still the case that the only goal that the egoist seeks is his own good. Following the rules is not a goal; it is just something that it is not morally possible to avoid doing.

We can draw a comparison here with the game of chess. There are many reasons for playing chess: for a diverting pastime, for the intellectual benefits it can bring, or for the exquisite pleasure of watching your opponent squirm as you ram your passed pawn down her throat. However, once you're playing there is but one goal—checkmate. Of course there are lots of rules of chess. You can't achieve checkmate just by picking up your queen and placing it next to your opponent's king, if that move is not a legal move in the actual position. This does not mean that the chess player has some other goal than checkmate, for instance checkmating in accordance with the rules. Checkmating when in breach of the rules is not checkmating at all, for then you are no longer playing chess. Similarly, the egoist will insist that obeying the rules and acting against his self interest does not mean that he is no longer an egoist. A concession has been made: what makes an action right is no longer determined wholly by self-interest, since you must also refer to the rules. However, your ultimate aim is still just to maximize your own good.

An egoism amended along these lines to incorporate some moral absolutes, and which expands the ego to include friends, is actually more in keeping with common sense than other ethical theories which insist that you should treat everyone the same, whether they are complete strangers, friends, or even yourself. Barney is a stickler for rules: as Ted puts it, "I'm sick of all the rules. There's too many of them: the Hot-Crazy Scale, the Lemon Law, the Platinum Rule. If everyone in the world followed every one of your rules, the human race would cease to exist" ("The Platinum Rule"). So Ted's not a fan; but there's every reason to think that Barney would find this version of ethical egoism appealing.

And the Moral of the Story Is . . .?

Our look at egoism has taught us something important about Barney. When we first meet him, he can come across as a bit of a jerk, entertaining when viewed from a distance, but hardly someone we would choose as a close friend. Early on, Ted admits that he had no idea why he hung out with him ("Sweet Taste of Liberty"). However, as the series progresses, he quickly develops into its breakout character. We end up sympathizing with him and liking him at least as much as any of the others (something the writers evidently grew to realize, as his story becomes ever more central).

Our burgeoning affection towards Barney is not due to a relaxation of his selfish principles. In fact, we'd be disappointed if he compromised. What does become apparent is that he is no run-of-the-mill egotistical merchant banker. Part of what's attractive about Barney is his intellectual consistency. Everything he does can be seen to flow from a system of principles for guidance in practical affairs, or what is colloquially called a philosophy. And that philosophy is best captured by the sort of ethical egoism that we have described.

It's not just that a proper understanding of ethical egoism gives us a more profound insight into Barney's character. The reverse is also true. Barney is no moral monster. It is not merely his cleverness that makes him so likeable. If he were so alien to our own ethical world view, we might find him amusing, but we would not care about him. Barney's moral exemplar encourages us to revisit an ethical position that we might otherwise too quickly dismiss. Once we realize that egoism is consistent with treating the interests of friends as ends in themselves, and with recognising certain moral absolutes, the view immediately becomes more palatable.

Of course, I would never encourage anyone else to become an egoist. However, the next time you're considering faking a heart attack to get an ambulance to take you across town ("Subway Wars"), maybe it's something you'll bear in mind.

4

The Most Amazing, Strong, Independent Woman Barney Has Ever Banged

AMANDA YPMA

Kids, you're familiar with Dreamhouse Barbie and Career Barbie. Those are the images of women children have been presented with for generations. To this day, you can ask any seven-year-old girl and she'll tell you the difference.

Dreamhouse Barbie is a wife and mother. She's caring and warm, and her home and family are the number one priorities in her life. Career Barbie is all about the workplace. She business-suits up, and her career always comes first. She's childless and single. If she does have a Ken in her life he's a low priority, more of an afterthought really, because she doesn't need him anyway.

Just like with toys, the rest of pop culture follows suit. Movies and television almost always give audiences these same two options, and at first glance it appears *How I Met Your Mother* is doing the same with its two lead female characters. Lily is the traditional, nurturing wife and mother. She met her husband at eighteen, has only had one sexual relationship, and just for good measure she's also a kindergarten teacher with a shopping addiction. In other words, she could have been pulled straight from any romantic comedy. Then there's Robin. On the surface, particularly when we first meet her, she seems like the typical feminist career women who doesn't need a man and turns her nose up at love, but with Robin the writers throw us a curveball because the viewer soon discovers she can't be so easily defined.

"I wish you hadn't taught me how to hunt and fish and smoke cigars and drink scotch because that's not what girls do.

And, you know, the reason I throw like a girl, Dad, is because I am a girl," Robin laments in "Happily Ever After," and that in a nutshell is the inner struggle facing her character. What is expected of her as a woman? Can she be free to live however she wants without the need to stick to any pre-set path? Or, as ethical psychologist Carol Gilligan contends in her book *In a Different Voice*, are there certain traits all women fundamentally share and therefore certain rules they all must inherently follow?[1]

Without completely Tedding-out, a 'no' answer to the last question in philosophy is known as non-essentialism. Non-essentialist feminists like legal ethics professors Deborah Rhode, author of *Justice and Gender*,[2] and Drucilla Cornell, author of *Beyond Accommodation*, believe that women—including former Canadian pop stars turned journalists—cannot be boxed into one set of defining characteristics because all women and their experiences are unique and no two women's paths in life need to look the same.[3]

Since television lives in stereotypes, the playground of essentialism, we're virtually never shown this concept. Women are either traditional—pick a solid husband, get married, have kids—or they are classic feminists, focusing on their career while maintaining their single status. We're rarely shown the middle ground, but that is where Robin Scherbatsky lives. She's a woman, like many of us real women watching at home, who's torn between the two worlds. She feels the need to be strong and hide her emotions and live for her career, but at the same time she's lonely and yearns for love and companionship. She requires both sides of the coin to truly satisfy her yet she's told it must be one or the other. That's what causes Robin's series-long struggle that only ends when she learns the lesson of non-essentialism. That same lesson is there for the audience too simply by going along on Robin's journey from a career-obsessed woman who didn't believe in marriage and couldn't even use the term 'we'

---

[1] Carol Gilligan, *In a Different Voice* (Harvard University Press, 1982).

[2] Deborah L. Rhode, *Justice and Gender: Sex Discrimination and the Law* (Harvard University Press, 1989).

[3] Drucilla Cornell, *Beyond Accommodation: Ethical Feminism, Deconstruction, and the Law* (Routledge, 1991).

to a successful journalist on a major international network who also happens to be the bride of one of the biggest womanizers in television history.

Am I Wired Wrong or Something?

When we're first introduced to her, Robin views a woman's future as taking one of two paths, and she adamantly sees herself taking Path B, that of a career woman—or in her words "a serious journalist." She doesn't want children and she doesn't want marriage, end of story.

Even after entering into her first ever long-term relationship, episodes like "Brunch," "Moving Day," and "Something Blue" make it clear that Robin's views have not changed. She still wants to maintain her independence. Above all else, she still wants to take that career path. She still wants to travel the world and have adventures that do not include children or a husband who wants her to stay at home and raise them. She may be open to dating but not at the expense of compromising her own unique identity.

But while it's clear that Robin does not want to travel Path A that Lily has taken, her feminist side is constantly pressured to bend to these traditional things. This is illustrated best in the episode "Slutty Pumpkin" where Robin openly wonders if there's something deeply wrong with her because she doesn't want that world of lovey-dovey, picture perfect couples for herself.

Calling Slut

Robin may be preprogrammed to be Career Barbie, but the writers very purposefully place her into a group of close-knit, co-dependent friends, three of the four of whom staunchly believe in that fairy tale, Rom-Com, Dreamhouse Barbie ending and therefore push Robin towards it in addition to the coercion she already feels from society as a whole.

As early as Season One's "Nothing Good Happens After 2 A.M.," Robin feels the stigma of remaining single and choosing her career and independence over love and tradition. When she attends Career Day at Lily's kindergarten class the children mock her for having no fiancé or husband and compare her to a lonely old cat lady. One child even questions her sexuality. It's a vivid example of the pressure Robin feels to bow to that conventional lifestyle.

At the same time that Robin has everyone lining up to tell her what she should be they're also constantly pressuring her to avoid what they feel she shouldn't be. From her character's introduction, Robin's always had a free attitude towards sex and one-night stands. She's not only able to separate the physical from the emotional, that's actually her involuntary response. She views sex as a physical desire, a need that's totally separate from romance or love and therefore does not require any sort of emotional connection. In other words, she approaches sex in the same no-strings-attached, Path B way that Barney does.

As a man, Barney's liaisons are overlooked and sometimes even applauded by his friends, but not so for Robin. Instead she's judged for her open attitude towards sex divorced from love. She's called 'cold' or sometimes far worse. In "The Naked Man," Marshall announces he's "calling slut," labeling Robin in an extremely derogatory manner because the group discovered she had a one-night stand with a man she has no interest in seeing again. It's clearly sexism at its height, but rather than take up the feminist torch Robin quickly succumbs to peer pressure. She feels so badly about herself that she attempts to seriously date the man and pretend to have feelings for him just to save face until Marshall takes back his claim that she's a slut.

"The Naked Man" illustrates the double standard that exists for men and women, but more specifically it highlights how even Robin, a woman who presents herself as a forward-thinking feminist, still feels compelled to conform to the traditionally approved path for women.

Daddy Issues

Just so we won't miss the ideological war happening within her, the writers compound Robin's struggle with the history of her upbringing. With a domineering single father who wanted a son and raised her as a typical boy, Robin was automatically pushed into feminist thinking from a very young age. The abnormal, exaggerated experiences of her youth set up immediate turmoil for Robin as to gender roles and what a woman should want out of life.

In "Happily Ever After" and "Who Wants to Be a Godparent?" Robin talks about the horrors of her young life and how all signs of traditional femininity were punished. In "Mystery vs. History" she even tells of how she was literally left alone in the wilderness and forced to become independent and self-reliant simply to survive the ordeal. Those are just a few of the episodes that in sometimes comical, sometimes heartbreaking, but always unmistakable ways demonstrate how Robin has been programmed since childhood to believe that all "girly" traditional things are bad, and has instead been shoved down a path of unrelenting self-sufficiency with a complete focus on career.

Do we all have a maniacal father who forces us to burn our feminine clothes in an oil drum, pushes us out of a plane over a wolf-infested forest, and sends us off to military school if we're caught kissing our crush? Do all of our friends "call slut" and instead promote saying "I love you" on the very first date? Of course not, but by placing Robin squarely in the middle, caught between the two opposing philosophies, the writers create the instantly recognizable struggle facing countless modern women over which version of themselves they can and should be.

I Never Said Never

At the same time that Robin is tugged in opposite directions by friends, family, and society both to remain a stanchly independent, career-focused feminist and to bow to the time-honored love and marriage lifestyle, her dilemma is further complicated by the fact that she feels a secret desire for some of those traditional things herself, leading to an increased sense of guilt and confusion.

In the second half of "Nothing Good Happens After 2 A.M.," when Robin goes home to her empty apartment, she realizes that those kindergarteners were right; she is lonely. It's that loneliness that compels her to start a relationship with the very conventional Ted in the first place, something she's avoided for months.

As the series goes on, that side of Robin begins to increasingly escape the hold it's been under since childhood, and her longings for love and a long-term relationship become more and more apparent. A third of the way through Season Two, in "Atlantic City," Robin's reaches the point of willingness to admit that she actually might consider marriage someday.

By the time the show is in its third and fourth season, Robin has the chance to experience firsthand the life of a single, independent, globetrotting journalist, but she quickly discovers she doesn't like it at all. "Wait for It . . ." and particularly "We're Not from Here" reveal that, while living in Argentina, Robin was sad and lonely and the first thing she did was take the very traditional step of starting a long-term relationship with a local man she even brings back home with her. Once she settles into her normal life again, she finally admits how unhappy she is and that Island Robin isn't who she really wants to be.

Similarly, in Season Four, when her career starts to take off and she's offered her dream job overseas, Robin doesn't want to go. By her own words in "Intervention", what she really wants is to cling to the creature comforts of home and family. When she moves to Japan anyway she's miserable there all alone and winds up quitting her job and coming back home after only one episode. Repeating the same pattern, it's later revealed that in her short stay in Japan, Robin once again turned to the reassurance of the traditional by starting a relationship with a man there too.

Throughout the rest of Season Four it's increasingly apparent that there's much more to Robin than just the independent, professional attitude her dad foisted on her. In "Woooo!" Robin admits to being just like one of the sad, lonely, and confused career women that she and Lily befriend. In "Shelter Island" Robin confesses her wish to have Ted there as a fallback so she won't have to end up single and alone for the rest of her life. In "The Front Porch" she takes it a step farther by making a "forty pact" with Ted to marry each other when she turns forty if they haven't found anyone else. Three episodes later in "Mosbius Designs," Robin's openly disappointed with herself when she realizes she was settling for a guy simply because he was physically there in her apartment.

What it all adds up to is that Robin is one very adrift woman because complete self-reliant feminism doesn't appeal to her any more than a cookie-cutter housewife lifestyle, but she still believes those are the only two options open to her.

Catching Feelings

Around this same time period, Robin begins to earnestly fall in love with Barney very much against her will. The connection between their characters is evident as far back as Season One, particularly in "Zip, Zip, Zip" where it's first demonstrated that Barney truly sees Robin as she is and likes her exactly that way. "How Lily Stole Christmas" and the aforementioned "We're Not from Here," where Barney is the only one who can bring Robin out of her identity crisis, further strengthen their bond. Their special connection is on full display throughout all of Season Three, ultimately leading up to "Sandcastles in the Sand." In that key episode, Robin acknowledges that she misses the freedom to simply follow her heart and so she does just that, finally giving in to her attraction to Barney. It's the first sign of a chink in her emotional armor and what will become a shift in her priorities.

Not only is "Sandcastles" the episode that officially begins their romance, it also highlights what becomes an ongoing theme of the show, that Barney loves Robin for exactly who she is without compromise. Unlike the rest of the people in her life who are pushing or pulling her one way or the other, Barney tells Robin she doesn't have to conform to any standard and should just be herself, reiterating the non-essentialist moral of Robin's story.

That theme continues in Season Four episodes like "Do I Know You" and "The Possimpible." The attachment between Robin and Barney continues to intensify, and more importantly Barney establishes a pattern of repeatedly encouraging Robin's career pursuits whereas Ted and the others generally regard that aspect of her personality as the enemy.

Non-essentialist feminism is wrapped up within all aspects of the Robin and Barney love story. Barney always embraces all parts of Robin, including those that don't fit any specific, pre-existing standard of traditional femininity, making their romance unique to any of her other love interests. He doesn't care or object to the fact that she was raised as a boy, she smokes cigars, she drinks scotch, she has a free attitude towards sex, she never wants kids, and she still struggles profoundly with anything openly emotional. Rather than encouraging her to change, Barney loves and accepts all the varying parts of who Robin is, but sadly that's something she still has to learn to do herself.

Maybe I Want the Trouble

When Robin eventually does enter into a relationship with Barney, neither one of them's ready. There are too many personal demons they each need to work out privately. Nevertheless, the relationship forever changes them both and marks a major shift (salute) in her thinking. When Robin was first introduced she was a hardcore feminist who suppressed her inner longings for a relationship and love because she felt embarrassed and ashamed of them. She outwardly reveled in her single status. There was always casual sex to be had if she wanted it and if she got lonely she could repeatedly date a guy, though she was fondest of taking the three-week relationship exit.

Robin discovered over time that the free-thinking feminist lifestyle didn't completely suit her, but it's only through falling in love with Barney that she realizes once and for all that she wants and even needs that sort of love and connection in her life and she begins to openly embrace her conventional desires.

After their breakup, Robin tries to return to that independent woman whose career was her all-encompassing desire, but it doesn't work. Her career alone no longer fulfills her. She wants love and a meaningful, traditional relationship. "Slapsgiving 2: Revenge of the Slap" reveals early hints of this when Barney debunks Robin's aloof, untouchable, fiercely independent facade by telling her he knows she secretly dreams of marriage and a classic church wedding with a little white dress and a husband who will love and care for her. Robin's extreme reaction shows that his statement touches a definite nerve.

As Season Five progresses, now that those traditional longings have been fully unleashed in Robin, she can no longer manage to keep them tamped down. Months later, in "Of Course," she's still jealous and hurting, crying her eyes out over Barney, yearning for that love she had with him. At this point Robin truly jumps ship and progressively crosses over to the opposite side, becoming a woman who absolutely does *not* want to be single and is determined to land the "proper" guy.

This shift in Robin starts to aggressively take hold when she throws herself into a relationship with the first suitable man who comes along, Don. After that doesn't work out, she repeatedly struggles with the notion of being alone throughout all of Season Six. In "False Positive" she bemoans her continued single status but states that it's too painful for her to even think about. She tries her old standby of turning to her career for comfort, but she's still lonely and conflicted. Four episodes later, in "Desperation Day," Barney is able to easily see through Robin's claims that her career alone is enough.

Then in "Doppelgangers" and later in "The Stinson Missile Crisis," Robin makes the definitive leap from feminism to tradition by actually choosing a relationship over her career, something she has never before done. In both instances she turns down a prominent job opportunity in order to stay close to a man she wants to be involved with. In doing so Robin is fairly openly demonstrating that her career by itself cannot sustain her and isn't even her number one priority anymore.

By Season Seven's "Mystery vs. History" and "The Slutty Pumpkin Returns" Robin seems like a different woman. Six years after the original "Slutty Pumpkin," Robin has gone from a complete inability to be part of a pair and utter revulsion at the idea of couples sharing food and wearing matching costumes to doing just that with Barney, frequently referring to the two of them as 'we' and 'us'. These episodes make Robin's shift from the feminist to the traditional path complete.

What's That Saying? Two Wrongs Don't Make a Right?

In late Season Five through Season Seven, Robin may have switched paths but she's more conflicted than ever before because she continues to see it as an all or nothing decision. Since self-reliant Path B didn't make her happy, she goes overboard into Lily's extremist version of traditional Path A at the expense of not only her feminist side but of what her heart truly wants. While actively seeking out love and marriage, Robin repeats the mistake of seeing things in black and white and now goes too far to the other end of the spectrum. The result is equally destructive to her life, translating into an all-out identity crisis.

Where she was once assured and self-confident, Robin now doubts virtually everything about herself. In "Big Days,"

"Unfinished," and "Subway Wars" she sees rejection by a man as a negative reflection on herself. Further still, in "Baby Talk," she believes Ted when he tells her that her independent nature and self-sufficiency are directly at odds with any hope of ever finding love and so instead she needs to become a stereotypically weak, needy, dependent woman if she ever wants to make a relationship work.

Barney continues to be the sole voice of reason, echoing the message of Robin's story. He's the only one to tell her that the very qualities that traditional thinking puts down are part of what makes her uniquely awesome and she should embrace them rather than try to change herself because there's absolutely nothing wrong with her exactly as she is.

But Robin persists in shifting too far into conventional thinking. Time and time again she makes traditional choices she views as proper and acceptable but she hates it all the while because she's fighting her true nature. She's so conflicted that for much of Season Seven Robin is barely holding it together. In "The Stinson Missile Crisis" she's reduced to hysterically crying under desks and tables, and by "Tick Tick Tick" she vocally wonders why any man would ever love a mess like her.

Can You Believe We Almost . . . ? Good Thing We Didn't

Nowhere is the mistake of denying her true nature while going to the traditional extreme clearer than in Robin's relationship with Barney. Her attempts to mold their romance into a traditional, Lily-esque idea of what love and commitment must look like rather than just being their true selves is one of the main factors that leads to their initial downfall.

Robin's very feelings for Barney are an embodiment of her entire struggle. Her love for him and the relationship they have, much like her own identity, doesn't fit into either philosophy. It's a bad idea from a feminist perspective and an equally bad idea from a traditional perspective. Whichever side she chooses, both dictate that she must bury that love and conform to set standards.

Robin loves Barney and desperately wants to be with him, but he doesn't fit into the traditional idea of what's safe and acceptable in a husband and what she should therefore want.

Conventional principles mark him as a risky choice that will never work out. This is highlighted over and over again, exceptionally so in "Challenge Accepted" and "The Best Man." In both episodes Robin longs to be with Barney but feels like she can't start something with him because of his womanizing and the failure of their first relationship that never could fit into either box.

Her indecision about Barney reaches a turning point in "Tick Tick Tick." Kevin fits the classic idea of a safe and appropriate mate and Robin falls heavily into that trap. She's convinced that if she wants love and marriage she has to have it in an all-around traditional way.

Robin's inability to leave Kevin is just part of a pattern of willingness to settle for men she doesn't even love simply because she thinks they're suitable. She tries to sell herself these relationships that tradition regards as the "right thing" but it never works and she's never happy because her place, much like her love for Barney, lies somewhere in the blurred lines of the middle.

Kids, I'm Glad You Guys Aren't Real

No matter which side she chooses Robin continues to experience longing for the other, leaving her confused and feeling like she's betraying both philosophies. This is never truer than in Robin's brush with motherhood.

The only thing Season One Robin was firmer about not wanting than a long-term traditional relationship was that she never wanted to be a mom, but even the issue of children becomes murkier over time. "Little Boys" is the first example of this. Robin dates a single father in answer to a challenge set by the group. She ends up bonding with the man's young son and actually enjoys spending time with the child.

Almost exactly a season later, in "Not a Father's Day," Robin's caught with a stolen baby sock in her purse and finally admits she doesn't know what she wants out of life but she might be warming to the idea of having children someday.

It all comes to a head in Season Seven's "Symphony of Illumination" when Robin believes that she actually is pregnant with Barney's child only to discover that she's not having a baby now and in fact she's physically unable to ever do so. At first she reacts as early series Robin would by insisting that she never wanted children anyway so it's for the best, but right away it's clear that Robin's masking a deep sadness over her inability to have a biological child.

This confusing pain she feels only adds to Robin's inner turmoil. She sits alone on a park bench in the snow imagining her potential children with Barney and how a traditional life with him could have been. She ends up weeping inconsolably, and weeks later in "Tailgate" she continues to refer to her diagnosis as the event that forced her to give up a dream she never knew she had. Yet, while mourning the loss of any future children with Barney, Robin simultaneously experiences guilt for feeling that sadness in the first place when the feminist career ambitions she still possesses continue to dictate that kids would only hold her back.

On the one hand, the guarantee of no children means there will never be any restraints on her career. On the other hand, tradition has a hold on Robin too. In "The Drunk Train," she feels less than whole because of her infertility and she fiercely worries that no man will ever want her without the ability to give him that traditional marriage with two point five kids. Just like with her career and love life, Robin is caught between the two worlds with her infertility as well.

A Little Ways Down the Road

The Robin who's a self-described mess, hiding under desks and crying while swilling wine directly from the bottle, is a far cry from the Robin we see in the flashfoward at the end of Season Eight's "The Pre-Nup." Here Robin is a self-assured woman with a beaming smile who's taking a break from her high-powered, international lead anchor job to meet her fiancé for lunch. That Robin just oozes with happiness. So what accounts for the striking difference?

From mid-Season Eight onward, beginning in the episode "Splitsville," when after a declaration of love from Barney she breaks ties with yet another boyfriend she isn't truly interested in, Robin slowly begins to accept that she doesn't have to settle for a guy she doesn't love for the sake of tradition, nor does she have to settle for being single just to maintain her independent self and career.

For years she was untrue to herself and the future she really wanted by trying to choose only one limited path. Doing so left her miserable and conflicted because she isn't entirely one or the other. Recognizing that she doesn't have to fully accept or fully reject either ideology is the final piece in the puzzle of Robin's character development. The key to her happiness lies in finally accepting that there's no singular definition for women and how their lives must go. She's allowed to make her own personal blend of the two styles that best suits her individual needs and in that way custom tailor her own happy ending that doesn't have to look like anyone else's.

If she wants to get married, that's okay. If she wants to be forever single, that's okay too. If she wants to travel the world alone, that's fantastic, but if she's lonely there's nothing wrong with that either. What she wants and what she needs, not what anyone else tells her she should be, is the fundamental goal. She can do and be anything she wants in whatever relationship she wants without worrying about falling in line with some rigid design of how things must look at "The End."

It's okay to not want kids, and it's even okay to falter a little from time to time. It's okay to fall in love, even the head over heals, beyond your control kind of love, and even if it defies all the rules. Robin can be a strong, successful journalist and business woman who also happens to never be alone because she's very happily married to an extremely non-traditional guy who is the farthest thing from "husband material" possible.

By allowing Robin to marry instead of remaining the forever single career woman, and just as importantly by letting her choose to be a wife but not a mother, the writers are telling us that there is no essentialism when it comes to women and what path their lives take. There is no one shining example that we all must strife for. Lily can be a traditional wife and mother but Robin doesn't have to be. Robin can be a feminist, independent career woman but also fall in love and get married.

Robin Scherbatsky is the poster child for the modern non-essentialist woman. Very few women are actually Lilys, who have it all fall into place at such a young age. For most of us it's not that simplistic and straightforward; most of us do exist in that middle ground. By featuring a female lead like Robin, who's dealing with this very same thing, *How I Met Your Mother* acknowledges the inner struggle that women face but it also gives us a solution. A woman should embrace what Robin has done: make whatever happy ending best suits her, and in Robin and Barney's "Robin 101" style give a thumbs up to anyone who doesn't like it.

5
Barney's Magical World of Self-Deception

CARTER HARDY

Kids, Barney Stinson is not as awesome as he seems. He's a trick of the light; a man trying to be himself and failing. He's like one of his own magic tricks: flashy and fun to watch, but after seeing it a dozen times, it becomes old and predictable. We all know who Barney is. His entire persona can be summed-up in a few consistent, self-defined, lifestyle choices. Barney is:

- **A businessman (though what exactly he does is a mystery)**
- **A lady's man who can get any girl into bed, even if it requires some intricate plan from his playbook**
- **A bro who worships the bro code**
- **A suit enthusiast**
- **An opponent of marriage and relationships**

In defining himself in these ways, he is forcing himself to be predictable. But everyone makes lifestyle choices, right? Ted chose to be an architect, Marshall chose to love Lily, and Robin chose to stop being a Canadian pop star. Isn't everyone predictable to some extent?

It's not just that Barney is predictable. It's that he's unknowingly forcing himself to be predictable. Aside from Ted saying "I love you" to any girl he dates, Barney is the most predictable character in the group, and this is no one's fault but his own.

Barney is doing something very special with regards to his own freedom. He is warping his entire world, making it perfect for him to be the way that he is. He is locking his actions and personality into a stagnant state. This magical world that Barney has created for himself is the greatest of all self-deceptions. It's legen-wait-for-it . . . deception!

I Dare You Guys to Dare Us to Make Out

At the core of this issue of self-deception is Barney's freedom of choice. We can't claim that Barney is deceiving himself unless he was free to not deceive himself. While there are many philosophical views about the nature of freedom, one that particularly rings true with Barney is the theory of Jean-Paul Sartre.

Sartre was a French existential philosopher, which means that he examined philosophical issues beginning from the standpoint of the individual. Unlike some other schools of philosophy that look for objective information about the world, existentialism is a cultural movement that is interested in the world as experienced by the individual. For an existentialist, individual existence and subjective knowledge are the most important.

In his book *Being and Nothingness* (Citadel Press, 1974), Sartre says that we're completely free to do whatever we want (p. 429). He doesn't mean that we're free to break the laws of physics by flying or walking through walls. Rather, he means that Marshall is free to make the jump to the adjoining roof (if he can build up the courage). Nor does Sartre mean that we're morally free to kill and steal. Even though Lily is physically free to steal when exacting her own brand of justice, that doesn't mean that it's moral to steal. She simply has that choice available to her, and she is free to choose it if she wants to.

This goes for everyone. We are all free to choose any action that is physically possible for us in any situation. For example, when Ted met Barney in the bar, Ted could have taken any number of actions in response to Barney:

- **Ted could have left the bar in order to avoid Barney**

- He could have told Barney to leave

- He could have ignored Barney until Barney left himself, or

- He could have even poured a drink on Barney's suit!

The possibilities are endless. However, Ted chose to put up with Barney (despite Barney being "kind of a jackass") and that was Ted's free choice.

There was a time when Barney was also presented with a life-changing choice. When his girlfriend left him for a suited-up businessman, he had a number of choices before him:

- He could have continued as he was, gone to Nicaragua, and hoped to find love again

- He could have broken down, depressed by the situation, and moved back in with his mom

- He could have fought the guy, whether he thought he could win or not

Again, the possibilities are endless. Barney was free to make a choice, and he chose to become a stereotypical, suit-wearing businessman. By becoming his enemy, he could get everything that he thought would make him happy.

The problem of self-deception arises when we start to choose actions as if they're our only options. When we deceive ourselves into thinking that there is only one possible action that we can choose, we have denied our freedom. Sartre calls this denial of our freedom "living in bad faith," but this is essentially just a special kind of self-deception (p. 44). We're deceiving ourselves and thereby denying our true freedom.

Barney made the choice to wear a suit, work for a corporation, and try to pick up women, but none of these actions is the problem. The problem is that Barney is acting as if these are the only choices that will bring him happiness. In performing these actions continually and consistently, he is deceiving himself that he can't do otherwise.

Of Course You're Living in Bad Faith, Take a Look at Yourself, You Dumb Bro

In choosing the specific persona of a stereotypical business-man, Barney is illustrating one of Sartre's most famous examples of bad faith. In his *Essays in Existentialism* (Citadel Press, 1993), Sartre uses the example of a waiter, rather than a businessman, so consider Wendy the Waitress (p. 167).

Imagine that Wendy was not being her normal, friendly, hates-Marshall-for-making-her-carry-out-the-recycling self. Instead, imagine that Wendy is trying to walk around with perfect posture, excellent manners, and catering to her customers' every demand. This would not be Wendy acting freely; this would be Wendy play-acting and pretending to be a waitress. In other words, this would be Wendy being a waitress, not a waitress who happens to be Wendy.

The difference is subtle, but important, like the difference between encyclo-PEE-dia and encyclo-PAY-dia. On the one hand, we have the Wendy who we're familiar with from the show. Here, Wendy is being herself, but also being a waitress. She is being a waitress in a way that does not conflict with her freedom to be herself.

On the other hand, we have the Wendy from the waitress example. Here, she's play-acting and trying to be a stereotypical waitress in spite of herself. The "trying to be a waitress" is a form or self-deception because Wendy is denying herself the other options available to her. In deciding that her only options are those that make her a stereotypical waitress, she is ignoring all of the other possible actions.

It's the same with Barney trying to be a stereotypical businessman. When he decided to become like the man who stole his girlfriend, he started play-acting as a businessman. He went out, got cleaned up, and bought himself a suit. He got a job at a corporation and he detached himself from committed relationships. Barney began acting as we would expect a businessman to act, curving all of his possible actions to support his new persona.

However, not all of Barney's decisions are actions. Often, he will simply deny the reality of a situation. Take for example that time Barney simply tuned-out when the group was suffering from a breakdown of their relationship-blinders. Lily chews food like a blender full of rocks; Robin is too liberal with the term "literal;" and Marshall sings nonsensical (yet, let's face it, really awesome and catchy) songs. When it's Barney's turn to have his flaws listed, everyone has something to contribute:

- **He sometimes talks in a weird, high-pitched voice;**

- **He uses lame catchphrases, and**

- **He often spaces-out, ignoring what others are saying**

Barney tunes back in just in time to retort, "See, you can't think of anything because I'm awesome!" If something is going to contradict part of his persona (in this case, his perfect awesomeness), then he ignores the situation entirely. To acknowledge the situation would require him to choose an action, which is the kind of freedom he is trying to deny.

Sartre's own example of this is one that Barney would love. It's an example that Barney can take to heart, or at least to bed. To explain how the denial of a situation can be a form of self-deception, Sartre uses the example of a woman who is being hit on by a man (p. 160). In this case, the woman is the one who is in bad faith, while the man is someone like Barney.

Imagine Barney trying to pick up a girl and he's following all of his rules of seduction. He's saying the girl's name a lot, subtly putting her down, and making physical contact. Now, when Barney is touching her knee, the girl notices that he is touching her knee and ignores it, while at the same time not stopping it. Here, the girl is deceiving herself because the girl is denying the true nature of the situation. In doing so, she doesn't need to make a decision about either rejecting him or accepting his advance. She is deceiving herself about her possible actions and remaining in a neutral state where she has no free choices.

Choosing not to act may seem uncommon for Barney. We've all seen his video resume. He is a man of action. We may not know what he does, but he is always doing something. However, like the girl from the example, there are times when he ignores the situation. At one time, he was at risk of being fired, but continued to act as if everything was perfectly normal. He simply chose not to acknowledge the situation. That way, he would not need to make a choice that could contradict his persona. This denial effectively deceived him as to his possible actions.

One final example concerns a man who is trying to decide who he is, such as when Barney is grappling with his feelings of love for Robin. If he thinks that he can't be in love because he is the kind of man that has one-night stands and doesn't settle down, then he is deceiving himself based on his past. That is, he is limiting his present options based on his past decisions. He's trying to be consistent to his persona, in spite of his freedom to act however he wants.

On the other hand, if he says that he's the kind of person who does fall in love, then he is also deceiving himself. In this case, the deception is from the future, rather than the past. Barney is essentially saying, "I am now going to be the kind of guy that falls in love and will base my actions on what that kind of person would do." This is no different from the other option. Either way he chooses, Barney is not doing what would come naturally. He is denying his own freedom to act as he pleases.

Barney desires consistency in his life, so he defines himself in a specific way and follows those guidelines. That is why he is living in bad faith, and that's why he is so predictable.

The Magician's Best Friend

It's tough to blame Barney for wanting a little consistency, especially since his real life is lacking in it. His father left him when he was a child. His first love broke his heart. Not to mention that, when he does admit that he loves someone, it always fails. Barney has not had an easy life, and yet he continues to be perfectly happy in his day-to-day life. This happiness with his current persona is the problem. Along with other emotions, it's the reason he falls so easily into self-deception.

As Barney's dad says, "a magician's best friend is a drunk audience." Drunken people are less attentive to the trick, and therefore much easier to fool and entertain. It's the same thing with emotions and self-deception. When in an emotional state, people see the world in a way that makes it easier to act in a certain way. Barney may not be physically drunk like Beercules, but he is definitely drunk on his emotions and ready to be tricked.

In his book *Sketch for a Theory of the Emotions* (Routledge, 1962), Sartre defines emotions as magical transformations of the world (p. 39). He says that we use emotions to perceive the world in ways that we want it to be—ways that make the world easier for us to deal with. Emotions are not just how we react to the world; they are ways of structuring our world.

Remember the way that Marshall becomes obsessed with the "best burger"? The thought of that burger makes him so happy, while the thought of other burgers being equal to it makes him sad or angry. In feeling this way, Marshall is constructing a magical world where there is only one burger like the "best burger" and all other burgers are just poor imitations. This limits freedom because it limits options. By only allowing for the one "best burger" he eliminates the options of all other burgers.

Barney's whole world is magical like this. As a child, his mom told him that Bob Barker was his father and he was more than happy to believe it. It explained a lot. If Bob Barker was his father, then his father would always be busy with *The Price Is Right*, which would explain why he was never around. It would also give Barney an excuse to not contact him, as well as someone to look up to.

At its core, Barney's happiness was an escape from the truth, because the truth would mean that his real father was still out in the world. If Barney were to accept this, then he would need to make a choice about whether or not to find his real father.

This would be too hard to do, so Barney settled into his happiness. Using his emotions, he constructed a magical world where Bob Barker was his father and there was no confusion. Barney never needed to go searching for his real father. His happiness restricted his freedom to do so.

When he met Bob Barker, Barney had the perfect opportunity to tell him that Barney was his son. However, he chose not to. His fear that he may be wrong, and his happiness with the answer that he already had, led Barney to keep the information to himself. He preferred the magical world where he was happy, rather than the real world where he would need to make a difficult decision about finding his real father.

It's not just this decision that Barney wants to avoid. He wants to avoid almost all of them. He doesn't want to make complicated decisions about how to dress, so he always chooses suits. Suits make him happy, everything else disgusts him, and it supports his view of himself as a businessman. The decision is easy.

He doesn't want to choose someone to be with for the rest of his life, so he just picks up women for one-night stands. The idea of having his heart broken again makes him sad and scared, so he eliminates all the possible actions that could lead to heartbreak.

Barney's world is constructed to support who he thinks he is and who others expect him to be. However, he could be otherwise. Sometimes he is.

Not the Purple Dinosaur

Barney's world doesn't need to be a magical escape from reality. He allows it to be that way. Like any other action, Sartre says that emotions can be freely chosen or denied (*Sketch* p. 40). When Barney gets mad at Ted for breaking up a catfight between Robin and Lily, it's because he thinks he should get mad about such things. He could easily choose to be happy when people break up catfights, but he doesn't. By thinking he needs to get mad at the end of a catfight, Barney has chosen this specific way to limit his own freedom.

Barney says, "When I feel sad, I stop being sad and be awesome instead." He can freely choose his emotional states, and he does, but only in ways that support his persona. If he is feeling one emotion, there's no reason that he couldn't change to feel another emotion. He just chooses not to.

Sadly, the truth is that Barney's deceiving himself more often than not. He's happy when he womanizes and sad when he breaks the Bro Code because that's the type of person he thinks he's supposed to be. He allows himself to adopt emotional states to support that version of himself—emotional states that deceive him about his true freedom.

However, the real proof of Barney's self-deception is that he's not always deceiving himself. Sometimes he acts in ways that are not consistent with his self-image. On occasion, he is a few other things that I did not mention earlier. Barney is:

- **A laser tag enthusiast**

- A magician

- A loyal friend who would fly all the way to California just to help get Lily and Marshall back together

- Someone who desperately wants a true friend, to the point that he despairs when Ted says he has outgrown Barney

- In love with Robin, to the point where he cannot convince himself otherwise, no matter how hard he tries

At times, Barney is so compelled that he throws caution to the winds and makes a choice in spite of himself. In this way, he exercises his freedom and chooses an action among all of his possible actions. He's not doing it because he feels he needs to. He's doing it because he wants to.

When he realizes that he loves Robin, it shakes him to his core. It doesn't fit with his image of himself. He's not the kind of guy who falls in love and commits to one woman. He's the kind of guy who sleeps around. Loving Robin is not a choice that's usually available to him in his magically constructed world.

When he actually chooses to pursue that love, he is acting freely. He is doing what he wants to do, despite the damage it does to the consistency of his persona.

The same goes for when he tries to reunite Marshall and Lily. In his normal view of himself, he would never support a lasting, monogamous relationship—especially one that is about to be bound by marriage. However, when his friends were in trouble, he acted outside of his magical world of limited choices. He helped bring them back together and didn't even take credit for his actions. Barney may be the most predictable character in the group, but when he chose these actions, I admit that I assumed wrong.

Wait for It . . .

It's true that Barney is, more often than not, living in bad faith. He defines himself in a very specific way and he play-acts in ways that reinforce that definition. This makes him very predictable because we expect him to act in the same way that he expects himself to act. He could always act differently, but that would be difficult. He has emotional connections to the world that make it easy for him to be the way he is.

He's happy to wear suits, womanize, and uphold the Bro Code. That's the way he wants to be. The way that his emotions have structured the world is only helping him be that way. Yet there's always hope for Barney.

He has broken out of bad faith before and he can do it again. As time goes on, he's becoming more and more unhappy with his created persona. Most importantly, it is getting harder for him to be happy with one-night stands, when he knows that he is in love with Robin. More and more often, he is realizing other options that are available to him. It's getting more difficult to predict what he will do next. As his emotions change, his magical world will start to break apart, and it will become progressively easier for him to act freely. All we can do is . . . wait for it.

II

True Story!

6

The Bro Code as a Relational Starter

FRANK G. KARIORIS

Kids, in the nineteenth century famous bro Mark Twain remarked "To get the full value of joy you must have someone to divide it with." And here is Friedrich Nietzsche: "Shared joys, not shared sufferings, make a friend."

Bros have existed for millennia and have remained a constant necessity. It is high time that Barney is given a place amongst history's great bros and is recognized for his brilliant contribution to relationships, embodied with the publication of *The Bro Code*. But Barney's contributions may not be all positive and one should question whether this is negated by the harm done with *The Playbook* and its fixation on conning women into bed.

Throughout the years, Barney has told countless stories, and elaborated on more than his fair share of rules ("I only have one rule . . .") and theories, from the Lemon Law to the Platinum Rule to the Mermaid Theory (necessarily covering all the bases of legal, regulatory, and theoretical rules). Amongst these countless theories and laws that Barney has put forth, there is a particular set of rules which form the basis for men's relationships with each other. These rules, together, form the Bro Code.

The Bro Code is a series of rules and laws governing the behavior between two or more bros. It is, in essence, the Bible for relations between men. And, much like the Bible, it's full of many useful pieces of wisdom as well as some not so helpful ones. And also like the Bible, there are inconsistencies, errors, omissions, and some items which are just plain stupid. As almost an exact biblical reference, Article 60 states that one should honor thy mother and father—of course giving a vastly different reasoning for such a rule ("A Bro shall honor thy father and mother, for they were once Bro and Chick").

While first set down in writing in 1776 by Barnabus Stinson on the back of the Constitution ("The Goat"), the Bro Code has a long history stretching back to biblical times. Pulled together from various fragmentary sets of rules, the Bro Code aims to strengthen the bonds of brotherhood between men, and to assist men in getting laid—the most important challenge society faces according to the Bro Code.

The most important contribution of the Bro Code has nothing to do with getting laid. The true importance of the Bro Code is the realization and strengthening of the bonds of 'brotherhood'—between men, and between men and women.

Much like one contextualizes earlier authors for racism, political beliefs, or other opinions which we in the twenty-first century have moved beyond, it is with a similar notion that we should approach the Bro Code. For there is certainly sexism in various parts of the Bro Code (let's just admit it). Just as we can look past the fact that George Washington had slaves, I hope you will look beyond the sexism as I show how the Bro Code can be used as a starting place for improving men's relations with other men, and, surprisingly, women.

To Bro or Not to Bro

There's a distinct difference between a bro and a friend, though the exact nature of this difference might not always be clear. The Code says that a bro is someone who will "give you the shirt off his back . . . a lifelong companion you can trust will always be there for you."[1] It's with this that we start to see the difference, and it's here where it's important first to understand in some small way ideas of gender and masculinity.

Masculinity in America today is defined most often in relation to others. This creates not only a public identity but also a sense of competition. One need look no further than when Ted, Barney, and Jim argue over who can be with Maggie in "The Window" or the literal fight between Ted and Marshall in "The

---

[1] Barney Stinson and Matt Kuhn, *The Bro Code* (Simon and Schuster, 2009), p. 1.

Duel." This overt competitive spirit is not just something that men do, but is part of their identity through which they interact with others.

The notion that men compete is, I'm sure, not something new to anyone reading this. The real question is: why do men compete? While there isn't one exact answer, it's due in part to the tentative nature of masculine structures which are bound up in the maintenance of hegemony. Hegemony is the idea of dominance over other groups which are subordinated and oppressed. In this case, hegemonic masculinity creates a situation where all other versions of masculinity are forced to compete socially with the dominant. Hegemony is the school bully who makes everyone else give them their lunch money. It is a similar situation, on a broader scale, of how hegemonic masculinity pushes other men around, as well as pushing women around.

Men's Relations Now

Competition creates a situation where men feel attacked at all times and need to be on guard for fear of loss or losing. The harsh reality is that in a competition between men, which in the spirit of masculine rivalry is the only true competition, there must almost always be a loser.

As Barney so eloquently puts it to Marshall in "The Scorpion and the Toad," the world is "a lawless post-apocalyptic wasteland. I may be your best friend, but in this world it's every hombre for himself." This is the mentality that men frequently approach situations, and relationships, with—not what one would call healthy.

This is the basis of many male relationships, overly competitive and unfriendly. It should not be shocking then to realize that this is how men see relationships, and how they continue treating relationships. Another ramification of this is that men's relationships with women frequently are treated as spaces of competition as well.

As male relations have been made to be competitive and combative sights of interaction, this discourages them from connecting emotionally with each other and with women around them, which in turn makes their relationships seem less personal and thereby more competitive.

These cyclical negative relationships are premised on societal ideas about how men should act, but there are situations where they can be overcome. Renowned philosopher and social scientist Michel Foucault talked about how the relationships and bonds in times of war and conflict connected and sustained men through the most destitute conditions, putting men in a situation which made it possible to move beyond the taboos stopping men's affections and emotionally healthy relationships. In an interview entitled 'Friendship as a Way of Life' Foucault shows not only the conditions which allow for healthier male relationships, but also the effect they can have.

While this has, in some way, described men's relations with each other, we must come back, continually, to the fact that men don't exist outside of their relations with women, and it is therefore crucial to see that these relations between men point to men's relations with women as well.

A Bro Always . . .

While *The Bro Code* doesn't give one fixed definition of what a bro is, by looking at the various articles it becomes clear. There are more than a few articles to the Bro Code, and some of them are written in a fashion which disguises the true intent of the article, but we can extract from the Code the five top qualities of what it means to be a Bro.

The Five Top Qualities of a Bro

1. Loyalty (Articles 1, 13, 147)

2. Friendliness (Articles 17, 46)

3. Equality (Articles 22, 37, 134)

4. Strong bonds with friends (Articles 13, 127)

5. Generosity in all things (Articles 65, 90, 114)

These qualities, I think we can all agree, are important and worthwhile values. While pointing out some of the better

---

"Friendship as a Way of Life" in *Ethics: Subjectivity and Truth* (Penguin, 1997).

aspects of the Bro Code, it is also important to realize that much of it is not as positive. Much of it is actually downright sexist. I've compiled the five most seemingly sexist things in the Bro Code.

The Most Sexist Things in The Bro Code *(in No Particular Sexist Order)*

1. When a Bro meets a chick, he shall endeavor to find out where she fits on the Hot/Crazy Scale before pursuing her (Article 86).

2. A Bro never cries (Article 41).

3. A Bro keeps his booty calls at a safe distance (Article 92).

4. A women's lust for gossip is matched only by her passion to have babies and accessorize (Article 101).

5. When on the prowl, a Bro hits on the hottest chick first because you just never know (Article 31).

These sexist comments, while not the only ones, represent some of the sexist thought that infiltrates the Bro Code. Some of this stems from an attempt to distance men from close relations with each other, as well as close relations with women.

Women, or 'getting laid,' is used as a way to allow men to have more affectionate relationships with other men. In this way, women become placeholders for the true purpose, or the true meaning, of relationships with other men. Distancing men from women creates a way that men can relate to each other more without seeming 'affectionate,' or any other trait deemed effeminate.

Yet for all the sexual bravado (or 'bro-vado') that the Bro Code claims, sex is a topic which the Bro Code sees as something not meant to be discussed publicly or in any detail (see Articles 48 and 146), and could be seen not to be used as a measure of masculinity.

The unattainability of masculinity pushes men into a conditional identity, one which is always at risk and in contest. Men must always fight for their masculinity, needing it to be validated by other men. In psychoanalytic terms, while women lack the phallic (the symbolic representation of male reproductive potency—virility), men are always in fear of lack of the phallic. It is this need to secure their masculinity which drives men away from close relationships with other men, and to degrade women and their relationships with them as a way to fortify their own masculinity.

Much like masculinity in America, the Bro Code is filled with inconsistencies and contradictions. Men are supposed to be strong, powerful, and unemotional, yet must simultaneously be loving fathers and husbands. A Bro can take a woman as a Bro or wingwoman, but will eventually want to sleep with her (according to "The Mermaid Theory"). These inconsistencies present men today not merely with a challenge, but also with an impossible task.

The Playbook

The Playbook makes no qualms about its goals, making it very clear what it intends. Its stated aim is that "you'll be able to approach any beautiful woman you want and trick her into sleeping with you." A bold statement, made more reasonable by the fact that Barney designed it and that he has "slept with enough hotties to overbook a commercial airliner" (p. xv).

The Playbook states that there are four things that women are sexually aroused by: money, fame, vulnerability, and emotion and spiritual fulfillment (p. xvii). While these may sound outrageous, and even sexist, you'd be surprised to find how many 'scientific' (that's to say, pseudo-scientific) studies claim to have demonstrated the same conclusion.

"Other seduction methods preach 'social dynamics' in which you insult women in an attempt to attract them. I find that approach both demeaning and offensive. Rather than degrade women, *The Playbook* centers on the profound, positive, and personal changes you can make to trick hot sluts into sleeping with you" (p. xvi). Barney elaborates on this, stating that the *Playbook* "focuses on transforming you" (p. xviii). It's this transformative approach that, in some ways, supposedly separates the *Playbook* from the trickery of other methods of attracting women, specifically the 'pick-up' artist community.

Just as I picked out the most sexist things in *The Bro Code*, I figured it was important to do that for *The Playbook* as well.

The Most Sexist Things in the Playbook

1. Pretty much everything

Sexist to Men as Well?

While *The Playbook* is blatantly sexist to women, sexism is directed at men as well.

"Recent evidence suggests that women enjoy sex [as well]" (p. xvii). Though it is in no way wrong to suggest that women have an empowered sexuality, there are still issues with this when seen from the male perspective. While empowering women to have their own sexuality, it simultaneously maintains and perpetuates the notion that men are always horny.

In this way, while freeing women, it maintains a strict idea about men and sexuality that can be seen throughout both *The Bro Code* as well as *The Playbook*. This can also be seen in the caricatured way Barney celebrates sleeping with two hundred women. It's shown clearly after Barney and Robin separate, in musical form, in the song "Bang Bang Bangity Bang" or the over-the-top Bangtoberfest and accompanying motto "This Time it's REALLY Not Personal."

This caricature of men's sexuality is only further played up in the *Playbook* for Chicks, where the one play in it says that any woman can pick up any man, anytime, anywhere, just by being a woman (*Playbook*, p. 65).

Aside from overly sexualizing men, it also attributes to them a callousness towards love. The "Fall in Love" Play (p. 113), while allowing that men could fall in love, also makes it seem as if it is a passing thing that is easily forgotten and neglected.

Bro to Bro

This focus on men's relations and implicitly discussing 'bro' as connected to men is due to the fact that this is how it is shown and seen. I would like to, as we continue forward, begin the process of transforming this vision of the Bro Code. Rather

[3] Barney Stinson and Matt Kuhn, *The Playbook: Suit Up, Score Chicks, Be Awesome* (Simon and Schuster, 2010), p. xiii.

[4] For amazing insight into this community, see Neil Strauss, *The Game: Penetrating the Secret Society of the Pickup Artists* (Regan, 2005).

than simply being about men's relations with each other—which it is also about—it's connecting to men's relations with women as well.

First, men's relations with each other, what we might call 'homosocial relations'. The Bro Code is put forward as the formation of a set of guidelines for male homosocial relations. In its own way, it seeks to give men some definition to their relationships. Though it is offered as a set of guidelines merely for men's relations with each other, the way these rules are enacted can also be seen as positive ideas about men's relations with women. Throughout the show, the characters seek to find themselves and define their lives. Most of the time it's through their relationships with other characters that they start to define who they are.

In "Sweet Taste of Liberty" Barney tells Ted that "Without you, I'm just the dynamic uno." It's the relationships (and in Ted's life, the stories) that structure who they are. It's because of this that our relationships with others are so important, and so, how we define a bro is critical.

The five attributes of a bro are loyalty, friendliness, equality, strong bonds with friends, and generosity. Throughout the show these qualities shine through in the relations between Barney, Marshall, Ted, Robin, and Lily. Even in cases where they contravene other articles in the code, these rules take precedence.

All of these traits are embodied in the competition for who could be Marvin's guardian. Ted, Barney, and Robin all want to be the guardian, while Marshall and Lily realize that they have been bad friends ("Who Wants to Be a Godparent?"). This is a perfect case in point of everyone in the group embodying the five important traits of a bro.

Wingwomen

Famous (literal) wingwoman Anne Morrow Lindbergh said that "men kick friendship around like a football, but it doesn't seem to crack. Women treat it like glass and it goes to pieces." Though this may not be entirely true, it gives us a statement about the roughness of men's relations with each other, and how this callousness can be both good and bad.

In the first season, as Ted and Victoria are beginning their relationship, Barney is left wingman-less, and turns to Robin in his need of a bro for his 'bro-ings on'. Not only does Robin take over Ted's spot as Barney's bro, she is by Barney's admission a better bro than Ted ever was ("You've already flown higher and faster than he ever did" and "You're a better Ted than Ted").

Robin, throughout the show, is shown not merely as an equal, but frequently as more masculine than any of the male characters. She hunts, plays hockey, drinks whiskey, loves guns, and altogether does what we might consider 'manly' things. So besides being Barney's bro, she can also be seen as a character pushing past traditional gender roles for women and men. Just as Robin pushes gender boundaries and roles, so do other characters on the show. Lily, while loving shopping and shoes, is also a hot dog eating champion.

While Barney acts as if he is a 'man's man', one sees him in a very masculine conflict with Robin's father choosing not to shoot a rabbit ("Band or DJ"). Ted and Marshall, in similar fashion display vast amounts of 'unmanly' or 'effeminate' qualities throughout the show (Ted's fear of spiders, Marshall's unwillingness to fire Randy).

All of the male characters, while projecting a masculine persona, at one point or another, display behaviors and traits which set them outside of 'traditional' masculine roles (though not always for long or in huge ways).

These gender transgressions, by both the male and female characters, further the idea that the relations between genders is crucial, and that, in a way, the Bro Code can be inclusive of not only these transgressions, but also of equality.

The inclusion of women as being equally able to be wingmen is crucial for a variety of reasons. First it speaks to the idea that the Bro Code is not meant strictly as a segregationist tactic to separate the spaces of men and those of women. It also builds on feminist struggles for equality and the ability to "sit at the same table as men."

While very few feminists might say that the Bro Code should be seen as promoting equality between the sexes, it is a first step. In finding a relationship which men and women can participate in equally and outside the realms of sexual relations, it can help build positive relationships between men and women (by using the positive aspects, while leaving behind the negative aspects).

Bro as the Gold Standard

The Bro Code, just like any other set of rules, is full of contra-dictions, inequities, and negative elements. But as can be seen, it is also meant to be broken, altered, gone against, and at times tossed out. This flexibility puts it above those guidelines which demand a strict following.

Aristotle says that friendship is a situation where both friends are equal in moral development, and at the bottom of it possess an element of mutual co-operation and benefit. Another way of putting the second part would be the ancient Roman phrase: quid pro bro.[5]

There's certainly something to be said that relations between bros contain strong elements of mutual co-operation and support, but the moral development of the bros in this case is seemingly less important. Take a look at Barney and Ted. You could hardly find two more morally dissimilar people—which may be part of the reason Ted, for a period, stops being Barney's friend and bro.

But true bros, regardless of their differences, are bound by their love and affection for each other. So in Ted's time of need, Barney runs all the way to the hospital—even wrinkling his suit!—to be there for his bro. Similarly, we see Ted rush to Lily's aid when the Fiero has a flat tire ("Milk") and Marshall helping Robin feel at home in New York by finding a Canadian bar for her ("Little Minnesota"). All of these situations display loyalty, friendliness, treating people as equals, a strong bond with friends, and generosity.

If we see the Bro Code in the right light, it can provide a way forward for all of our relationships in our lives. In so doing, we can see others as our equal, importantly seeing women as equal to men. Whether you identify as a feminist or not, women's equality is a crucial issue for all of us—men, women, and otherwise. To quote Karl Marx: "Social progress can be measured exactly by the social position of the fair sex, the ugly ones included."

We're More than Friends, We're Brothers

"Whether we know it or not, each of us lives a life governed by an internalized code of conduct. Some call it morality. Others

---

[5] The Broman version of 'Quid Pro Quo', meaning 'this for that'.

call it religion. I call it 'The Bro Code.'" This is how it starts, and it seems a fitting thing to return to at the end of this discussion.

The Bro Code is not perfect and has many flaws (thanks, Barney!), but it is also the beginning of a discussion about how we can view homosocial relations between men, and relations between men and women.

As discussed earlier, the displacement of male-to-male affection through the utilization of women as sexual objects creates a situation where men feel unable to have true intimate friendships and must construct a barrier to fend off the advances of supposed femininity. In this case, that shield is the elaborate structure of the bro, with all of its rules, in the form of the Bro Code. As Ted says so clearly, it is "a list of do's and don'ts for all bros. Some were basic. Some were unbelievably complicated. And some were just plain disturbing."

As we move further and further into the twenty-first century and become more individualistic (with more people living alone), we're more connected than ever through Facebook and the internet, but what is the impact on our relationships of all this? While I don't think it is as doom and gloom as some would have you believe, I do think it is still critical to value our personal, and in-person, relationships with friends.

With all of this in mind, I would like to propose an amendment to the Bro Code. Amendment VII: A Bro should at all times act in such a way to show his devotion to his Bros, committing himself to acting with the virtues of: loyalty, friendliness, equality, strong bonds with friends, and generosity in all things.[6]

---

[6] This chapter is dedicated to the amazing brothers in my life, most especially those who helped with this chapter (Ron, Dan, and Dorian), and my father, grandfather, and Pappou—the men who showed me what it means to be a good man.

7

Ted's Cockamouse Flies at Dusk

M. CHRIS SARDO

Kids, in the opening scene of Season Three, "Future-Ted" tells his children, "Kids, there's more than one story of how I met your mother. You know the short version, the thing with your mom's yellow umbrella, but there's a bigger story, the story of how I became who I had to become in order to meet her."

Ted is not simply telling a linear narrative detailing the events prior to meeting and falling in love with his wife, but a story that has a progressive logic to it. For Ted the episodes of *How I Met Your Mother* do not depict random events but necessary events, without which he never would have met his wife. Ted, then, is not only telling his children the story of how he met their mother, but is also attempting to teach them a lesson on Georg Hegel's philosophy of history.

For Hegel, history has a universal, guiding principle, or idea, that directs historical events towards some final purpose. Thus, history is not a series of random or haphazard happenings organized chronologically, but follows a rational design. As Hegel writes, this rational purpose of history can be discovered in a "final end" which "governs and alone consummates itself in the events that occur to peoples, and that therefore there is *reason in world history*."[1] In other words, we can and should judge history by looking at its final results, and not the particular events that lead to the eventual purpose of history. If this final end can be justified, then the events leading to this end are

---

[1] G.W.F. Hegel, *Lectures on the Philosophy of World History*, Volume 1 (Clarendon, 2011), p. 144.

justified, regardless of whether their functions are understood as leading to this end at the time of their happening.

For Hegel, the movement of history is governed by the development of human freedom, which he views as "the way in which the idea brings itself forth" (p. 146). In his lecture courses on the philosophy of world history, Hegel traces this development throughout world history. He begins with what he calls "Oriental World," in which only the tyrant is free, and ends with the "Germanic World," or nineteenth-century northern Europe, where all human beings are free in virtue of their being human. Between these extreme, Hegel traces various stages of historical and human development.

No less laudable, Ted's organizing principle of history is the development of his love life leading to his eventual marriage. Like world history, Ted's dating life similarly goes through various stages. In the first episode, he is happily single with no thought of marriage until Marshall's proposal to Lily pushes him to start seriously looking for the woman of his dreams. In "No Tomorrow," Ted tells his children that their mother was at the same St. Patrick's Day party but they didn't meet, and "it's a good thing I didn't, because if I had met her I don't think she would have liked me." Though actively looking for "the one," Ted had not yet reached an appropriate level of emotional maturity to meet her.

In Season Seven, after another Robin-relapse that leads to her moving out of his apartment, Ted tells his children that "in my own crazy way, I was kind of happy. For the first time in years there was no little part of me clinging to the dream of being with Robin, which meant for the first time in years the world was wide open." This closure with Robin was another key step in the development of Ted's emotional being that brings him closer to meeting his kids' mother. Ted's love life is not simply a parade of, in Robin's words "dubious conquests," but a series of relationships, each of which developed him in ways that were necessary for him to become the man he needed to be to meet, woo, and marry his future wife.

For both Hegel and Ted, the events that constitute history are not merely haphazard occurrences. Instead, they are necessary elements in the development of an idea, whether human freedom, in Hegel's view, or that Ted's true love is out there. Though some of these events may seem terrible at the time, whether the numerous deadly wars throughout history or the litany of heartbreaks Ted suffers, they all serve the advancement of history. They are then in a sense redeemed by the achievement of the final end of history, as each event serves a particular purpose and are necessary to reach the final end. Ted and Hegel are not merely relating a series of events in chronological order, but showing how these events are necessary for the development of a given history. Their goal is to show that every event in history, no matter how minute contributes to the progression of history and is a necessary prerequisite for history's final purpose.

Ted Mosby's Reflective Logic

While Ted's and Hegel's shared understanding of history has both a rational purpose and a guiding organizing principle, this idea of a "guiding principle" must be clarified. As Hegel famously wrote:

> Philosophy . . . always comes too late to perform this function. As the thought of the world, it appears only at a time when actuality has gone through its formative process and attained its completed state. . . . When philosophy paints its grey in grey, a shape of life has grown old, and it cannot be rejuvenated, but only recognized, by the grey in grey of philosophy; the owl of Minerva begins its flight only with the onset of dusk. (*Elements of the Philosophy of Right*, Cambridge University Press, 2010, p. 23).

While this argument may seem difficult to grasp, once the Hegelese is translated, its main claim is very clear: we can only know the organizing principle of history *after* history has reached its culmination. Philosophy cannot know ahead of time what the final end of history will be, and therefore it cannot know what the guiding logic of historical progress is. It's only after the end has been achieved, that philosophers, and philosophically inclined architects, can reflect back upon history and see how the various events fit together in a series of necessary relationships. Only reflection can transcend the various particularities of history, the myriad wars, revolutions, elections, cultural changes, blind dates, one night stands, and broken hearts and see how they fit together in service of a higher goal.

This Hegelian insight—necessity can only be achieved through reflection—forces us to think with more nuance about necessity and the unfolding of history. It's tempting to read Hegel's philosophy of history as claiming that history has built-in rules and functions on auto-pilot until it reaches its destination. Such a view of history would deny any meaning to human action; all actions would be predetermined, leaving no room for human freedom. If Hegel's argument is that history is essentially the development of human freedom, then this account of necessity is ultimately unsatisfying. However, such an account of history fails to take into account Hegel's claim about the untimeliness of philosophical reflection. When the philosophy of history is read in context of this logic of reflection, it becomes clear that the necessity Hegel is talking about is always a belated necessity.

By reflecting on history, and not simply narrating a series of events in time, one can attribute necessary relationships to these events. This is because, according to Hegel, the rules and concepts that are required to claim that events are necessarily related are not given in advance but emerge only through the development of some system, whether a history, a logic, or a philosophy. As Hegel says, "Logic, therefore, cannot say what it is in advance, rather does this knowledge of itself only emerge as the final result and completion of its whole treatment."[2]

Similarly, history does not announce its final end in advance, but we can look back at history and trace how certain events form a coherent logical whole. At any given moment I cannot know in advance what effects my actions will have for my future development, but years from now I can reflect on how these actions have brought me to where I am. This is because I can connect where I am now to where I came from, in effect reading back into a history the final end that it has achieved. "Reflection," according to the Hegelian inspired philosopher Markus Gabriel, "retroactively creates its own starting point, and this starting point is thereby always already related to what follows from it."[3]

While Ted begins his story with Marshall and Lily's engagement, he could have begun his story with his first day of col-

---

[2] *The Science of Logic* (Cambridge University Press, 2010), p. 23.

[3] *Transcendental Ontology: Essays in German Idealism* (Continuum, 2011), p. 132.

lege, and the causal relationships, and unfolding logic, between the events leading to his marriage would have taken a different form. The sequence of history does follow an inherently necessary relationship but this necessity is imposed on these events after their culmination. Hegel can read history as the development of human freedom only after human freedom has been realized universally; Ted can tell us the story of how the events of his life led him to his wife only after he has met her.

Deciding What the Universe Decides

Lily and Marshall must have not listened carefully to Ted's overly-enthusiastic explanation of Hegel's philosophy of history, as their views of history represent an example of the first reading I have described. Viewing history as completely pre-ordained, Marshall and Lily often simply "let the universe decide." In the episode "Doppelgangers," they base their decision on whether or not to start a family on the universe's signal. Lily tells Marshall, "When we finally see Barney's doppelganger, that's the universe telling us its go time." When Marshall expresses some concern that having a baby shouldn't be left up to the universe's whims, Lily retorts that "it's so much easier to let the universe decide." Upon believing that they had seen Barney's doppelganger driving a cab, they decide that the universe has approved their decision to start a family. When Marshall discovers that Barney's doppelganger was in fact Barney, he refuses to tell Lily, as she is still waiting for the right signal from the universe.

Similarly, in the Season Seven episode "Rebound Girl," when deciding on whether or not to move to Long Island, they judge that Lily's pregnancy precludes them from making a decision, and instead choose to let the universe decide. Immediately upon being challenged by Robin, a man with a "For Sale" sign offers to purchase their apartment. Just as their decision to have children was governed by a sign from the universe, they rely on a signal to make another life-changing decision. Marshall and Lily recognize that they must reach a certain level of development in their relationship, but they believe that the universe has also built in certain road signs that exist purely to guide the development of history. Marshall and Lily believe in a logic of history, but believe that the universe will inform them of this logic before its culmination.

Ted, who studied philosophy at Wesleyan before taking up architecture, has a better understanding of Hegel's philosophy of history. While history unfolds according to a rational logic, Ted understands that he is imposing this logic upon history. The entire narrative structure of the show follows this idea. Ted is reflecting back on the events that shaped his life before he met his wife, and narrates this account of his progression to his children. Now that Ted has reached his own end of history, he can organize the events of his life in such a way that every single one is in a necessary relation to others, culminating in his marriage and family. While "Future Ted" clearly understands how these particular events fit together into a coherent whole, he's oblivious to this unfolding narrative while the events themselves transpire.

For example, in "Doppelgangers" Ted's view of the universe's sign stands in strict contrast to Marshall and Lily's. Where Marshall and Lily view the universe as following a rational course of development that can be known in advance, Ted recognizes the reflective nature of such historical judgments. "Future Ted" narrates at the end of the episode, "Kids, you can ask the universe for signs all you want, but ultimately we only see what we want to see when we're ready to see it." In one sentence, Ted explains the idea of belated necessity.

First, we can't know the course of history in advance, because the universe does not provide signs for us to read. Second, through reflection we impose certain rules that order seemingly happenstance events into a historical narrative of progress, as we "see only what we want to see." Third, and finally, we can only understand this logic belatedly, after the culmination of the progress of history, or "when we're ready to see it." Rather than viewing history either as a series of unrelated events or as a book already written with no room for choice, Ted follows a Hegelian approach to history. While this is evident in the general structure of the show, it is made even more explicit in certain episodes.

Lucky Penny

In the Season Two episode "Lucky Penny," Ted and Robin are debating why they're late for a plane to Chicago, where Ted has a job interview. In typical Hegelian fashion the cause of their tardiness depends on where they begin the story. By reflecting back, they string a set of seemingly random events into a coherent story that explains how they miss the flight.

In the first version of the story, the blame lies with Barney, who after running the New York City Marathon finds himself unable to get off the subway. Ted, attempting to come to his aid, jumps a turnstile, is issued a citation, and must attend court, making him late for his flight. Here, two completely isolated events, Barney running the marathon and Ted being late to his flight, can be united through an act of reflection that ascribes a necessary relationship to the two.

However, Ted and Robin aren't finished with their philosophical reflections yet. Ted pushes the starting point back even further, attempting to find the cause of Barney running the marathon. Ted states that Barney only ran the marathon because of a bet with Marshall, who was unable to run because of a broken foot. Marshall only broke his foot because, while addressing his t-shirt chaffing with petroleum jelly, Robin startled him. He then slipped and broke his foot, and was thus unable to run the next day. When starting the narrative here, Ted is able to lay the blame on Robin.

Yet their reflections still remain incomplete, as Robin argues that she was only in Ted and Marshall's apartment because she needed to take a nap, having spent all night with Lily camping out for a bridal sale. Pushing back even further, they discover that this only occurred because Ted and Robin discovered the sale while eating hot dogs from a street vendor. Even further back, Ted realizes that they were only eating hot dogs because he had found an old penny. Promising Robin that it was a valuable collector's piece, he pledges to buy her dinner with the money he receives from it. As it was worth one dollar and fifty cents, they can only purchase hot dogs for dinner. From this penny a chain of events is set off leading to Ted and Robin missing their flight.

Thus, through an act of reflection, Ted is able to apply a necessary, albeit belated, relationship from two disparate events: him finding a penny on the subway and him missing a flight to Chicago. The historical progression also depends on where the story is started, which always is arbitrarily imposed, but is nonetheless a significant determinant to the unfolding of the sotry. As Robin points out, "I don't think we can go back any further than that unless you know who dropped the penny," implying that the story could potentially change even more. Thus the progression of history itself always mirrors the logic employed to connect its various events. Furthermore, while the Ted of the present is able to connect this lucky penny to missing his flight, "Future-Ted" is able to connect the lucky penny to the final end of the narrative, his marriage. "Future-Ted" knows that Ted missing this interview kept him from relocating to Chicago, which would have prevented him from meeting his wife. Eventually, at the end of history's progression, Ted is able to connect a single penny left on the ground to him marrying his wife. This narrative could never be known in advance; only through the idea of belated necessity can one connect something as miniscule as a penny to finding "the One."

Right Place, Right Time

In the episode, "Right Place, Right Time," Ted accomplishes another feat of reflective logic, explaining how a number of haphazard events led to him being on the same street corner as Stella, the woman who left him at the altar. Looking back, Ted realizes that he was only on that street corner because of a number of unrelated decisions made on a walk that day, and that without running into Stella and her fiancé Tony, Ted never would have met his wife.

Again the narrative starts with a trivial event: Ted lacks architectural inspiration, and Robin tells him to go for a walk. Ted decides to grab a bagel, but remembers that Robin got food poisoning from his favorite bagel shop. He therefore turns left out of his apartment and goes to his second favorite bagel place. On the way, he stops to purchase a copy of the magazine *Muscle Sexxy* to see Barney's two-hundredth sexual conquest, who was featured in the magazine. Next, he stops to give a homeless man a dollar.

In another flashback, we learn that Marshall, having discovered the GNB graphics department, developed an endearing, yet annoying, fascination with charts. In retribution, Ted threw all of his charts out of the window, only to learn that some were for an important presentation at GNB. When Ted goes to retrieve them, he finds them in the possession of Milt the homeless man, and Ted agrees to pay him one dollar a day for one million days in exchange for the charts. Ted then arrives at a street corner only to be tapped on the shoulder by his ex-fiancé.

In this episode Ted not only shows that historical narratives depend on where they are chosen to begin, but also how his own life was affected by the apparently unrelated actions of his friends. Without Barney trying to meet a challenge of sleeping with two hundred women and Marshall's fascination with charts, Ted would not have been at that street corner at that particular moment. As we learn in the next episode, Tony was concerned with Ted's emotional well-being after their meeting and offers him a job as a university professor. As we'll see in the next section, this event plays a critical role in Ted's life. Only upon reflection, Ted sees how Barney's love-life and Marshall's professional life are necessary to him meeting his future wife.

In addition to telling his children how he met their mother, he attempts to give them a lesson on Hegel's philosophy of history in this episode. He tells them:

> The great moments of your life won't necessarily be the things you do, they'll also be the things that happen to you. Now, I'm not saying you can't take action to affect the outcome of your life, you have to take action, and you will. But never forget that on any day, you can step out the front door and your whole life can change forever. You see, the universe has a plan kids, and that plan is always in motion. A butterfly flaps its wings, and it starts to rain. It's a scary thought but it's also kind of wonderful. All these little parts of the machine constantly working, making sure that you end up exactly where you're supposed to be, exactly when you're supposed to be there. The right place at the right time.

Thus only "Future Ted" can see how these apparently unrelated events play necessary roles in him finding his wife. While Ted appreciates the majesty of the universe unfolding towards a final purpose, he also maintains the space for the human freedom. It is the unique combination of Ted's own decisions and actions and the events that happen to him that move him closer and closer to meeting his wife. Though he can see how these fit together at the end of this process, he is completely on his own while in the midst of them. The universe's plan is always created belatedly; until "Future Ted" can reflect back upon history the stages of this plan appear to be unrelated contingent events.

The Leap

In "The Leap," the finale of Season Four, Ted wrestles with whether or not he should take Tony's offer to become a professor of architecture or whether he should continue working as an independent architect. While designing a building for a rib restaurant, Ted wrestles with, and loses to, a goat that Lily has taken home from school. Later, Ted learns that the restaurant has decided to go with the design offered by the Swedish architectural group "Sven."

Lily attempts to cheer Ted up by telling him to just give in and let the universe make his next move. Again, Lily seems to misunderstand the Hegelian lesson of history. The universe's decisions only become apparent through an act of reflection; the universe can't act for us, as it's through our actions that history progresses. Ted and Marshall take the correct Hegelian approach, however, and both of them decide to act, even if these actions are conditioned by the unfolding of the universe, and neither can know the outcome of their actions. Marshall decides to literally take "the leap" and jump from the roof of Ted's apartment to the neighboring roof. Ted accepts Tony's job offer, and becomes a university professor.

At the end of the episode, "Future Ted" tells his children:

> That was the year I was left at the altar, it was the year I got knocked out by a crazy bartender, the year I got fired, the year I got beat up by a goat, a girl goat at that, and damn it if it wasn't one of the best years of my life. Because if any one of those things hadn't happen, I never would have ended up with the best job I ever had, but more importantly, I wouldn't have met your mother, because as you know, she was in that class.

Again, only "Future-Ted" knows how these events conspired to bring Ted to his wife. While in the present, Ted understood them as simply minor, accidental events. However, here "Future Ted" nuances the familiar Hegelian lesson. Here, it's not simply that the necessary relationships that guide history to its final end can only be discovered at the culmination of the process. Instead, Ted shows how the final end of history, him meeting his wife, redeems all of the terrible events of his life.

Meeting his true love did not merely make getting left at the altar, getting beat up by a bartender, getting beat up by a goat, and failing as an architect worth it in the end. Indeed, each one of these events, despite seeming dreadful at the time, played necessary roles in the unfolding story of how he met his wife. As he states, without any one of these events, he never would have met her, and his children would not be subjected to his now eight-year-long story. Just as for Hegel all of the violence and deaths throughout history are redeemed by contributing to the development of free political and social institutions, all of the negative events of Ted's life are finally understood as playing critical roles in a history that brings him overwhelming happiness.

A Love Story, Told by Hegel

Ted Mosby didn't become a professional philosopher after college, but he has mastered at least two arts of the trade. First, even though his first and only lecture has lasted for eight years, he still attracts many auditors for his weekly evening sessions. Second, and more importantly, he has found a novel way to teach Hegel's philosophy of history. He has limited Hegel's scope both temporally and geographical from world history to the history to his own adult life in New York. He has also shifted the purpose of history from the development of human freedom to him meeting the love of his life. Yet the key tenet of Hegel's philosophy remains the same: history has a rational purpose, but this purpose must be imposed through an act of reflection. This act establishes necessary relationships between seemingly unrelated events, placing them in service of a final end.

For both Hegel and Ted an interesting relationship between necessity and contingency emerges, that of the "necessity of contingency." History is made up of contingent, random events, yet they become necessary through reflection at the culmination of them. The universe, despite Lily's protests to the contrary, does not impose a pre-established harmony between all happenings. Instead, only Ted can impose this belated necessity on his life, showing how these contingent events necessarily made him the man he became, and led him to his wife.

Hegel symbolized this idea with the "owl of Minerva." The goddess of wisdom's pet owl only flies at dusk, just as a philosophical understanding of the necessity of history always comes belatedly. While the flight of the cockamouse that lived in Ted's apartment may not provide as majestic an image as Hegel's owl, *How I Met Your Mother* serves as an excellent introduction to Hegel's philosophy of history.

8
Smoking Subs and Eating Joints

MIGUEL ÁNGEL SEBASTIÁN AND
MANOLO MARTÍNEZ

Kids, we've seen many times how Ted, Marshall, and Lily, while in college, would eat from a two feet long sub that they would pass from one to another. But wait a minute, passing a sub around? Look at their faces and their laughs; this is not a sub, it's a joint. Or is it? Well, it depends on who you ask.

How I Met Your Mother is a fictional show. That much is clear. And we know many things about it: that our five friends live in New York; that Robin is Canadian; that Barney wants to nail Ted's mother (but hasn't, *wink*); that the Sasquatch is as real as the Loch Ness Monster, and both *very* real (at least if you ask Marshall). We know these things because we're told so in the show. But not all the things that we're told in the show are true in the story, especially when it comes to Barney's words. In spite of his indisputable awesomeness—he can even stop being sad and be awesome instead!—it's not true (not even in the fiction) that he has an additional awesome gland where others have a shame gland or that, when it seems that his nose is running, it is just overflowing with awesomeness that has to come out. Even though Barney tells us these things, we're sure they're not true even in the fictional show itself. How do we know that these things are false in the story?

Furthermore, there are plenty of things that are true in *How I Met Your Mother* which we are never explicitly told. We know from the very beginning that Ted's children's mother has a face and that Quinn was once a toddler. What makes those things true?

Bimbos Do Not Pop into Existence in MacLaren's (and Out Again After Sleeping with Barney)

Ted, Lily, Marshall, Robin, and Barney are having a drink at MacLaren's. We see how Barney targets a beautiful (say) brunette. He walks to her, whispers something in her ear and off they both go to Barney's apartment. Next day Barney tells Ted that they had (by Barney's standards, at least) sex that just about made the awesomeness threshold. For all we see in the show, the girl might have just popped into existence in MacLaren's and popped out of existence again after sleeping with Barney. This would probably be Barney's dream, but (just this time) Barney's dream must go unfulfilled. Unfortunately for Barney, it's false in *How I Met Your Mother* that chicks suddenly cease to exist after leaving his apartment. An interesting question is how we know that.

Well, in this case there's an easy answer. We know that the girls that Barney picks up are human beings and we know that human beings do not suddenly pop in and out of existence— they are born, they die, that sort of thing. In general, some things are true in fiction because other things are true: since both Barney and Ted's children's mother are humans, and because humans have faces but not awesome glands, we know that Barney does not have two awesome glands and that Ted's children's mother has a face.

What is true in any story depends on what the author tells us; in the case of *How I Met Your Mother*, these truths depend on the story that Ted tells their children and the images and conversations that illustrate it. But clearly, as the case of Barney's victims (and their existence before and after meeting him) shows, not exclusively on this. Some things are true in *How I Met Your Mother* because we're told so and we see so—we might call these "primitive" truths. But some things are true in the show merely because *other* things are true in the show—call them "derivative" truths. Examples of primitive fictional truths are that Ted's children have a mother, or that Barney was close to completing a perfect week. Examples of derivative fictional truths are that the Captain, at some point in his life, didn't know port from starboard, and that there was some wisecrack realtor that coined the name "DoWiSeTrePla" for the neighborhood in which Marshall and Lily live.

The interesting philosophical question at this point is how the latter, merely implied, derivative truths about the show are generated from the former, explicit, primitive fictional truths. Unfortunately this is not the only problem that we have to solve (neh, *fortunately*: problems are awesome.) We also need to get clear about what are the primary truths in a story. We're told that Lily, Ted, and Marshall used to pass around subs while in college, but we don't think that this is true. Why is it true that Robin is Canadian but not true that Ted, Marshall, and Lily, while in college, ate from two feet long subs that they passed from one to the other? Let's start with derivative truths.

Why Barney's Dream Isn't True

Barney's *one-night stands* are not always clear about the time-window that Barney has allotted for their relationship: one night. In Barney's dreams girls would disappear right after crossing the door of the apartment or even better right after a crazy night—committing to oblivion those that insist on having a long breakfast in the morning. Unfortunately for Barney, this is not what happens in *How I Met Your Mother*, and he has to deal with girls calling back and not understanding that the best night of their lives has already gone; but why is Barney's dream not fictionally true?

Barney's dream is false although we are not explicitly told so. We're told in the series that some girls call back trying to get Barney, but in some cases we're not told what happens with them. Nonetheless, we know that it's not the case that they pop out of existence. The girls he landed during his "almost" perfect week kept on existing after meeting him: this is a derivative truth. It is true because it is fictionally true that they are girls and that girls do not pop out of existence. The first one is a primitive fictional truth, we are explicitly told so in the series, the second is not. The problem of derivative truths is the problem of determining which truths we're supposed to keep fixed, in the process of generating derivative truths.

If It's True There, It's True Here

Well, there's this: in general, when we watch a fictional TV show or read a novel we do not believe things that are *inconsistent with what we know is true in the real world*, unless this is required for understanding the story. We don't go around saying things like "You know, for all we know, two plus two might very well equal five in *How I Met Your Mother*—after all, this is a *fictional show*, maaaan." That would be pretty stupid: nothing in the show suggests that math might be fundamentally different in the *How I Met Your Mother* universe; so we simply assume that math is just the same as we know it in the real universe.

And we're not required to suspend our belief that Barney is a human when we watch *How I Met Your Mother*—even if it's hard to believe that a human being can be that awesome. Along these lines, the most straightforward attitude towards *How I Met Your Mother* is to deem true all the things that *really* are true, if they're not incompatible with the primary truths in the show. We know that people do not pop out of existence, that they have kidneys and faces, and that's why it's true in the show that Lily has kidneys, Ted's children's mother has a face, and Barney's dream is false. On the other hand, we know that no one can be as awesome as Barney, but we give up this belief when following the show because it's incompatible with what we're told in *How I Met Your Mother*: Barney is as awesome as Barney!

There's a catch, though: if we take this idea too seriously, we end up generating the wrong kind of fictional truths: there are *way too many* things that are compatible with *How I Met Your Mother* primary truths, which we do not want to count as true in the show. It would be true in *How I Met Your Mother* that at three in the morning on the Third of November 2008 there was no one eating gazpacho in Brighton Beach, Brooklyn, or that, I don't know, something really random was taking place, or not, in some really random corner of the world. It's unreasonable to take *How I Met Your Mother* as being concerned with those things. It's a show about important stuff, people. Also, if such things were to be counted as true in the show, no one, not even the screenwriters, would ever come to know whether it was true in *How I Met Your Mother*. And we like to think that screenwriters have some kind of control on what is true in the story they are writing (even if many of us have watched *Lost,* but let's not go there).

If We All Believe It, It's True Here

One way to avoid this absurdly-random-fictional-truths conclusion is to appeal to the beliefs that are openly shared by the community in which the story is written. There are no openly-shared beliefs about gazpacho consumption in Brighton Beach in November, and therefore those things do not count as true in the show.

This proposal is not free of problems. For example, we are not willing to count as true in the show everything that most people believe in contemporary North America. Apparently, a majority of Americans believe in God, but it's weird to take that as a reason to believe that it is true in *How I Met Your Mother* (as opposed to, say, true in *Bruce Almighty*) that there is a god.

Now we can consider the case of Lily, Marshall, and Ted eating from the two-feet-long sub that they're passing around. While they are doing that, they are laughing and they look stoned. We all know that they are high and that they are not passing a sub around. We conclude this because we all believe that those are clear symptoms of smoking dope. (We're not accusing the reader of having experienced these effects though—on the other hand, how else does the reader know about those symptoms? Will the reader start respecting us, the writers of this chapter, as the discerning adults we are and come clean? Or are we to continue playing little ambiguity games with the reader? Geez, the reader should give us a break.)

So, it's reasonable to think that at some point fifty-something Ted became—he probably always was—a bit prudish and that he doesn't want to tell his children that he used to smoke grass when he was younger. The problem now is that, in the show, we're explicitly told that Lily, Marshall, and Ted gather together to eat subs and therefore this should count as a primary fictional truth. But, come on, it's perfectly clear that they gather to smoke grass and not to eat subs; that is, it follows from what we believe about the behavior and looks of people smoking grass: a derivative fictional truth.

There you go: a derivative fictional truth that contradicts a primary fictional truth. Should we, in this case, not hold fixed those beliefs that brought us to derive this truth? We expect the reader's head to be spinning at this point. Even without smoking dope.

They Used to Smoke Dope, Didn't They?

In *How I Met Your Mother* Ted tells his children the story of how he met their mother. In doing so, we learn many things about the gang and some of the characters surrounding their lives, Ted tells us that Lily and Marshall have been together since college, that Victoria is a pastry chef, and that Barney is (for lack of a more awesomer word) awesome. Those are primary fictional truths.

We have seen that there are more things that are true in *How I Met Your Mother* than the things Ted explicitly relates— what we have called derivative fictional truths. Primary fictional truths together with certain background beliefs entail derivative truths like that Robin has two kidneys (we also learn that Doogie Howser gave up his brilliant career and that Chris Peterson didn't pass away after meeting Spewey but it is not clear that those are derivative truths in *How I Met Your Mother*).

One would think that primary truths are easy peasy: in *How I Met Your Mother* they are the things that fifty-something Ted, who is the narrator, tells us. As the philosopher David Lewis has suggested, the author of a fictional story pretends to be a narrator, so when Ted tells us about their lives during their early thirties, the screenwriters are pretending to be Ted giving us accurate information about Lily, Ted, Marshall, Robin, and Barney. Since Ted tells us that Robin is Canadian, this will count as a primary fictional truth.

Yeah, not so quick. (That should be the *motto* of all philosophers: Gothic letters inside a laurel wreath reading "YEAH, NOT SO QUICK." When you see the T-shirt, remember: you read it here first.) The Ted-as-narrator account of primary truths has some flaws. For example, we believe that Ted might tell things wrongly, that he is not infallible; in fact, and to judge by the way he handles his personal life, he is *far* from infallible. Ted's fallibility in turn requires that things in the fiction are allowed to be different from the way in which Ted presents them and therefore, that there are primary truths that differ from what Ted tells. Maybe some of the goofs and mistakes of the show (some of the continuity errors, say) can be explained by older-Ted's unreliability. A further problem is that there are more primary truths than what Ted tells us. For instance, as Ted is fighting that evil goat we can see that there is a striped carpet in the floor. This seems to be a primary fictional truth but hardly something that Ted is telling his children: *Kids, in May 2009, my living room was furnished as follows: . . .*

The philosopher Gregory Currie has proposed a theory of truth in fiction that attempts to solve this kind of problems. Currie proposes that each fiction has a *fictional narrator*, who is neither the author nor the narrator *in the fiction*—the screenwriters and Ted respectively, in our case. Such a fictional narrator, as opposed to Ted, is supposed to be reliable; he is telling us known facts of the story. When we engage in the fiction what we do is reconstruct the beliefs of such a narrator.

We can see how such a fictional narrator is helpful in stories-with-narrators: in *Sunset Boulevard,* for example, the story is told by Joe Gillis, but (leaving aside the fact that he is dead) it's impossible that Joe remembers (let alone narrates) all of the details that are portrayed in the film—everything Norma Desmond says, word by word, how every shadow falls on her face, and so on. That's where the fictional narrator comes in handy: *that thing* can remember and narrate everything with Terminator-like attention to detail. Yay the fictional narrator. The highest of fives for them.

In *How I Met Your Mother*, the fictional narrator is particularly useful: it is the entity that narrates, as a truth of the *How I Met Your Mother* world, that Ted is *lying* to his children about his (and uncle Marshall and aunt Lily's) grass-smoking days in college. In other words: *How I Met Your Mother* all but forces us to introduce the figure of the fictional narrator. More than just a neat problem case, our show is *evidence* in favor of one particular family of views.

On the other hand Currie's fictional narrator is not enough to solve the sub-versus-joint controversy, though. This guy (not Currie, the Terminator guy) is supposedly telling us about Ted's story to his children, making it true that Ted is lying to his kids in order not to encourage pot-smoking and filling in the details that Ted cannot or will not remember: exact furniture, exact dialogues, exact positions of goats, exact Laser Tag high scores, exact brand of Lithuanian beer. One could go on, and that's precisely where things go south: exact aspect of two-feet-long sandwich, exact ingredients . . . Hey, if the fictional narrator tells us these things they must be true. That's what the fictional narrator is for. So they *were* eating subs after all. Case closed. Everyone please go home. Take that goat with you. Leave the Lithuanian beer, though.

Yeah, not so quick. The fictional narrator is simply a methodological fiction designed to help us reconstruct what counts as true in the show. And we are pretty (make this a very long "y") certain that they were smoking, not eating—indeed, the fictional narrator was supposed to make *this* fictionally true. Smokitty smoke, fictional narrator, you are not fooling us with the lavish detail of those subs.

One could maybe go all Currie on this, and postulate the existence of *yet another* narrator, one that is telling us about the other Currie-fictional narrator who is in turn telling us about older Ted (who is in turn . . .). Some philosophers (one of us, but not the other, for example) enjoy this kind of complicated theoretical construction with a lot of fictional narrators, and narrators-in-the-fiction, and real narrators, each nested inside one another. But one cannot shake the impression that describing how come that certain things are true in *How I Met Your Mother* should not turn into an exercise in near-Medieval near-theology.

And the Moral Is . . . Okay, There's No Moral

We're all more or less clear about what's true in *How I Met Your Mother* and what's not true.

It's fictionally true that Robin is Canadian, Ted's children's mother has a face, Barney's disappearing-girl dream is just a dream, and Lily, Marshal, and Ted used to smoke dope while in college.

It's not true (nor is it false) in *How I Met Your Mother* that at three in the morning on the Third of November 2008 there was no one eating gazpacho in Brighton Beach, nor that there is a god. More tricky, as we have seen, is to get clear about *why* it's the case that those things are, or are not, truth in the fiction.

This is one of the situations that make philosophy fascinating: we have this mostly unproblematic, fun, enjoyable thing that is *How I Met Your Mother*. We *know* how to watch it, what it means, what events transpire about its fictional universe. And we, quite reasonably, assume that explaining how come that we know these things should be equally simple. *Yeah, not so quick.* When it comes to theory, we need to make all sorts of strange moves, invent all sorts of weird entities that somehow or other must be there, if the way in which we describe our everyday experience with shows such as *How I Met Your Mother* is even approximately accurate.

In fact, *How I Met Your Mother* is pretty (short "y" this time) great in that this mismatch between experience and theory is particularly striking. So, hey, if you do philosophy you get double the fun out of the same show. Sort of like a sub doubling as a joint. Not that we know anything about subs.

9
Telling Each Other *Everything*

Jordan Pascoe

Kids, in the Season Eight episode "The Lobster Crawl," Marshall reveals that he knows all about Robin's attempt to seduce Barney—he knows about the purple and black lingerie and everything. "Lil, feel free to disregard that 'Don't tell anyone, ever,'" Robin says. And Robin is right to feel betrayed: she made Lily *promise* that she would keep her secret, and Lily told Marshall.

Did Lily break her promise to Robin when she told Marshall about it? The answer depends on whether we think Lily *can* promise to keep secrets from Marshall, given that Lily has already promised to tell Marshall everything. Marshall and Lily's relationship involves a level of truth-telling that few of us achieve in our relationships, and one that often poses problems for members of their group. "In a real relationship, you share everything," Lily says. "That's why Marshall and I don't keep any secrets."

But of course, Marshall and Lily don't always meet the standards of honesty they set for themselves. Lily, it turns out, has a shopping problem and racks up thousands of dollars worth of credit card debt, and she keeps this from Marshall for over a year after their marriage. This lie seems like an obvious betrayal—but we sympathize with Lily's reticence in coming clean about it: no good can come from Marshall knowing about her mistakes.

One way of understanding Lily's and Marshall's promise to tell each other everything is to say that they have promised never to lie to one another. And this, most philosophers would

103

argue, is a commendable promise. The German philosopher Immanuel Kant is particularly strict about the duty to tell the truth we *never* have the right to lie—even when the lie is for good reasons. "By a lie," Kant says, "a human being throws away and, as it were, annihilates his dignity as a human being." And while Barney willingly "annihilates his dignity as a human being" on an almost nightly basis in his quest to sleep with as many women as possible, Marshall and Lily generally hold themselves to high standards of honesty—standards that even Kant might agree with.

Even Kant, however, might have issues with the level of honesty Lily and Marshall require of each other. Lily and Marshall, Ted reminds us, tell each other *everything*: they tell each other the minute details of what they do each day, even down to what they have eaten that day. "They don't just tell each other *everything*. They want to *know* everything," Ted tells Barney, and flashes back to sitting on the couch while Marshall tells Lily about his day. "So after the shower I was brushing my teeth and I was like, Oh man I wanted to have some orange juice I should've done that first! But I already had the tooth-paste on the toothbrush so I just went ahead a brushed them anyway," Marshall says. And Lily, clearly in suspense, asks anxiously, "What happened next?"

Though Kant is rigid in his requirement that we not lie to one another, there is reason to believe that he would think Marshall and Lily tell each other *too much* for a healthy relationship.

So what's a good level of honesty for a marriage like Lily's and Marshall's?

Adventures in Dowisetrepla

Kant tells us that lying is wrong for a number of reasons, all of which come back to his conception of the moral law—the universe's supreme Bro Code. First, the moral law requires us to never treat ourselves as exceptions to the rule: if we think that telling the truth is generally the right thing to do, and that everyone ought to tell the truth, then it's not okay for us to lie.

In the same way, if we would prefer that people not litter, we shouldn't litter ourselves, even occasionally. It's hypocritical for me to say that I value not littering, to hold others to that, and then to litter myself. And so, similarly, it's hypocritical for me to say I value truth telling, and to then decide that it's okay for me to lie—even if I'm lying for what seems like a really good reason. So, when Lily lies to Marshall about her credit card debt, she's wrong in part because she's violating a more general rule of their marriage: Marshall and Lily tell each other the truth. (In fact, they tell each other everything). It's hypocritical for Lily to expect Marshall to abide by their shared rule to tell one another the truth, and then to break it herself. (And Lily, of course, knows this—she feels epically guilty about lying to Marshall. And about racking up incredible credit card debt. So guilty, in fact, that it's all she can do to not go on a crazy shopping spree).

From Kant's perspective, though, Lily is wrong to lie to Marshall about her credit card debt for a second, more serious reason: when Lily lies to Marshall in this way, she fails to treat him as an end in himself. Kant tells us that morality consists largely in the basic requirement that we treat others as "ends in themselves" rather than "as means to an end," and this really just means that we have to respect others and not use them as a means to our own ends. So we probably shouldn't, as Barney does, construct entire fake identities in order to get women into bed and then abandon them freely the next morning.

Part of respecting someone as an "end in themselves" is respecting their right to choose their own actions, goals, and projects. And when we lie to someone, Kant argues, we fail to fully inform them of their options, and we deny their right to make these choices freely. So, if Robin asks Ted to lend her $100, and she promises to pay him back, knowing all along that she'll never actually pay him back, Robin does more than lie to Ted: she denies him the right to decide, on his own, whether he wants to give Robin $100. It's entirely possible that, if Robin really needed the $100, Ted would just give it to her, no questions asked. And he'd get to feel good about it, too—he'd be helping a friend in need. But when Robin lies to him, and says she'll pay him back, she takes away his opportunity to choose for himself, and to do a good deed for a friend in need. By lying to Ted, Robin treats Ted as less than a fully rational, independent person. She's making his choice for him, and denying him the space in which to think for himself.

We see this play out pretty clearly in the episode "Dowisetrepla," where Lily lies to Marshall about her credit card debt. Marshall and Lily are looking into buying a home, and Lily knows that her bad credit is going to get in the way of their application for a mortgage. Marshall is weighing whether or not to buy a place—he's taking into account the cost of real estate, the burden of his student loans, and his and Lily's shared income. Without the piece of information Lily is hiding from him—the amount of her debt, and the fact of her shopping problem—he's not able to make a fully informed decision.

Marshall and Lily's apartment hunting adventures are shaped by another kind of lie. The apartment they're looking at is in the "trendy, new" Dowisetrepla neighborhood, which no one has ever heard of, but which the real estate agent assures them is "*the* up-and-coming neighborhood." But the real estate agent only shows them the apartment on a Sunday, while extolling the virtues of the neighborhood. It's not until Marshall and Lily have bought the place that they discover the true meaning of "dowisetrepla": downwind from the sewage treatment plant. The real estate agent has purposely omitted this fact from her description of the neighborhood, and in doing so, has led Lily and Marshall to make a poorly-informed (and quite smelly) decision about buying their new home. The real estate agent has treated Lily and Marshall as a means to her end (selling the apartment) rather than as ends in themselves, capable of making reasoned choices.

We tend to expect this sort of betrayal from real estate agents and others whose livelihood depends on selling things to people, and who benefit from selling those things for more than they're worth. And it's hard to fault the real estate agent too much for her deception, since Lily and Marshall asked her frighteningly few questions, and never bothered to check the accuracy of her description. ("It should have gone like this," Ted tells us in voiceover, showing Marshall asking canny questions about the place. But instead we see only Marshall's childlike enthusiasm—"We love it! Sell it to us! We will give you *so much money!*") It's harder to excuse using lies to manipulate people in interpersonal relationships—something Barney does with alarming frequency.

In the same episode, Barney uses the empty apartment Lily and Marshall are trying to buy in order to deceive his latest conquest about his interest in commitment. His lies, in this encounter, are many: he lies about his name and his address, to lure Meg, the girl in question, back to the apartment and into bed; he falsely tells her that he's looking for a committed relationship and a "woman's touch" around his "home," and he even tells her—blatantly falsely—that he's falling in love with her. In the morning, he offers to make her waffles, only to abandon her alone in the apartment, where she will discover that nothing that she'd learned over the last twelve hours was true.

Barney lies to get girls into bed all the time, but the extent of this lie—involving, as it does, an entirely fake set, fake self, and fake proclamation of love—is especially troubling. It offers us a particularly clear example of how lies are an instance of treating someone else as a means to one's end (in this case, getting Meg into bed), and how, in doing so, we block the other person's capacity to achieve their own ends. Meg can't possibly make an informed decision about her interaction with Barney, because she knows nothing at all about the decision she's making. By presenting her with such a well-constructed deception, Barney lulls her into believing that she's choosing for herself, all the while drawing her into a situation from which she would likely have run screaming. Barney treats Meg as if she were a thing not because he wants to sleep with her once and never see her again—lots of women would willingly sleep with Barney, or at least, Neil Patrick Harris, and then never see him again—but because he refuses to give her the choice to do so.

Barney's lie, like Lily's lie about the credit card debt and the real estate agent's lie about Dowisetrepla, is designed to make someone else do what he wants her to do, without presenting her with a full account of the choice she's making. Kant warns us that when we lie in this way, we not only fail to respect the person we're deceiving—we also make ourselves responsible for the unforeseeable consequences of the lie we're telling. We force the other person to act within the framework of our deception, which denies them the ability to take full responsibility for their choices. By lying, we become, in some sense or another, responsible for those choices. We can try to avoid this responsibility by dissolving our relationship with the person we've lied to, as Barney and the real-estate agent do, but in a marriage, like Lily and Marshall's, there is no way out. When Lily lies to Marshall about her credit card debt, and Marshall, who believes they have more disposable income than they do, then applies for a mortgage they can't afford, it is Lily, rather than Marshall, who becomes morally liable for their terrible choices.

What Doppelganger?

Unlike Barney and the real estate agent, Lily's motive for lying to Marshall isn't vicious: she's not really trying to manipulate him for some end of her own. She's trying to protect him, and herself, from an unpleasant truth. Is it okay to lie to someone for really, really good reasons?

In "Doppelgangers," Lily and Marshall make a deal: they will be ready to have a baby when they find Barney's doppelganger. They've found doppelgangers for the rest of the gang— Robin's is a lesbian, Lily's is a Russian stripper, Marshall's has a mustache, and Ted's is (awesomely) a Mexican wrestler. So Lily and Marshall, unable to decide whether they're ready to have a baby, agree that they'll start trying to get pregnant when they find the fifth doppelganger. ("Stands to reason," Marshall says when Lily proposes this solution.) When Marshall finds the doppelganger —a taxi driver—Lily turns to Marshall and says, "Marshall Eriksen, put a baby in my belly."

But Marshall discovers, shortly thereafter, that it wasn't a doppelganger at all: it was Barney himself, in disguise as part of a plot to sleep with a woman from every country in the world. (The hitch: it turns out women don't want to sleep with cab drivers.) And so he agonizes over whether to tell Lily the truth. His motives are good ones: he and Lily are genuinely overjoyed that the universe has told them it's time to make a baby, and Lily feels safe and supported in her knowledge that the appearance of the fifth doppelganger is a sign from the universe that they're ready to undertake this adventure. And it's not like anyone is harmed by this lie—they were planning to have a baby anyway, and the true identity of the doppelganger is really just a symbolic thing. But, silly as it is, it's an *awfully* big lie: if Marshall lies to Lily about this, he's lying to her about the very premise of them becoming parents.

So is it okay for Marshall to lie to Lily about something so silly and inconsequential in order to help her feel happy and secure in her decision to have a child? Kant says no—even the best motives can't make up for the fact that he's failing to treat her as an end in herself, capable of making a fully informed decision. Kant is so strict on this point that he infamously argues that lying is *never* okay, even when you're lying to a murderer who's shown up at your door to seek the whereabouts of your friend, who's hiding in your closet. Even if you *know* the guy at the door is out to murder your friend, Kant argues that it's still not okay to lie to him.

Kant's critics thought this was crazy—surely, they argued (sagely), the murderer doesn't have a right to the truth in this case, and surely, you have an obligation (because of the Bro Code, if nothing else) to protect your friend. But Kant claimed that everyone, simply by virtue of being human, has "a right to the truth"—we can't go around distinguishing murderers from friends. And if we do, Kant says, we've already proven ourselves to be liars. If we stop and ask ourselves whether, in this case, it wouldn't just make more sense to lie to the murderer and protect our friend, if we ask "permission to think first about possible exceptions" then we are "already a liar," according to Kant. Telling the truth is a duty, Kant says, and not something to be decided on a case-by-case basis.

Although the whole telling-the-truth-to-the-murderer bit seems like a questionable piece of advice, there's something to be said for Kant's insistence that we shouldn't decide whether or not to lie on a case-by-case basis. On the night that Marshall and Lily are supposed to start making a baby, Marshall must decide whether or not to tell Lily the truth about Barney and the doppelganger. In the moment he hesitates before kissing her, we can almost imagine what's running through his head: *is there really any reason to tell her? What's the worst that could happen? We're ready to have a baby, anyway! It* could *have been a doppelganger. Baby Eriksen!* And, in the face of awesome consequences (Baby Eriksen!) and minimal downsides (*what's the worst that could happen?*), Marshall decides to go for it. And it's possible that—if Barney hadn't shown up a minute later and told the truth—he'd have gotten away with it. Because there are lies like that—lies we can get away with, lies with good consequences all around, lies that bring peace and comfort to all involved.

Except that Marshall has a duty to his relationship with Lily: they tell each other *everything*. And this thing—this silly, symbolic, the-universe-told-us-it-was-time-to-have-a-baby thing—is a pretty big betrayal of that duty. Telling Lily this lie would mean that Marshall let his desire for a baby come before his marital obligations, and it would mean that he had taken from her the right to make this decision for herself.

Telling Each Other *Everything*

But Marshall's motive for telling Lily the truth about Barney's doppelganger in the end hinges less on a concern about failing to respect her than about the damage it would do to their relationship: that lie would mean he would always know something she didn't. And that small, meaningless deception would, over time, eat away at them. For Marshall and Lily, truth telling is an important form of intimacy, and both worry about the ways in which even the smallest lies might undermine the strength and openness of their relationship.

One of the ways Marshall and Lily practice marital intimacy is by telling each other, as Ted puts it, *everything*. They end each day by telling each other what they've had to eat that day—"An everything bagel, a chicken breast, celery sticks, and a spoon of peanut butter," Lily tells Marshall in "Three Days of Snow." Their friends find this compulsive, detail-oriented truth telling rather bizarre. In "Slap Bet," Barney challenges Lily's claim that Marshall tells Lily everything, quizzing her on Marshall's darkest secrets: (Barney) "Bill's bachelor party in Memphis?" (Lily) "Oh, when they had to pump out all the nickels from his stomach?"

Surprisingly, despite his insistence on the immorality of all lying, I suspect that Kant might be a bit worried about the level of truth-telling Marshall and Lily engage in. If lying prevents us from respecting others, too much truth, too, might undermine respect. For Kant, the critical ingredient in friendship is respect: moral friendship, he tells us, involves the "complete confidence of two persons in revealing their secret judgment and feelings to each other, as a far as such disclosures are consistent with mutual respect." And this description of friendship, with its emphasis on mutual respect and confidence in one another, sounds an awful lot like Lily and Marshall's relationship.

Kant worried about what too many confidences and too much openness in relationships might do to our capacity to respect one another. In a letter written in 1792, Kant offered advice of this sort to a young woman seeking his opinion about her romantic relationship. She had lied to her lover, and he had abandoned her; Kant, predictably, told her that the lie was wrong and that she needed to repent for it. But he then suggested that, while lying violated one sort of duty, perhaps she had nonetheless shared too much with her lover to be deserving of his respect. "We can't expect frankness of people, since everyone fears that to reveal himself completely would be to make him despised by others," Kant wrote, assuring her that "this lack of frankness, this reticence, is very different from dishonesty." Indeed, he suggests that reticence may in fact be a virtue of friendship: we should avoid telling friends things that may cause them to lose their respect for us.

Barney gives Ted a strikingly similar piece of advice in "Slap Bet," when Ted agonizes over a secret Robin is keeping from him. "You should be grateful Robin has a secret," Barney tells him. "The more you know about someone, the closer you get to hitting the fatal "Oh" moment." But Lily, predictably, disagrees: "In a real relationship, you share everything," she says. "That's why Marshall and I don't keep any secrets."

Even Lily thinks that a little reticence is essential to a healthy marriage In "Zip, Zip, Zip," Lily and Marshall find themselves trapped in the bathroom while Ted has a romantic date with Victoria. After an hour of hiding out, Lily says to Marshall, "Baby, there's something I have to do, and if I do it in front of you, it will change the entire nature of our relationship." Lily drank a Big Gulp of Mountain Dew before they got stuck in there, and she has to pee. But Lily and Marshall have kept the bathroom door closed in their relationship: in nine years, Lily has never peed in front of Marshall. And this, she argues, is part of keeping some of the "mystery" alive in their marriage.

We might think it odd that Lily and Marshall tell each other *everything*, but still keep the bathroom door closed. But this apparent contradiction highlights the tension between respect and intimacy present in committed romantic relationships. Kant thought this tension was impossible to manage—he suggests that marriage is an intimate relationship and that in this sense it is quite different from the "mutual respect" involved in a moral friendship. And no wonder, given his concerns with reticence: sex is rarely a reticent sort of activity.

Sex, for Kant, involves an unacceptable sort of use of another person, and this use tends to undermine respect. Kant doesn't think the respect involved in friendship is enough to overcome the disrespect that sex entails, and so he argues that sex is permissible only within marriage. In marriage, partners have a legal obligation to respect one anther, and they become, before the law, one person. And this means, Kant says, that married partners have "a right to each other akin to rights to things": married partners can use each other *as if* they were things (crazy monkey sex). Married partners promise to *share ends*, and so when they use one another for sex, they're doing it for shared ends.

As a married couple, Marshall and Lily function, from certain perspectives, as a single moral entity, with a single set of ends. So the sort of sexual use Marshall and Lily make of each other is fundamentally different from the sort of use Barney makes of the women he sleeps with. Barney's ends are his own, and he's using these women as a means to his own ends, while Marshall and Lily have shared ends, and they can use one another however they want to to achieve those ends.

But because Marshall and Lily share ends, and use each other for those ends, they've failed at all that reticence and respect that's key to a Kantian account of friendship. So, because marriage is an intimate (and sexual) relationship (and because he didn't have terribly high opinions of women) Kant doubted that one could be friends with one's wife.

And this is, of course, ridiculous. *Of course* you can be friends with your wife. Marshall and Lily refer to one another as "best friends" all the time, and it doesn't seem as though all that sex has seriously undermined their respect for one another (although Lily does occasionally objectify Marshall when they're not having enough sex). Their friendship is, in fact, the great strength of their marriage. But this isn't to say that striking a balance between intimacy and respect is always easy, as their escapades in the bathroom suggest. Even more challenging is striking a balance between their intimacy with each other and their obligations to respect their friends' secrets.

The Canadian Mall Marriage 6000

There's another problem embedded in Lily and Marshall's practice of advanced truth-telling: sometimes they find themselves telling one another truths they've promised to keep as secrets. So, in "Slap Bet," while Marshall tells Lily what he's eaten that day, he also inadvertently reveals that he went to the library and discovered that Robin had never been married—a fact he'd *sworn* to Ted he'd keep secret. We've established that Marshall has an obligation to tell Lily the truth—but what is he supposed to do when he also has an obligation to keep Ted's secret? Does the general obligation to be truthful with one's spouse trump specific promises to keep secrets?

One answer is that Marshall and Lily shouldn't ever promise to keep things from one another. But, in a circle of friends as tight as theirs, this isn't going to work. Robin needs to trust Lily to keep her secrets (even though Lily is a self-admittedly *terrible* secret keeper), and Marshall sometimes needs to abide by Barney's Bro Code and not tell Lily everything the guys discuss.

A second answer is that no one should tell Lily or Marshall anything they wouldn't want the other to know—and Marshall and Lily, similarly, should refuse confidences they can't share with the other person. But this solution faces the same problem as the first: it's impractical, in a friendship circle so small, to simply refuse to hear the secrets our friends want to tell us, and these refusals would put them in danger of becoming bad friends.

So this seems to leave us with the notion that Marshall and Lily should keep secrets for their friends, and should, if necessary, lie to one another about them.

But this solution poses another problem, one thrown into particularly sharp relief by the radical forms of honesty and intimacy that Marshall and Lily more regularly engage in. Marshall and Lily have, after all, promised to tell each other *everything*, and so any promise they make to a friend to keep a secret from each other, is a violation of that first promise. And this leads to all sorts of tricky moral calculations. In "Slap Bet," Marshall finds himself caught between his specific promise to Ted that he will keep Robin's secret, and his more general promise to Lily to tell her everything.

We might say here that the specific promise outweighs the general promise, since the terms of the specific promise (to keep Robin's secret) are clear and limited, while the terms of the general promise (to tell Lily everything) are somewhat fuzzier. (What is "everything," anyway? If Marshall tells Lily that he had a bagel for breakfast, but not that he almost had chicken salad on it and then wound up with scallion cream cheese, is he failing to tell her "everything"?) In other words, if Marshall was going to "lawyer" us about this promise, he might be able to get away with the claim that he met the terms of both promises by keeping his promise to Ted, since telling Lily "everything" is a vague promise to make.

Marshall might even take this a step further, arguing that telling Lily "everything" isn't a promise he's qualified to make (I mean, who has the time to actually tell someone *everything*?) And, if keeping the promise isn't *possible*, then we might say that it's not a permissible promise to make. We make promises like this all the time, and no one expects us to keep them. So, if Marshall were to promise Lily that he would give her the sun, moon, and stars, we don't seem to think Lily has the right to hold him to it: giving her the sun, moon, and stars isn't actually possible. It's a sort of metaphorical promise, and he might find himself bound by the "spirit" of the promise, without being held to the specific terms it dictates.

So maybe Marshall is bound by the "spirit" of the promise to tell Lily everything, without actually being required to tell her every single thing that happens in a day. And so, maybe he can abide by the spirit of his promise while not telling her Ted's secret about Robin.

It seems, however, that Lily really does expect Marshall to tell her everything, or at least everything important. When Barney challenges this, she's able to cite multiple cases of Marshall telling her things Barney assumes he's kept secret— like the time Marshall was in Trenton and a donkey ate his pants. So it seems unlikely that Marshall can keep Robin's secret from Lily while still holding to the spirit of their promise. Instead, I think that Marshall might not be able to promise Ted that he'll keep a secret from Lily: to do so would be to violate a prior agreement. It's also practically impossible, since Marshall can't walk Lily through the normal adventures of his day without letting the secret slip.

Kant's account of the distinction between marriage and friendship may be useful in understanding why Marshall's promise to tell Lily everything outweighs his promise to Ted. From a Kantian perspective, as a married couple, Marshall and

Lily share ends. And this means not only that crazy monkey sex is okay, but that they operate within a kind of moral bubble. From an outside perspective, Marshall and Lily are sort of like one person.

Lily gets a taste of this in "Dowisetrepla," when she and Marshall apply for a mortgage, and the loan officer demands her social security number along with Marshall's. Lily, still trying to keep her credit card debt a secret, resists, arguing that Marshall's financial information must be enough, since "he's the breadwinner" and "can women even own property, anyway?" And of course, once upon a time (Kant's time, in fact), this argument would totally hold up: one way in which married couples operated as a single unit was in the fact that married women couldn't independently own property, and so all marital property was owned jointly by the couple. And though Lily, in the twenty-first century, totally *can* own property independently, neither she nor Marshall can apply for a loan without taking the other's financial well-being into account.

Lily tries to protect Marshall from her financial failings, going so far as to suggest that they get a divorce "on paper." But Marshall refuses, arguing that when he married her, he married her problems, too. Her problems became his problems, just as his ends became her ends. There's no other sort of relationship (except, possibly, parenthood) where we so completely join our selves, our problems, and our interests to another persons'.

This joining together, says Kant, creates a new sort of moral space. In this moral space, we're allowed to do all sorts of things we aren't allowed to do outside it—including (and maybe especially) crazy monkey sex. We aren't in danger of using one another in unacceptable ways in marriage, because we've fused our ends together. We're like one person, and so the things we owe each other are no different from the things we owe ourselves, honesty included.

So, in marriage, respect doesn't require us to be reticent the way that friendship does (and, Barney, let's hope you've already had the "Oh" moment with the girl you marry). Intimacy and frankness are okay—they are maybe even required. So Marshall and Lily are supposed to tell each other everything, not just because the "Oh" moment is long past, but because they need to be informed of each other's wishes, needs, and credit card debt in order to successfully share ends.

This doesn't necessarily mean that Marshall and Lily can't keep secrets from each other. There are good secrets, like Christmas presents, surprise birthday parties, and sexy lingerie (as long as it's not Robin's lingerie). And there are harmless secrets, like Robin's crush on Ted. But it seems as though Marshall and Lily can't be *required* to keep secrets from each other: any secret that threatens to undermine their capacity to share ends must be shared. And Barney, Ted, and Robin come to expect this: over time, they learn that to tell Lily something is to tell Marshall, and vice versa.

III

Wait for It ...

10
Why You Should Never, Never Love Thy Neighbor

R ADU U SZKAI AND E MANUEL S OCACIU

K ids, there are many neat, well-rounded, and inspiring stories about morality out there. Great thinkers in the history of philosophy have taught us that morality is about timeless principles, or about developing the virtues of a beautiful character, or about bringing as much happiness as possible to as many people as possible.

And then there are a few messier stories told by equally great thinkers who just couldn't swallow any of those elegant formulas. Among these eccentric few we find two of the most intellectually engaging thinkers of modern times, whose doctrines show remarkable, if sometimes disturbing similarities: David Hume and . . . wait for it . . . Barney Stinson.

Hume's Awesome Approach to Morality

David Hume tries to explain the task of the moral philosopher via a metaphor. Approaching the topic of morality (or, more generally, that of human nature), one could proceed "either as an anatomist or as a painter; either to discover its most secret springs and principles or to describe the grace and beauty of its actions" (letter to his bro Francis Hutcheson in 1739).

Or, to update the metaphor, we might choose either Barney's approach, or Ted's. While the job of the painter is surely important and not to be dismissed, it has to rest upon the foundations carefully laid down by the anatomist: even using the richest colors and conveying the most appealing attitudes, we couldn't do justice to the beauty of a Helen or Venus without paying attention to the structures and proportions of the human body. Because it is impossible to employ both perspectives at the same time, the moral philosopher would have to choose the more fundamental, anatomist approach to morality. In other words the philosopher should be a keen observer of human realities and, as far as possible, an experimenter.

Still, Hume sees that doing that can be painful: "The anatomist presents to the eye the most hideous and disagreeable objects" (*An Enquiry Concerning the Principles of Morals*, Introduction). We might not like what we stumble upon. And Hume himself found out quite a few things using his method. In a much-quoted place he relegates Reason, arguably the flagship of almost any philosophical armada, to the role of a shabby little fishing boat anchored in the shallower part of the harbor.

Starting with Plato, philosophers usually teach us that moral action is always guided by reason, and its goal is to overcome passions, viewed as obstacles. Shockingly, for Hume it's the other way round: reason alone can never be effective in motivating actions. It always has to be guided and ruled. "Reason is, and ought only to be the slave of the passions, and can never pretend to any other office than to serve and obey them" (*A Treatise of Human Nature*, Book 2, Part 3, Section 3). Kinky!

This disconcerting and rather BDSM picture of the interaction between reason and passions is the first of the two major hallmarks of Humeanism in moral philosophy. It fits the bill that the title of a wonderful book written by one of the most well-known Humean moral philosophers of our time (other than Barney Stinson, that is), is *Ruling Passions*.[1] But to argue that Barney is a Humean in this sense is a bit too easy, as obviously his world is ruled by passions.

The second, and less discussed major hallmark of a Humean approach to moral philosophy concerns the theory of norms. It wasn't terribly new, even for his time, to just say that moral norms govern, at least partly, our social behavior. But usually philosophers who focus on norms tend to regard them as displaying some sort of objective or intrinsic quality that lends

---

[1] We refer to Simon Blackburn. Actually, focusing on passions allows Humean moral philosophers to give highly enticing titles to their books. Another one of Blackburn's is called *Lust*.

them special value. In religious ethics, norms are God's commandments; for Immanuel Kant, norms are deduced from a supreme principle of morality which is universal and discovered by pure reason, independently of any particular context or experience; utilitarians think that the moral norms are the ones conducing to the greatest amount of overall happiness; and so on. In all such typical cases, norms are out there waiting to be *discovered*: through revelation, or pure reason, or calculus.

Well, not for David Hume! Norms are just human conventions, like money or language. They are *invented*, rather than discovered. But wait, does this mean that Hume was a relativist? Not quite. In an important passage in the *Treatise of Human Nature*, he tries to answer this possible objection. Moral norms might be artificial, but they are by no means arbitrary. "Mankind is an inventive species; and where an invention is obvious and absolutely necessary, it may as properly be said to be natural as any thing that proceeds immediately from original principles" (*Treatise*, 3.2.1.19)

Okay, how does the story go then? How do norms arise? Why would they be necessary and how could we avoid relativism? Instead of imagining a social contract through which everybody agrees to establish a bunch of rules to be followed, Hume gives a strikingly original explanation, framed in evolutionary terms. Norms, although invented, are *not designed*. Just like his great bro Adam Smith did with economics, Hume gives an invisible-hand explanation to social morality.

The argument starts from identifying the function of norms. They are around to facilitate co-operation between humans. We all know co-operation is mutually beneficial. At least, we become painfully aware of that when we encounter non-co-operators (that is, when we get crossed). But in order for co-operation to be even possible, there has to be a reasonable degree of predictability concerning the future behavior of others.

Would you take as wingman a dude that always behaves randomly, with a fifty-fifty chance of denying that you are a SNASA astronaut who just returned after climbing the Everest for fun, without an oxygen mask, during the Thanksgiving holiday? Neither would we and, for that matter, probably anybody (except when the dude is the only available option and the lady you want to mix it up with is really, really hot). So humans need some kind of a problem-solving device in their social interactions to make co-operation more likely, and this is the job of norms.

A likely to-do list for Hume's evolutionary approach to norms is the same as for any other evolutionary theory: to explain the emergence of norms (how they appear), their relative stability over time (why they don't change daily) and their variability over longer periods (why our current morality is not exactly the same as, say, the one in the Broman Empire).

We'll skip the details about how Hume and his followers today take up this challenge. The key notion, however, has to be mentioned. It's reciprocity. Here is how norms come about, in Hume's own words describing the mechanism for a specific case, the rules of property:

> I observe, that it will be for my interest to leave another in the possession of his goods, *provided* he will act in the same manner with regard to me. He is sensible of a like interest in the regulation of his conduct. When this common sense of interest is mutually expressed, and is known to both, it produces a suitable resolution and behaviour. And this may properly enough be called a convention or agreement betwixt us, though without the interposition of a promise. (*Treatise*, 3.2.2.10)

But, again, the results are not random. The process selects norms based on something similar to what contemporary biologists would call "evolutionary fitness" (their capacity to reproduce, forming patterns of behavior). Norms do compete, warns Hume. The winners are the ones that best match human nature (a combination of self-love and limited generosity) with the circumstances of the external world (most importantly, scarcity of resources).

To wrap-up: in Hume's approach, moral norms are just context-dependent problem-solving devices for human interactions, that evolve over time. Now it's time to see how Barney applies and enriches this morsel of wisdom.

An Enquiry concerning the Bro Code

Philosophers tend to imagine a whole lot of wacky things. For example, Thomas Nagel invites us to imagine, if we can, what it's like to be a bat. Not that a personal in-built radar wouldn't come in handy at times, but let's face it, being a bat is not anybody's dream.

Let's start this time from a more pleasant scenario: you're in a bar, having some beers with your bro, when, suddenly, a hot chick appears. Moreover, at a first glance, judging through the lenses of the Hot/Crazy scale, she appears to be, unlike Vicky Mendoza, hot enough to be only a little bit crazy. If you were Barney Stinson, for example, your first thought would be how to come up with a scheme, maybe from your *Playbook*, which would allow you to. . . . Unfortunately, your bro stops you short and tells you: "She's my sister, bro!". Well, so what, you might reply? Is there some rule against having a legendary night with her?

If you're really a bro, you know there is! And if you didn't, maybe we should stage a trademark *How I Met Your Mother* intervention for you. It's in the *Bro Code*! References to this great human achievement are scattered throughout the show, but where could we find a full version? Fortunately, Barney and his bro Matt Kuhn published it with a preamble that gives very useful insights into the nature and function of the Code. Writes Barney: "Whether we know it or not, each of us lives a life governed by an internalized code of conduct. Some call it morality. Others call it religion. I call it the Bro Code."[2] And it wasn't passed on to humanity in stone tablets by the Supreme Bro, or even discovered by other philosophical devices such as Reason. It's actually the result of repeated interactions between bros all throughout history.

Why did Cain kill Abel and commit the first broicide or why did the Trojan War over Helen take place between a bro from Sparta and a bro from Troy? Simply because the Bro Code, as a piece of Humean morality, didn't exist in the beginning of time. It was invented to solve these kinds of problems in interactions between bros. And it survives and develops because it fully respects Hume's criterion: it best matches bros' human nature (we all know what's there!) with the circumstances of the external world, namely the scarcity of good things (be it beer, hot ladies, or Superbowl games).

---

[2] Barney Stinson and Matt Kuhn, *The Bro Code* (Simon and Schuster, 2008), p. ix.

Historically, as shown in the episode "The Goat," it was Barnabus Stinson, one of the lesser known delegates to the Continental Congress, who drafted the first version of a bundle of moral rules from past interactions between Bros. Carefully observing the bickering between Benjamin Franklin and George Washington over "codpiece blocking" a bro who "called dibs first on some wench," he proceeds to "inscribe" this set of rules on the backside of the Constitution, in order to save paper and impress a young damsel next to him. And all this happened in 1776, the year David Hume died, exactly twenty-five years after he published his *Enquiry Concerning the Principles of Morals*. You *must* see the connection here! Still not convinced? Let us tell you then that David Hume and Ben Franklin were bros, with Hume actually introducing Franklin to French intellectual high-life. True story.

To paraphrase German philosopher Heidegger though, why is there a Bro Code, rather than nothing? To put it simply, if we properly understand the Bro Code as a bunch of socially evolved norms, then we could see it as the social glue holding us together as Bros. Norms such as "Bros before hoes," "No sex with your Bro's ex (unless granted permission)," or "Bros cannot make eye contact during a devil's threeway " have a specific function in our life: that of better co-ordinating our actions and resolving co-ordination problems so as to avoid unpleasant outcomes (especially the one regarding the threesome). In the words of Robert Nozick, "the function of ethics, of ethical norms and ethical beliefs, is to co-ordinate our actions with those of others to mutual benefit. . . ."[3]

For example, what's the function and justification of Article #150, which prohibits you, as a Bro, doing the hanky-panky with one of your bro's ex-girlfriends (unless he grants you permission, of course)? The answer is quite simple: just look at Barney's reaction after first having sex with Robin, Ted's ex, in Season Three. He desperately tries (even hires the unemployed Marshall as a lawyer) to find a loophole in the *Bro Code*. Why so desperate? Because he's aware of the fact he has done something wrong: he violated the principle of reciprocity between two bros. Furthermore, he also wants to escape from a possible

---

[3] Robert Nozick, *Invariances* (Harvard University Press, 2001), p. 240.

punishment from Ted, namely losing his bro and wingman status. Unfortunately though, as awesome as he may be, by the end of the episode Ted decides to penalize him even harder, by breaking up with him as a friend (and eventually revoking the punishment). Bluntly put, the function of a rule which prohibits any sex between a bro and a bro's ex is that of reducing the possibility of such co-ordination failures and increasing the chance that the two will remain bros. Before hoes.

Neighborly Love in Eight Easy Steps

To avoid any appearance of questioning anything said by the awesome Barney Stinson, let's just accept here that the Golden Rule actually is "Love thy neighbor." Compare it with the Platinum Rule, Article 83 of the *Bro Code*: Never, ever, ever "love" thy neighbor! While the first would be the article of choice for all the painters of morality (remember Hume's metaphor!), it takes the clinical approach of the anatomist to fully understand and appreciate the merits of the latter.

The Platinum Rule was first mentioned in the show by Barney in Season Three, as an attempt to dissuade Ted from pursuing the catastrophic intention of taking his doctor (a tattoo remover and, eventually, a heart remover) out on a date. Remarkably, Barney proceeds in purely Humean fashion, not by inferring the rule from a higher abstract principle, but by presenting it as the result that emerged from countless repetitions of similar interactions.

A little difficulty appears here. If the moral thinker has to be a bit of an experimentalist, the number of available options is quite limited. We don't have access to other peoples' minds, so it's hard to know what they really think. Introspection is no good either. Empathy, in the sense of trying to place yourself in the situation of others wouldn't work because it would still be us in the imagined situation, with our own luggage of commitments and biases.

The only reality that we have experimental access to is the way people act. So, says Hume,

> we must therefore glean up our experiments in this science from a cautious observation of human life, and take them as they appear in the common course of the world, by men's behavior in company, in

affairs, and in their pleasures. Where experiments of this kind are judiciously collected and compared, we may hope to establish on them a science, which will not be inferior in certainty, and will be much superior in utility to any other of human comprehension. (*Treatise*, Introduction, 10)

In making the case for the Platinum Rule, Barney is a textbook Humean gleaner of observations about peoples' behavior "in company, in affairs and in their pleasures." Three particular case studies are invoked to point at the co-ordination disasters that result from failing to follow the Platinum Rule: his own mix-up with Wendy the Waitress, the couples version of dating that Marshall and Lily had with their neighbors across the hallway, Michael and Laura (involving brunches, dinners and charades, of course, don't go all Barney Stinson over it!) and Robin's romance with her co-worker and former hockey player Curt "The Ironman" Irons.

But what makes someone a neighbor in the Platinum Rule sense of the word? According to Marshall, neighbors are all the people you see on a regular basis and you can't avoid. So co-workers are, in this sense, neighbors. Your classmates in college are too. And, of course, actual neighbors are definitely Platinum Rule neighbors. But, as Lily emphatically points out, it actually gets worse when it's a neighbor that you also pay like, in Ted's case, his doctor Stella (though the same applies to the milkman, the newspaper guy, or the waitress in your favorite pub).

The Eight Stages

In all cases of "loving" one's neighbor, Barney was the first to notice the same succession of eight stages: attraction, bargaining, submission, perks, tipping point, purgatory, confrontation, and fallout (to which Ted adds one more in the end, but we'll come to that later).

Obviously, the attraction stage is necessary in order for the Platinum Rule to apply. There isn't, however, a universal recipe for attraction in neighborly situations. Robin, for example, feels irresistibly drawn towards Curt "the Ironman" Irons because he was a hockey player and she's Canadian. In Marshall's and Lilly's case, it's the sharing of the same favorite pastimes. And Barney, well, Wendy just looked interested. And, be it triggered by a whim or by deeply shared interest, it's not the attraction alone that's the problem in case of the Platinum Rule, it's actually acting upon it in the context.

The next step is bargaining. Interestingly though, it's not a bargain between the attracted and the "atractee," but between the attracted and his or her friends, who try to discourage initiating a relationship. The most interesting negotiation takes place in the first case, namely Barney's. The gang had only vague hunches about something being seriously wrong in this situation. They even expected that some rule should apply, which Barney, out of all people, should already be aware of and have a catchy name for. But Barney wasn't. Confronted with their amazement, he replies: "what rule is there that says I can't seduce the waitress in my favorite bar?" This is a typical situation which philosophers would call "anomic" (that is to say, not governed by any norms). Moreover, this would be exactly the kind of scenario in which Hume would expect a norm to emerge, or be invented, because the costs of failure would simply be too high. What would the gang do in a hostile bar?

But everybody thought it would be okay. And so the next stage develops: submission. As it turned out, they all succumbed to temptation: Barney found a creative use for soda, Lily and Marshall had the time of their lives throwing dinner and charades parties with the Gerards, while Robin enjoyed a hockey game without paying to much attention to what happened on the ice.

And why wouldn't they give into temptation? They seemed to have all the incentives in the world to do it. Let's face it, the perks can be awesome. Just look at Lily and Marshall: always searching for a couple to do couples stuff together. And when your best friends are always in the business of screwing up every relationship, that's not that easy to find. Then, the Gerards moved across the hall! Pretty convenient, huh? Or so it seems to the untrained eye.

Perks, however, come with costs. Even worse, the same things that make perks possible also produce costs which might become unbearable. Consider the opportunity costs (all the alternatives that you have to give up) in pursuing a course of action. Barney suddenly found his bar off-limits for picking up other girls. His own bar! Lily and Marshall quickly discovered that "dating" their neighbors across the hall made other plans impossible. Robin, on the other hand, was dating a co-worker, so in her case, considering her well-known fear of commitment, the tipping point came more swiftly and bitterly.

When becoming fully aware of the costs, the sixth stage begins: purgatory. The slogan for this phase, for all of them, becomes: "God, I'm such an idiot!" The realization of the mistake they made dawns on everybody. However there's a difference between Dante's Purgatory and the gang's: while the first one is filled with popes, kings, and poets, the latter is populated with loving neighbors. It's like the Universe is shrinking on them. As Barney explains, "What was once my jungle is now my Zoo. And I am forced to mate with the same old lioness again and again and again." Why would he be "forced"? Break-ups are as old as relationships, so isn't there an exit option available? There might be, but not easily available. What makes the neighborly purgatory special, compared with things going bad in a "normal" affair, is the absence of a post break-up safe haven. This makes enduring a viable strategy, at least until it becomes really unbearable.

And when it does, it's time for a "relationship-ectomy" (told you, Barney Stinson is a Humean anatomist!). The confrontation stage marks the end of the neighborly "love," In other, typical relationships, that would be all. In this one, there's still another step, namely fallout. Since you're doomed to run into your neighbors constantly, their opportunities to retaliate or to punish you are considerably higher than in a normal post-break-up situation. Things do not just revert to the the pre-submission scenario. What once was a pleasant and cozy surrounding has now all the attributes of a cowboy movie standoff.

In Robin's case, the punishment exacted by Curt amounts to a live outbreak on TV that puts both in a professionally awkward position. For Marshall and Lily, the penalty is being stalked by the Gerards. Even when they try to get out of the building using the fire escape, they end up with Michael and Laura waiting for them at the bottom of the stairs. Yet, once again, Barney's conundrum is the most interesting. Even though there's seemingly no retaliation from Wendy the Waitress, he still gets the fallout. He naturally expects to be punished in one way or another, maybe by having his gin and tonic poisoned. The fear is terrifying. As Barney puts it, the succession of stages in neighbor-loving scenarios is a "rule of nature," so fallout is inescapable (even if actual retaliation might not happen).

Reciprocity is the main mechanism for enforcing cooperation in the Humean framework. To non-co-operators, people usually reciprocate with punishment (retaliation or revenge). Initiating a break-up in a relationship is an age-old example of non-cooperative behavior (or "defection," in a more pretentious and technical jargon). What puts neighbors in a unique position to retaliate is the multiplicity of means and opportunities at their disposal, given by the high probability of future interactions. That's why the Platinum Rule has to be invented as a moral norm.

What's so cool about using this method is that we don't have to rely on the natural goodness of all bros. Even if we start from a bleaker view of human nature, moral behavior can still emerge. Another major present-day Humean, the philosopher and mathematician Kenneth Binmore, makes this point in a plastic manner: "we therefore do not need to pretend that we are all Dr. Jekylls in order to explain how we manage to get on with each other fairly well much of the time. Even a society of Mr. Hydes can eventually learn to co-ordinate on an efficient equilibrium in an indefinitely repeated game."[4]

Still, there's quite a bit of a role to play also for the Painter towards the end of the story. Ted (incidentally an architect) reveals that fallout is not necessarily the final step in this type of scenarios. It is, at least sometimes, followed by a ninth stage: co-existence. The grudges can melt away, eventually. Robin and Curt, the Eriksens and the Gerards are living proof for this. Even Wendy the Waitress. In fact, everybody but Barney, who's still experiencing the fallout from really "loving" his neighbor. Quite happily ever after!

Thanks to Barney

As a piece of Humean morality, the Bro Code will surely evolve. Maybe, at some point, the Platinum Rule will be overridden by too many exceptions. Be it as it may, at any given time, it will

---

[4] Kenneth Binmore, "Reciprocity and the Social Contract," *Politics, Philosophy, and Economics* 3:1, p. 21.

still be based on the foundations selflessly laid out by the great thinkers who featured in our story. As modest scribes, telling this tale, it's a matter of courtesy to give the last word to the one and only Barney Stinson, because, yeah, he has another crucial point to make:

> . . . centuries from now, when a Bro applies the rudiments of the Bro Code to score a three-boobed future chick, the only thanks I'll need is the knowledge that I—in whatever small capacity—bro'd him out . . . though if he could figure out how to bring me back to life, that would be pretty awesome, too. (*The Bro Code*, p. xi)

11
A Tale of Two Feminist Icons

TINA TALSMA

Kids, compared to old shows like *Leave It to Beaver* or *The Brady Bunch* modern-day sitcoms have largely moved beyond traditional gender roles. This is because we now recognize that women are capable of doing more than folding laundry and cooking dinner, and men are capable of much more than simply "bringing home the bacon." In many modern-day sitcoms, there is much to be celebrated, especially for women who look, in some small way, to these characters as role models.

But what about one of the most successful shows on TV: *How I Met Your Mother*? Do the main characters embrace traditional gender norms or have they, like main characters in other competitor shows, such as *Community, 30 Rock* (Liz Lemon, at any rate)*, and *Parks and Recreation*, moved beyond those old traditions that hold us back?

When we focus on Barney, all hope seems lost. Though we've seen Barney change recently, what with his relationship with and elaborately planned engagement to Robin, his character is roughly a powerful corporate type who only values women so long as he can get sex from them. Furthermore, all three male characters have powerful, prestigious jobs compared to Lily who is a kindergarten teacher and Robin, who has spent most of her career as a ridiculous caricature.

But to dismiss *How I Met Your Mother* as embracing traditional gender stereotypes would be a mistake. Both Robin and Lily are strong characters who embody different, but equally important, feminist ideals and philosophical views. Even Ted

131

and Marshall show a level of complexity that tells against clear black-and-white gender lines.

The Strength of Each Is the Strength of All

Each member of Ted Mosby's gang demonstrates a personal strength unique to them. It's because each is seen as strong on his or her own that the group has such a fun, often highly comical, dynamic. And the viewer gets the impression that having such strong, admirable friends, each with strengths that the others lack, enhances the life of each of the friends. It's because they are each so strong, interesting, and unique that we, as an audience, want so badly to hang out in MacLaren's with them.

Ted soldiers on in spite of his overly dramatic, often comical, search for love. In spite of many failed attempts to find his wife, Ted remains hopeful. Barney is the typical corporate play boy who succeeds in everything he does, most notably in bedding a continuous string of women. Barney always exudes charisma and confidence. Marshall shows tremendous courage and strength in leaving a cushy corporate job to fight for a cause he believes in. And Lily is often the one who must enforce the rules of the multiple challenges, competitions and bets the others concoct, showing that the others look up to her and respect her decisions. But in many ways it's Robin's strength that outshines all the rest. She shares Barney's autonomy and independence, Marshall's courage in pursuing difficult career goals, Ted's hope in true love and the respect of the group like her best bud, Lily. Because of this inner strength she's a character who easily embodies feminist ideals and who serves as a model for women living in the twenty-first century.

Robin as Autonomous

The most obvious way in which Robin operates as an example to modern liberated women is in the focus she places on her career. One of the loudest calls for equality that has marked the last several decades, including modern times (following the initial call for the right to vote), was and remains the call for equality in the workplace. Robin is a great example of a woman who can do whatever she sets her mind to (though she must certainly slog through some rough patches to get there) and who can, like any man, place her career at the top of her list of priorities, if she so chooses.

In fighting so hard to be accepted as a top-rate journalist, and laughing in the face of adversity (or at least not minding when others laugh at her through the adversity), Robin demonstrates a great deal of autonomy. According to Marilyn Friedman, "autonomy involves choosing and living according to standards or values that are, in some plausible sense, one's 'own.'"[1] That is, an autonomous individual sets her own priorities and then lives according to them. She is not told what her place in life is or what dreams she may or may not have and follow. She is, in a word, "self-governing."[2]

Autonomy has been of such importance to women working in the feminist movement because it has been historically withheld from women and other oppressed groups. In fact, oppression often just is a lack of autonomy. In decades past, women have been unable to pursue dreams that take them out of the home. They have been unable to act on values that differ from those that society has dictated, in particular values that are different from being a good wife and mother. And women have often suffered in relationships in which they do not have a way to express themselves or that they are not free to leave. The struggle for personal autonomy is one that continues and one that Robin clearly embodies.

Robin's focus on her career is seen throughout the series. She fights through a few years working early morning shifts as the on-air talent at a local TV station. The only people who watch her are drunk college students who have turned her frequent use of the phrase "but, um" into a drinking game. Though she's often forced to work on projects that she thinks are ridiculous and even her best friends cannot stay awake to watch her, she never gives up and eventually works her way up to lead news anchor. To succeed in such a competitive environment takes a great deal of individual strength, determination and courage, all qualities that Robin possesses to the max.

---

[1] Marilyn Friedman, "Autonomy, Social Disruption, and Women," in *Relational Autonomy: Feminist Perspectives on Autonomy, Agency, and the Social Self,* edited by Catriona Mackenzie and Natalie Stoljar (Oxford University Press, 2000), p. 37.

[2] Sarah Buss, "Personal Autonomy," *Stanford Encyclopedia of Philosophy* <http://plato.stanford.edu/entries/personal-autonomy>.

In addition to being a career-oriented woman, Robin is fiercely independent in other aspects of her life. She's often seen leaving her friends to meet up with other groups of friends, showing that she can stand on her own two feet. She also finds clinginess and neediness in a boyfriend intolerable. And, though this is chalked up to her national heritage and the fact that her father raised her as a boy, she does not demonstrate stereotypically feminine traits. She is not quiet, respectful or afraid to voice her opinion. And she seems to love violence, as is seen in her favorite (or favourite!) hobbies of hockey, hunting, and bar fights and her embarrassment surrounding her past as a Canadian pop star. So, she ignores gender stereotypes and exists as her own person, whoever she wants that to be. If others think she should be something else, well then to hell with them!

This fierce independence is also seen in her lack of a desire to have a family. Many women feel that tug to be a mother, but for Robin, this is not something that she desires. It's not that she looks down on women who do (including her bestie Lily!) but she doesn't see herself as defined by her anatomy and the goals that other woman have. When she finds out that she can't have children, she's upset for a short while, but it seems that she is most upset by the fact that something external to her will has determined this choice for her, not that she actually ever wanted to make the choice to have a family in the first place. That is, she is saddened by the lack of autonomy that comes from her infertility, and not because she cannot ever be a mother. This further supports the idea that Robin is an independent woman who values her own autonomy above most everything else.

Robin as Multi-dimensional

Though Robin is a career-oriented woman, she is not one-dimensional. In fact, she is almost as much a sucker for love as is Ted. Robin seems to want both a career and a deep personal life that includes loving relationships. And there really seems no reason why she can't have it all.

Robin chooses love over her career on at least one occasion, when she is offered a job in Chicago as a lead news anchor and turns it down to stay with Don. This scene shows that while

Robin cares about her career, it's not at the cost of all else. And when Don takes the same job offer, leaving Robin behind, we view this decision as less admirable than Robin's choice. Why? Because we think that people who can balance their career and personal life are to be praised. Too much emphasis on career is not healthy nor does it lead to happiness. Happiness, as Aristotle argues, is achieved when you strike the right balance. Happiness or flourishing are not found by following any one emotion or activity to the extreme.[3] Being focused on making something of your career is a good thing, a value that Robin really embraces. But focusing on work to the detriment of all else is not desirable. The fact that Robin strikes this balance, following her dreams but also making sure her dreams are diverse and varied, shows that while she may get knocked down on occasion, she is a better person for it. In this complexity, there is a unique strength.

The multi-dimensional aspect of Robin's character is also played out in her national origin. Robin is Canadian, but has made America her home. With this mixture comes a complexity to Robin's character that the others often find charming and (even more often) hilarious. But from Robin's perspective, it also brings a confused sense of identity. In one episode, Robin feels estranged from both groups, lamenting that neither country accepts her and she no longer has a home.

This confusion about one's identity is familiar to many women who work outside of the home. Women have fought long and hard for the right to pursue a career outside of their family and be accepted as equals in that environment. While women can (in most cases) work where they want, they are still underpaid compared to their male counterparts and often overlooked for important promotions. They are thus often frustrated by a lack of equality and acceptance in their careers. On the other hand, they are also wives and mothers who find that they struggle to keep everything in order at home. The house is a mess, the kids have to go to daycare and dinner is a constant struggle. (Why many women feel pressure to take on all of the domestic duties on top of their full-time jobs is an interesting question I won't pursue here.)

---

[3] *Nicomachean Ethics*, Book II.

A common frustration for working mothers, then, is that they seem incapable of achieving perfection (or anything resembling it) in both spheres and so feel like a double failure. While Robin's frustration with her personal identity is of a different sort, she represents the real challenge faced by many women today: where do I fit in? Insofar as we, as a society, have not fully reached our goals in terms of gender equality, this is a very real challenge faced by women (and many men!) today.

It's Barney who puts the entire issue in perspective when he assures Robin that it's not that she doesn't have a country but rather that she has two. This assurance, that we can find our identity in multiple roles and in multiple different ways, can be extended beyond national citizenship to other facets of our lives.

Lily: A Feminist Model?

Where Robin is an obvious candidate for a role model for the women of today, Lily seems less obviously fit for the role largely because she is Robin's opposite in many ways. Whereas Robin is career-oriented, Lily works but isn't focused on her career. While Robin's job is in an exciting, traditionally male arena, Lily works in a traditionally female position, as a kindergarten teacher. Robin is independent and multi-faceted; Lily is defined more by her relationship with Marshall than anything else and seems to lack a certain level of complexity as a character. And while Robin rejects the role of motherhood, this is a role that Lily embraces.

Of course, Lily is arguably more sexually liberated than Robin, not afraid to ask for what she wants or embrace and admire the sexuality of both men and women. And she was raised by a staunchly feminist mother. But when compared to Robin, she seems the lesser candidate for a feminist role model on the show. But should we be so quick to reject Lily as a role model in favor of a strong, independent woman like Robin? To favor Robin over Lily or to think that she better epitomizes feminist ideals is, I think, a mistake. Lily stands in as an (admittedly different) role model for a very different approach to feminist theory: feminist care ethics.

Feminist Care Ethics

Feminist care ethics is a branch of virtue ethics that places its primary focus on care. It got its start in 1982 with Carol

Gilligan's book, *In a Different Voice*. Gilligan noted that men and women typically (though not always) approach ethical dilemmas and issues in different ways.[4] And while traditionally masculine ways of looking at ethics have long been favored, Gilligan argued that both have their strengths and a feminine approach to ethics is often preferable.

The study of ethics over the past several hundred (even several thousand) years has focused on such ideas as justice, rights, and equality. In fact, these ideas are often at the heart of feminist social criticism. But feminist care ethics offers a different approach, one that focuses on love, nurturing, and dependence. It is, essentially, a view of ethics modeled on a mother's love and care for her children. This is a radically different approach to ethics but it is one that women typically (though not always—no one's claiming that all women, or men, are alike!) take in everyday life. Feminist care ethics, while very different from typically feminist calls for increased equality, is a feminist view because it calls for the equal status of an outlook on life that is held by many women. It calls for values and ways of tackling problems that matter to women to receive equal respect and weight in ethical theory.

Russ Shafer-Landau explains that there are several key ways that feminist care ethics differ from more traditional (masculine) approaches to ethics. First, feminist care ethics emphasizes the importance of emotions in ethics. Where traditional ethical approaches focus on rationality and suppressing emotion so as to not let it cloud your judgment, feminist care ethicists insist that at the very heart of morality is a set of emotions that surround care, namely "sympathy, empathy, sensitivity, and love."[5] As Shafer-Landau notes, emotions like love and sympathy both keep us in tune with the needs and wants of others and motivate us to move to fill the need. Without care, we wouldn't know what we ought to do, nor would we want to do it even if we knew. Thus, it is a network of emotions that provide a framework for deciding how we should treat others and for inspiring us to action.

---

[4] *In a Different Voice: Psychological Theory and Women's Development* (Harvard University Press, 1982).

[5] Russ Shafer-Landau, *The Fundamentals of Ethics* (Oxford University Press, 2010), p. 266.

Second, feminist care ethicists reject the call for impartiality (p. 268). Many ethical views demand that we view all people as equal. We are told that to favor some over others is unethical. In fact, this is often the sort of reason offered for extending equal rights to oppressed groups. But if we take care to be our model for right action, we see that we absolutely may and even *should* show partiality towards some people, namely those with whom we have very strong, loving relationships. Thus, a mother rightly provides clothes, food and attention to her child over other children because her child stands in a special relationship with her.

Third, feminist care ethics emphasize co-operation over competition. The emphasis is on love, not winning. Hand-in-hand with this idea is a focus on interdependence such that we are not to see ourselves as largely independent beings who are in competition with others, but rather as dependent beings who flourish when we work together. And fourth, talk of justice and rights in feminist care ethics is pushed aside for more emphasis on what we owe one another (p. 269). When we insist on our personal rights, we set our interests against those of others. But when we focus on love and care, our own interests fade to the background because we are instead looking primarily to fill the needs of others. This is the appropriate moral stance to take, one that mothers exemplify in their interactions with their children.

Lily as a Mother Figure

But which character in *How I Met Your Mother* does this sound most like? It certainly doesn't sound like Barney or Robin. It seems to me that it most describes both Lily and her hubby, Marshall. The most obvious proof of this is not only that Lily's the only one in the group who actually *is* a mother, but also that she's seen by the other members of the group to be a mother figure even towards them. She's constantly looking out for each of her friends and goes over and above to make them happy (even when they do not want her to). She is always the one to reinforce the rules and give relationship advice because she wants her friends to find the happiness with their love interests that she has found with Marshall.

Lily demonstrates the specific traits associated with the feminine moral outlook that Shafer-Landau points out. She's probably the most emotional of the group. This is sometimes a bad thing, but often it's a good thing. She is motivated by her love of her friends to defend them, even to the point of violence and manipulating circumstances behind their backs. While she is at times misguided in her attempts to bring her friends happiness, and very often overdoes it, she is always motivated by her love for them and very often right about what it is that they need. It is because she is motivated more by certain emotions, such as empathy and concern, that she can see down to the heart of a situation or relationship and perceive more than what at first meets the eye.

We have seen this emotional, caring side of Lily come out on several occasions in the eighth season of *How I Met Your Mother*. Most notable are her reactions to her own son, Marvin. She and Marshall care deeply about his milestones and making sure that he is safe and happy. This is seen in their long search for a nanny, their obsession about Marvin's bedtime routine, their depression when they miss his multiple milestones and the trouble they have finding a balance between time with Marvin and time with the gang (and with one another). Lily reacts to many of the issues that arise for new parents with very strong emotions that demonstrate the depth of her love.

But Lily's love and care is not just directed towards Marvin. Lily is instrumental in helping Ted get through Robin's engagement to Barney. In fact, we find out that she has strong misgivings about becoming a mother and sometimes regrets having made this life decision. Rather than undermine our belief that Lily cares more for others than she does herself, this revelation further strengthens this view. Lily views this emotional reaction to motherhood as morally reprehensible and it would be easy for to keep it to herself. But she opens up to Ted in order to help Ted come to the realization that he's not dealing well with Robin's engagement. So, Lily does something that hurts herself in order to help a friend and in doing so demonstrates not only care and empathy, but also a commitment to co-operation. She and Ted are in this together, even when things get really messy. A few episodes later, it's Lily who supports Ted's unhealthy relationship with a stalker girlfriend, not because this is a good relationship but because it is what Ted needs. And she lets Ted know that when the relationship inevitably ends, she will be there to help him pick up the pieces.

Lily definitively favors her friends (and Marvin once he arrives) above strangers and will often go to comical lengths to ensure that they are happy. And she's rarely motivated by issues of fairness or impartiality. Lily often meddles in Ted and Robin's love lives, openly scorning their rights to determine their own happiness. She does this not because she doesn't care for Ted or Robin, or because she lacks respect for them, but because she wants them to have what she has with Marshall. It is because she loves them that she meddles. She is particularly active in Barney and Robin's on-again, off-again relationship, forcing them to come to terms with their feelings for one another. But for all of her meddling, we find this to be a charming quality about Lily, rather than something she should get rid of. And finally, Lily is constantly stuck in the middle of bets and competitions between her friends (can anyone say "slapbet?") and continually calls for co-operation and compromise, to no avail. She seems to value co-operation and the group dynamic more than any of her friends and it is Lily who often serves as the glue that holds everyone together.

Lily Is Complex

Lily does exemplify many of the values of feminist care ethics, but she is not a pure representation of the ideal. Lily is often very focused on justice and retribution when she is wronged, much more than any of her friends. For instance, when Ted co-opts many of Marvin's firsts, Lily waits years for her retaliation. She makes sure to exact revenge by bringing Ted's child to Santa for the first time.

Lily also often fails to consider how her friends might feel when she meddles in their lives. She acts from care for them, but often does not go far enough to consider their values and concerns. And she's always the one called on to enforce the rules in various competitions, showing that she has a healthy respect for justice and impartial rules. But, far from showing that she fails to be a feminist icon because she does not tow the party line on feminist care ethics, I think this complexity adds to her depth as a character. Lily shows an interesting mix of both a masculine and feminine moral outlook, something that many responding to feminist care ethics would embrace. That is, she embodies character traits that both groups of feminists embrace (care and empathy on the one hand, and an insistence on rights and justice on the other), adding a layer of depth and complexity to her character.

Actually, if any character most exemplifies feminist care ethics, it is Lily's husband Marshall. Not only is Marshall a caring individual, but he sacrifices personal gain to pursue an admirable career defending the environment. He cares so much about Lily that he feels guilty about fantasizing about other women and places her needs above his own at every opportunity. He cares deeply for his family, including most importantly his parents and his son. And he often calls for cooperation in his group of friends. While he participates in crazy competitions with Barney, he rarely gets vindictive like his wife Lily and will often bend over backwards to help out a friend (even though that often backfires and he is taken advantage of).

It's a strength of the show that a female character, Robin, best exemplifies personal strength and independence, and it's a male character who best exemplifies feminist care ethics. Lily bridges the gap between the two, as does Ted, who has a strong career-focus but is also driven by a search for love (in fact, the entire show is about the story of how Ted meets his wife and the mother of his future children). Only Barney truly embodies a gender stereotype (one that he's slowly growing out of as his relationship with Robin deepens), and insofar as he does, he comes off as ridiculous. And while Robin is a clear example of a feminist icon, Lily, both in her own character traits and in her choice of a mate, shows the importance of another side to the coin and serves as a second, albeit different, female role model. *How I Met Your Mother* deserves to be ranked as equal to other currently popular, obviously progressive, sitcoms such as *Community*, *30 Rock*, and *Parks and Recreation* as portraying and embracing the complexity of gender roles in the twenty-first century.

12
The Legen . . . wait-for-it
. . . dary Moment

MARYAM BABUR

Kids, *How I Met your Mother* is about a lot of things, and one of those things it's definitely about is the identity crisis, more commonly known as the mid- or quarter-life crisis. Even the sweethearts of the show, Lilypad and Marshmallow, have had their bouts of uncertainty and confusion.

Remember when Lily accepted an art fellowship in San Francisco, strangely conflicting with her and Marshall's original wedding dates? As Ted pointed out when he caught a $90 cab ride out into the middle of nowhere to change Lily's flat tire, . . . wasn't this all a cry for help? To move away from the center of art and culture to the other side of the country . . . for an art fellowship? Lily admits she's just going to try, it's just an application to see if she can get in, just a little experience, there's nothing to worry about! And she speeds off, leaving Ted behind at the side of the road.

After using two teenagers to get into a high-school prom just to get a chance to hear The 88, the band Marshall wanted to hire for their wedding, Lily remembered the girl she used to be and realized that she hadn't become all that she'd expected. In fact, she was becoming exactly the opposite of what she wanted: she was walking into being tied down. Her freedom was at stake. And she had to go. Now. And so Lily gets her fellowship and moves off to San Francisco, ready to breathe some newness into her life.

Marshall, on the other hand, was self-destructing in another way. His quarter-life crisis revolves around responsibility. He overburdens himself by taking an internship at Barney's notorious corporation, later to be known as Goliath National Bank. The monstrous corporation, going against all of Marshall's idealist environmental morals and aspirations, is giving Marshall the opportunity to offer Lily the whole package. (As if his isn't big enough.) He drags himself to the internship, and later, through a full-time job, unable to see his freedom. Only responsibility lies ahead.

So that's some of Lily and Marshall's bouts of confusion. . . . And yet in terms of confusion and identity crises, Barney, Ted, and Robin seem to be even worse off. While Ted and Robin seem to be floating from partner to partner, and mostly, as becomes repeatedly evident, from one mismatch to the next, Barney's string of one-night stands is exactly what he's about. Though Ted and Robin seem to be the unwilling victims of self-doubt and confusion, Barney seems to know *exactly* what he's doing. Even though Barney has some mother issues, some father issues, and what comes across as a very unstable home and family environment, when it comes to who he is, Barney seems to be stable and secure in his conception of himself. And yet, you probably still have the tendency to think that Barney's brand of self-certainty is not completely convincing. Isn't he just as confused as the rest?

Old White Balding Men and Their Identity Fetish

Midlife crisis, quarter-life crisis, identity crisis, confusion, call it what you may, the old (mostly dead) white balding men's club we call philosophers have pondered over it for centuries. The Greeks, the medievals, the Renaissance men, the existentialists, the Marxists, and even today, the branches of neuro-philosophy, political philosophy, social philosophy, ethics—everyone wants a piece of that identity pie!

And yet, although so many philosophers come to mind while I'm trying to filter everything that's going on in that awesome show we know as *How I Met Your Mother*, two philosophers step up more than the rest for me: Søren Kierkegaard and Martin Heidegger.

Kierkegaard was a bit of an odd philosopher. First and foremost, because he died young, *and* he had a really nice head of hair. Oh yeah: and he was a Dane (not a very philosophically fruitful country). He wrote many books and journals where some of the recurring themes are identity, existence, life, time, and that thing we call love. Ironically, his own love life was a shambles, he had father issues, and he kept publishing books he had written under strange pseudonyms, even though everybody already knew that he was the author (identity crisis anyone?). Also ironically, his first philosophical work, his dissertation, was on irony.

Heidegger became famous for his first book, *Being and Time*, which he republished seven times during his lifetime and never finished, always publishing it as a completed Part One, repeatedly stating that there would be a second part, and yet never writing it. In this book he focussed, much like Kierkegaard, on identity, existence, life, and time. He also published many other books thereafter on (amongst other topics) technology, art, and philosophy.

Heidegger led a controversial life. Besides having long-term mistresses, who just happened to be his Jewish students, this German also became a Nazi. And after the war was over, he never apologized for being a Nazi. He was definitely not a role model; something which can place his philosophy in a very negative light. I know it's tempting, but let's not focus too much on that.

Dude, Just Be Yourself

Returning to *How I Met Your Mother*. To my mind, just as *How I Met Your Mother* is all about midlife crises, it's also all about figuring it all out—"Dude, just be yourself!" seems to be the underlying message. Ted's narrating the story to his kids, so there's got to be some underlying lessons to be learned, right? Similarly, Kierkegaard's all about being who you are, as a 'singular individual', or as that unique person that you are. And Heidegger's all about the same, which he calls 'authenticity' (such a Ted and Karen word, I know).

We'll come to Kierkegaard, but let's start off with Heidegger. The strange thing is, Heidegger's whole book *Being and Time* is supposed to be about the universe, as explained through existence (being) and time. But right from the start, he claims that the only way to figure out what being is all about is to ask ourselves what do we always already know about being? For when we say something 'is' something else, we imply that we already know something about what 'is' is.[1]

By saying this, he rejects all the philosophers before him (yes, that's why they and we can be such an arrogant breed). He argues that philosophers shouldn't focus on what makes an object an object. What we really should be talking about is people. That's because we humans are the ones who actually reflect on existence in the first place, thereby making the existence of objects and even our own existence, a problem that needs solving. So studying what it means to be us is the best gateway to figuring out what being in general is all about (suspense killer: remember how Heidegger never finished his book? He never wrote part two where he was supposed to figure out the 'universe's' side of the equation).

So, You're Telling Me Women (or Men for That Matter) Aren't Objects?

Barney, reading this heading, would probably not be pleased! But that people aren't objects is one of the first topics Heidegger covers in *Being and Time*. He begins making his point by making a bold move as a philosopher. He doesn't launch his investigation with sky-high ideals, instead, he just focusses, first and foremost, on life as it is (warning: in really very convoluted terms. He even makes up words. But he should get credit for 'just keepin' it real' in the end). This type of approach is called phenomenology: he looks at the world, and claims that if he looks deep enough, and at the right things, or 'phenomena', something will reveal itself. These underlying secrets to life that are revealed, will actually end up always being things we already know, which he's just going to bring to the surface. He wants to express what's implicit in everyday life.

So what does he do first? He begins with a toilet (okay, actually it's a hammer, but toilets make more sense for all of us non-carpenters). He says that if we really consider it, we never really talk about the being of toilets. Really, we just use them. It's only when the toilet suddenly doesn't flush—that's when we actually start thinking about the toilet as an object rather than something we use. Unlike other philosophers, he's not going

---

[1] *Being and Time* (Harper and Row, 1962), p. 32.

to theorize about what it is about the toilet that defines it for what it is (made of porcelain, a certain shape, and so forth).

Heidegger goes on to argue that all the objects around us make up a network of equipment, and equipment isn't really anything concrete; rather, we could define 'equipment' abstractly as "something in order to" (p. 97). Toilets aren't really toilets, they're these, often porcelain, things that fit into our environment of a bathroom, which fits into our idea of a building, which fits into our idea of a place to live, which . . . If we continue that line of thought, we realize that everything around us really just fits into our network of ideas of our environment. And if we reach the end of that line of thought, we realize that it's all about us in the end; we are the 'for-the-sake-of-which' of the totality of equipment, as Heidegger would say (p. 116). We make objects what they are, giving them meaning; they're there for us, it would seem. I can just imagine Marshall and Ted in their dorm, eating a sandwich and thinking "Whooooaaaaaaaaaaaaaaaaaaa."

But Heidegger doesn't stop there. He says that we humans normally go on living life just doing what humans do. We rarely stop to think about who we are. We're just reading the paper as humans do, fantasizing about Robin as Teds do, buying bread from the baker—okay the supermarket—as people do. For the most part, we're in our instrumental mode of being: using things and in a different sense, using others. And we're doing so in the way everyone else does. Heidegger calls this *Das Man* or 'The They', which comes close to the hippy idea of 'The Man' telling us what to do all the time. And yet, no one's really telling anyone to do anything. Heidegger argues that we're mostly the 'not-I', or not ourselves: we're 'inauthentic' (p. 167). This, you can imagine, is a big problem for Heidegger, who, to my mind, is all about being yourself and being authentic. This 'they', it's not someone, not someone else, nor some people, nor the sum of all people—it's everyone and yet no one at all (p. 164).

And worst of all, this monster is a part of all of us, and who we normally are every day. And perhaps even worse or more monstrous, this thing that we all are becomes a way to shirk our responsibilities in life; specifically, it becomes a way to shirk our responsibility to just be who we are (p. 165). It's so easy to not be accountable for anything if it's not you who did it; I mean, c'mon, everybody's doing it! Yes high-fiving is back because James says it's back, and he's just doing what every-body knows is back in. Duh.

At the same time, Heidegger tells us something even stranger: authenticity is just a modification of inauthenticity (p. 224). Meaning, to my mind, that not-being ourselves is in some way essential to being ourselves. Even when we are who we are, we still have to read the paper and buy bread. We just can't think about who we really are all the time.

Anxiety

And what happens when we get wrenched out of our normal and somewhat necessary state of absorption in life (p. 220), and are suddenly surprised and confronted with the question: "Who am I really?" Anxiety happens. Yes, it's the stuff of midlife crises.

Heidegger realizes that at some point in time, we're bound to be confronted with *Angst* or anxiety. In anxiety, nothing really makes sense anymore, because we realize everything revolves around us. You realize that toilets are not just toilets, but rather some kind of bookmark of understanding this world you've been given. And really, you could just hang a toilet up on the wall and call it art and that would be okay. So why use them—defecate in them?!! In anxiety, nothing makes sense anymore and you feel detached. Suddenly who you are and your life as you live it lack meaning. And it can be scary, intim-idating, nerve-wracking. But what are you scared of in this free-floating diarrhea-like state? Heidegger says: you're shrinking back in fear of yourself (pp. 230–31).

At the prom, Lily's world suddenly breaks down and anxiety rears its ugly head. She realizes all the things she could have been, all of the possibilities of who she is and could be that she has neglected. In Heideggerian terms, this is an anxiety borne out of our capacity for 'projection' or 'possibility', or freedom. Lily's freedom is at stake, which is why she bolts off to San Francisco. But was this the 'authentic' thing to do? In being confronted by herself and her need for freedom, did she actu-ally confront herself and be what she had to be, or run away from herself instead?

Marshall, on the other hand, is burdened by another kind of anxiety in choosing to work at Goliath National Bank. In Heideggerian terms, this anxiety is one that aligns itself with the human side of being 'thrown', or Marshall's sense of finding himself thrown into a situation he can't control. He is far too aware of the passive aspect of being human, of everything in his life—every circumstance in his life that he just didn't choose, of the situation he's 'thrown' into . . . Lily's not earning enough, he has to provide for them both, the credit card bills, the rent . . . It all piles up. Marshall forgets about his freedom, and in his anxiety, settles for what the world is giving him. But then again, was this the 'authentic' thing to do? In being confronted by himself and his burden of responsibility, did he actually confront himself and become what he had to be, or did he run away from himself instead?

After dabbling a bit in Heideggerian philosophy, we can digest what Lily and Marshall are going through perhaps a little better. And when we ask if their choices are 'authentic', if they really are being who they truly are, we probably already know the answer, but it may seem hard to explain.

Before we can come to an answer though, we should be a bit weary of the fact that Heidegger's idea of being yourself is a little mysterious in terms of content. He doesn't really say what we're supposed to be in order to be ourselves. But in terms of form, I think he's more clear, framing being-yourself in terms of being absorbed in the world, and yet at the same time, also being a 'thrown possibility' (p. 183), or a free being that finds itself in a particular situation it can't control. Given this frame, his advice, to my mind, is to walk forward in your freedom while still be responsible for the situation you find yourself in.

So even though Heidegger uses the term 'authenticity', which may come across as meaning the one thing or being that you are and always will be, or some kind of essence, this idea is actually more fluid. The person you always already are is also a person that is free and not yet determined. So even though you find yourself in a certain situation, you always already are somebody with possibility (freedom in general), and possibilities (concrete things you could be). This means that being yourself, if you're to do so 'authentically', must be some form of openness to your freedom and possibilities as well as to your responsibility. And yes, that means taking responsibility for everything that ties you down to the life you find yourself living, even though it's often a plethora of circumstances you can't actually control and didn't actually choose.

Commitment, the Hardest Thing in the World

This idea of authenticity is what Heidegger calls 'anticipatory resoluteness'. It is probably the most difficult thing in the world. The task is to be yourself, as you are, in the present moment. But also, to commit to being yourself over and over and over again, always trying to remain in the present moment.

When Lily runs off to San Francisco, although she gets in touch with her freedom, she lets go of the responsibility she has towards herself. She says she's going off to find herself, but instead she violently displaces herself in order to not face the reality that she can't actually be and do everything she wants to be and do. Even her art teacher in San Francisco told her that her best work was the worst he had ever seen. The world can't give you all the freedom you would want.

And when Marshall drudges through life in Corporate America, he may say to himself that he's doing what's best for himself and Lily, but is that really the case? He's violently depriving himself of all that he could be as an environmental lawyer. The world is eating away at his bank account, but he also has more freedom than he's allowing himself. He has (much) more say in his life, even if the world seems to be indicating otherwise.

When Lily and Marshall snap back to their senses and out of their identity crises, they not only make a commitment to each other, but more importantly, to themselves. Of course, anything can happen, but they give it a shot anyways, and by doing so, they commit to an authentic being-themselves that is truly free.

What's Ti-i-ime Got to Do with It?

To my mind, Heidegger and Kierkegaard both see a certain idea of time as essential to being yourself. Kierkegaard captures the problem of time well when he writes in his *Journals*:

> It is perfectly true, as the philosophers say, that life must be understood backwards. But they forget the other proposition, that it must be lived forwards. And if one thinks over that proposition it becomes more and more evident that life can never really be understood in time simply because at no particular moment can I find the necessary resting place from which to understand it—backwards.

In being yourself, you need to reflect—you need to look back to your past. But if you want to understand all of yourself at once, or want to be who you are all at once, it seems that you would have to see your entire past before you, completed, or as a whole. But this suggests that you can only be yourself when you're dying. This doesn't really make sense, because when you're dead, you aren't yourself anymore. On the other hand, as long as you're living, it seems you're never really completely that being which you are. You still have a future before you, and anything can happen. So trying to be yourself as you truly are, right now, seems to be out of the question.

What Kierkegaard and Heidegger point out is that our normal conception of time is not conducive to a theory of being ourselves as we are. If we're speaking in terms of 'backwards' and 'forwards', then we're assuming that time is limited to being linear, as if it followed a straight line moving from the past into the future. If that's the case, then indeed, we can't ever truly be ourselves. Everything's already decided, and we're not actually free—we're simply flowing from one point in the line to the next. . . . Or rather, being pushed from one circumstance to the next. This would mean that we wouldn't have a say in being ourselves, or living our own unique lives, or being free.

Have You Met Ted?

Speaking of not having much say in the matter, have you met Ted? Ted Mosby, the architect. Ted has horrible timing, and is really altogether lost when it comes to time. Ted goes from one extreme of waiting for things to happen, to trying to force things to happen. And nothing quite works, . . . well sometimes it does, but that seems to have more to do with fools' luck than with Ted.

Here's the Ted who constantly waits for things to happen to him: Ted had to have Barney steal his identity for a night in order to make 'Ted Mosby, the architect' a hot catchphrase. Ted kept missing an opportunity to kiss Robin because he was waiting for her to give him the signal (loud and clear). Ted expects the universe to throw the woman of his dreams at him. And every time it does, he doesn't meet the mother of his children because he's too busy messing up his dealings with time in the other way.

Here's the Ted that messes up in the other way with time, trying to force something to happen: Ted plans everything out, especially when it comes to Robin. He starts out by planning to ask her out (on a date) without actually asking her out, which earns him the name 'Gatsby'. Every Halloween he goes up to the roof in search of the Slutty Pumpkin, trying to "get a second chance to make a first impression." He surprises Robin with a blue orchestra and an apartment full of roses and chocolate, and then presents her with an ultimatum. To which she responds that she, unlike Ted, doesn't plan everything out.

Ted never seems to get it quite right. And even if he does, it's for the wrong thing, the wrong woman. . . . Ted is mostly not in tune with the moment, nor is he in tune with himself. Either he pushes for something too much, or lets go too easily. When will he figure out the recipe for a legend-wait-for-it-dary existence? He seems to be a victim of time, being pushed from one moment to the next in an inevitable movement towards his destiny.

Suit Up!

Barney, on the other hand, seems to have everything under control. His timing is almost (ridiculously) perfect.

He's always prepared for a moment that will be legen-wait-for-it-dary. He does his research (sure, he makes up a statistic or two), he lays his plans (The Playbook), he comes ready with a pocket full of magic tricks, and of course, he arrives on the scene in a suit.

At the same time, he understands that the universe can and *will* slap back. It was Barney who was the voice of reason when Ted was frantically doing a Rain Dance on the roof. Barney knows that you have to wait for an opportunity to present itself. Not everything is in his hands. He may go to the airport in order to pick up women, but he doesn't know whether or not he'll succeed. He does know, however, that if he plays his cards right, something legen-wait-for-it-dary can happen. He doesn't know what, nor does he expect much either (at least a six, let's hope), he just knows that something truly new and unexpected can happen. And whaddya know, he ends up licking the Liberty Bell. It's no wonder he's slept with half of the city. Barney understands the limits of uncertainty and certainty.

Really, Barney's the One Who's Getting It Right?

Perhaps that goes a bit too far. Barney is a class A Sleazeball. Endearing, but a sleazeball nonetheless.

At the same time, we should realize that Barney's version of time is all about newness. Unlike being pushed from one moment to the next, Barney is actually making choices. He may not choose what's going to happen that night, probably after 2:00 A.M., but he's ready for something new nonetheless. He always suits up. He uses his freedom to choose to be prepared for whatever may come.

And yet, he's well aware of not being in control of the moment. Sure he's a schemer, but he'll accept almost anything that comes to him, or rather, any opportunity to find his way into the bed of any hot (enough) woman. As he always announces: "Challenge accepted!" And it is a 'challenge' because he's knows that he can't control the situation that presents itself. So in a sense, Barney takes responsibility for the situation that he can't control.

Barney freely prepares, he walks forward into the moment, he lets an opportunity present itself, and then in a state of alertness, he grasps onto what's been given to him in the situation and makes it his own. In this version of time, something truly new can happen. It's not wholly based on the logic of cause and effect. Instead it's some kind of alertness and acceptance of uncertainty, which means preparing yourself to make a choice despite all the other choices out there, and committing yourself to it (if only for one night). Just like the definition of authentic freedom we talked about earlier in the case of Lily and Marshall.

Barney Is No Marshall—He's Not Even Marshall's Best Friend!

That's right, there's something still twisted about Barney. When asking the question is Barney really confronting himself and being himself? We intuitively respond with a resounding 'No'.

He's just too manipulative. It's what Kierkegaard, in *Fear and Trembling*, referred to as the "demonic." Even in explaining the concept, Kierkegaard talks about a Barney-like womanizer.

But in order to understand the 'demonic' individual and where things get twisted, we should first understand what the opposite, not-twisted individual, would be like. Kierkegaard sees Abraham, from the Old Testament, as precisely the non-twisted type: an example of an authentic individual. Kierkegaard talks about how Abraham almost killed his son Isaac because he thought God had told him to. Abraham makes the leap of faith, offering himself to God, and yet gets himself (and his son) back. The leap of faith is a move tied to authenticity, here you become an individual by walking forward trustingly into the absurd unknown.

Abraham, when asked to kill his son in God's name, cannot communicate his worries to others, nor even begin to explain to others what he is about to do. Kierkegaard compares this to the Greek tragic hero, Agamemnon, who sacrifices his daughter. In that story, the audience can understand why Agamemnon is pushed to make the decision he makes. However, in this respect, the story of Abraham is terrifying. It almost seems like the story of a murderer; inexplicable to the masses. Abraham's wholehearted trust in God, in the absurd unknown that awaits him, goes beyond our normal conception of ethics. And yet, he is seen as an enlightened individual, not a murderer. Kierkegaard tries to show that this leap of faith that Abraham makes, into the absurd, beyond the realm of ethics, is one where Abraham really becomes himself. Through his complete trust in uncertainty, he becomes individualized to such an extent that he cannot even explain himself to others any longer. The result of this enlightened decision is that Abraham receives a new future, getting his son 'back' and a new meaning to his individual life.

It's this kind of trust, where whatever happens, you trust you will become who you are meant to be, that being authentic entails. You don't set this enlightenment as a goal, you simply respond wholeheartedly to the task at hand, ready to give up the person you are or have become, in order to be the individual you are meant to be. You're prepared to carry yourself forth in becoming the new you. As I've tried to show, this decision is tied to a certain conception of time where anything is possible.

Barney's not someone who is enlightened in his trust of the uncertainty and absurdity that life may bring. Instead, he's manipulative in such a way, that Kierkegaard would probably categorize him as 'demonic'. Although he seems to be aware of the leap into uncertainty, trusting that legendary things are going to happen, he manipulates this move to produce a certain result. Namely, he plays the game in such a way that new situations will present themselves, he latches onto them, but he never gives up his old conception of himself. Barney is closed off to becoming anyone other than who he wants himself to be. He's not open to becoming someone different (until perhaps Season Eight); his identity is not open to discussion. He's not Swarley, he's not Jennifer, he's Barney, and he always wears a suit. This makes him what Kierkegaard referred to as a 'demonic' figure. He understands newness and change, but manipulates these in such a way that he never changes himself; he never gives himself up. It's the ultimate identity crisis: the one that never ends.

Legen . . . wait-for-it . . . dary and the Midlife–Identity Crisis

"Legen . . . wait-for-it . . . dary" is a catchphrase that I think points to a conception of time that is open to newness and not limited to cause and effect. This concept of time, where anything can happen and you can be ready for it if you play your cards right, is something that I think is key to being yourself and getting out of midlife identity crises. It shows that there's an active aspect to being yourself and dealing with time—realizing that you're responsible for the situation you're thrown into, even though you didn't choose to be there, and accepting the opportunities that the past gives you, while at the same time realizing that you're free to move forward in life by preparing to orient yourself as open to your fully undecided and indeterminate future. You prepare to truly become someone new, repeatedly, over and over again. Legen-wait-for-it-dary also reveals the passive aspect to being yourself and dealing with time—realizing that if something new happens, it will present itself in the world, and not be a situation that you manufacture, create, or manipulate into existence. And in uniting the two, you get the possibility of something new in the present: legen (active preparation)-wait for it (passive, acceptance of a new moment)-dary (something new happens and you capture the moment).

And that's one of the many aspects of *How I Met Your Mother* that makes it so awesome. That it's all about those special moments when we're just being ourselves, when we make choices and are open to the world around us, and something simply extraordinary happens. . . . And Ted finally meets the mother of his children. . . . It's going to be legen . . . wait-for-it . . .!

13
Is It Irrational to Wait for the Slutty Pumpkin?

Tobias Hainz and Yvonne Würz

Kids, all of us know people who appear to be deluded, out of their mind, utterly crazy—perhaps not on all occasions, but in particular situations—and especially when those people are near and dear to us, we usually try to bring them back to normal.

Imagine that a good friend of yours spent Halloween at a roof party every year because he wanted to meet a particular woman he had met on this very roof years ago. You would probably try to talk him out of his plans because there are simply thousands of Halloween parties in your city, which is one reason why your friend's chance of meeting this woman is close to zero. If your best friend's fiancée suddenly called off the wedding, split up with him, and quit her job as a kindergarten teacher to pursue a career as an artist, you would probably believe her to be insane and call her a grinch. Some philosophers believe we can explain precisely what's wrong with behavior like this, behavior they call "irrational."

Many cases of irrational behavior are pretty straightforward. If your boyfriend suddenly expressed the desire to jump off a bridge, you would no doubt try to talk him out of this plan, and if you spotted your girlfriend running around naked in public, you would try to persuade her to follow you into your house, so that you can enjoy the view all by yourself. However, the case of the guy who attends the same Halloween party each and every year and the case of your best friend's fiancée are much more difficult to solve. Is it really the best choice to convince the poor guy on the roof to leave and accompany you to a

Victoria's Secret party? And is your best friend's fiancée really insane and deserving to be called a grinch?

Ted Needs Your Advice!

People do things to bring about states of affairs they want to prevail. So we can look at the desires people have and we can look at whether their actions really will bring about those states of affairs. Let's take a closer look at the Halloween roof party!

The Halloween roof party is featured in the episode "Slutty Pumpkin" (Season One). Ted attends this same party every year because he's obsessed with a woman disguised as a "slutty pumpkin" he met there years ago. We don't know whether Ted sincerely believes that he will meet her there, but we know that he hopes that she will show up, so that he can get another shot at trying to score with her. Barney, on the other hand, oscillates between incredulity in the face of Ted's seemingly foolish behavior, compassion, the desire to help his friend by inviting him to a Victoria's Secret party, and mischievousness—when he shows up disguised as a penguin and makes Ted believe that the woman of his dreams has finally arrived. Not surprisingly, the slutty pumpkin does not show up at the party, and Ted's desire is frustrated again, just as it was in the previous years. Now let's see how a philosopher might analyze this situation.

The major *state of affairs* involved in "Slutty Pumpkin" is that the slutty pumpkin actually attends the Halloween party on the roof—this would satisfy Ted's desire. Other states of affairs featured in the same episode are that Robin finally finds Ted on the roof, that Marshall dresses up as Jack Sparrow, and that Barney repeatedly changes his costume. A state of affairs can either exist—like the ones just mentioned—and can fail to exist—like the state of affairs that the slutty pumpkin attends the same Halloween party as Ted. So, you can imagine plenty of states of affairs, but we're concerned with these which do not yet exist, but play a role in the desires of people who want them to exist in the future.

Now imagine you were a friend of Ted, sitting right next to Barney, Lily, Marshall, and Robin at MacLaren's, being asked by him right before the Halloween party whether he should go there or not. Although you don't know whether the state of affairs that the slutty pumpkin attends the same party will come about or not, you do know that there is a certain *probability* that it will come about. Maybe you don't know the exact value of this probability—you are a philosopher, not omniscient—but you can estimate its value, and you know that it's extremely low. Millions of people live in New York, and there are plenty of Halloween parties, so you can roughly imagine the probability of the slutty pumpkin showing up on this night. This is the *subjective* probability of this state of affairs, with you being the subject, as opposed to its *objective* probability only known by God.

However, since it is not you who needs advice but rather, Ted, his subjective probability has to be determined. You should ask him, then: "How likely do you think it is that the slutty pumpkin attends the Halloween party on the roof this year? Just give me a number between 0 and 1, with 1 being absolute certainty that she will show up, 0 being the complete opposite, absolute certainty that she will not show up, and 0.5 basically resembling a coin toss." If you get an answer from Ted, congratulations, this is the first step to arriving at a philosophically justified piece of advice you can give to Ted.

Your next step should be to ask which *utility* he would assign to meeting the slutty pumpkin again, that is, how happy he would be seeing her in this astonishing costume. For simplicity, ask him which number between 1 and 10 he would assign to this state of affairs, with 10 being 'absolute bliss' and 1 being 'utterly depressed'. We can expect Ted to assign a very high number to meeting the slutty pumpkin, something like a 9 because a 10 would be reserved for entering a relationship with Robin. It's important that you don't assign a number to this state of affairs by yourself because you can't look into Ted's mind and because you yourself happen to be completely uninterested in the slutty pumpkin. It's Ted's utility that matters in this case, not yours, not Barney's, not anyone else's because we're trying to get at whether Ted's behavior is irrational or not.

Let's assume that he has given you a utility of 9 and a subjective probability of 0.1, that is, a 10 percent chance that she shows up—which is exceedingly optimistic. What you want to know is the expected utility of the state of affairs in question with regard to Ted, and you get it by multiplying his subjective probability, which is 0.1, and his utility, which is 9, so you end up with an expected utility of 0.9. That's it.

So what's our advice?

Why the Math Matters

We're still at MacLaren's, and Ted is waiting for the advice that you pretentiously claimed to be able to derive from a fairly simple mathematical operation. Barney is already planning to introduce you to the girl with the nerdy glasses over there, Lily has fallen asleep, Marshall's mouth will stay open for the rest of the evening, and Robin has already left for her date with Mike. Your triumphant smile, however, is an indicator of your ingenuity, so you tell Ted: "Be patient, my friend, and I'll tell you why this matters and what you should do. Remember, we have calculated an expected utility of 0.9, which you will receive if you attend the Halloween party on the roof and the slutty pumpkin shows up. Think of this as your reward—the higher, the better. But Barney here wants to go to the Victoria's Secret party, and he is so kind to take you with him if you wish to. Let's just play the same game again: Tell me how likely it is that you will meet a nice model and assign a utility to this state of affairs."

After a brief moment of reflection, Ted tells you that he estimates the chance of ending up with a Victoria's Secret model as being a coin toss of 0.5 (or fifty percent). Actually, Ted argues, he is a quite handsome guy, and Barney is an efficient wingman (though this may be hard to admit), so 0.5 is a justified guess. Furthermore, a random model may not be the slutty pumpkin and certainly not Robin, but it's also much better than nothing, so he assigns a utility of 5 to it. You quickly multiply 0.5 with 5 and shout: "Forget the slutty pumpkin and head to the Victoria's Secret party. If you attend the roof party, you get a feeble expected utility of 0.9, but if you accompany Barney, you end up with a much better expected utility of 2.5. It would be *irrational* to attend the roof party because rational people maximize their expected utility, and you do this by going to the Victoria's Secret party. Math doesn't lie, bro!"

Perhaps you can imagine Ted's reaction: "I thought you were a philosopher, not some math crackpot!" Fortunately, you have already prepared a splendid response: "It's actually very easy,

Ted. You really wish to end up with the slutty pumpkin, but you also think that meeting a random Victoria's Secret model is not too bad either. You also believe that your chance of meeting the slutty pumpkin at the roof party are actually quite low (one in ten) whereas your chance of hooking up with a model are quite good (fifty-fifty). So you have a good reason to go to the Victoria's Secret party and no good reasons to attend the roof party. My little bit of math is just more accurate than ordinary language, but both are based on your own desires and beliefs, and both tell the same story: Victoria's Secret is better for you than the roof party, so it's irrational to wait for the slutty pumpkin."

What have we learned from this? First, we know what it means to act irrationally and how to avoid it. An irrational person does not maximize her expected utility but rather performs actions that promise a lower expected utility than the possible maximum—in short, they do things that are not in their best interest given their present desires and beliefs. Second, it would be irrational for Ted to attend the Halloween party on the roof because attending the Victoria's Secret party holds a much higher expected utility for him. This is not simply an unjustified postulate, but based on Ted's own state of mind: Although his desire to meet the slutty pumpkin is much stronger than his desire to meet a random Victoria's Secret model, he should still try to satisfy his weaker desire because he believes that meeting a random model is more probable than meeting the slutty pumpkin.

Why Other Things Matter Too

Now we have an idea of what it means to act irrationally if we have certain desires and beliefs. However, there are further ways in which we can be irrational, not just by refraining from maximizing our expected utility given our desires and beliefs. We could also be irrational by acting upon *false* beliefs or upon desires that are *harmful* if they are satisfied. A false belief is a belief that does not correspond to any fact in reality, such as the belief that Earth is the planet next to the sun (which is in fact Mercury). A desire is harmful if its satisfaction would be bad for us, such as the desire to jump off a bridge, which will most likely result in our death.

When giving Ted advice on whether he should attend the roof party, you should not only ask him for his subjective probabilities and utilities and do some basic math, but also analyze whether his beliefs and desires are true and harmless, respectively. You already have considerable evidence that his beliefs about the chance that the slutty pumpkin will show up are much too optimistic because of the sheer number of people living in New York and the number of Halloween parties. Although you do not know its exact value, you are justified in believing that the actual chance of the slutty pumpkin attending the roof party is much closer to zero than Ted's subjective probability of 0.1. And if you were omniscient or had a crystal ball, you would know that Ted has assigned the wrong utility to meeting the slutty pumpkin because in "The Slutty Pumpkin Returns" (Season Seven), we learn that Ted and Naomi—which is the slutty pumpkin's name – make a really bad couple.

So it's not only irrational to choose an option that doesn't lead to your expected utility; it's also irrational to maximize your expected utility if your calculation is based on false beliefs or harmful desires, at least if you could have done better. These are the two additional ways you can be irrational: first, you could assign a probability to a state of affairs that is not the same as its objective probability, and second, you could assign a utility to a state of affairs while not taking into account the harmful consequences of your desire being satisfied. Ted could have done better in regard to the first way, but is innocent with regard to the second. Overall, our philosophical considerations so far still tell us that attending the roof party was not Ted's best choice because accompanying Barney would have been more likely to hold a pleasant experience for Ted.

Is this the final verdict on Ted? Is it irrational to wait for the slutty pumpkin each and every year, and should he rather enjoy other Halloween parties with his illustrious friends? Or might there be a mistake in our rigid philosophical analysis? If you have the gut feeling that we've ignored something utterly important in our analysis, you should take this feeling seriously because gut feelings—*intuitions*, as philosophers like to call them—can be the starting shot for a race towards some deep insight.

Rationality as a Roadblock

We fast forward into the gang's future, where Ted, after many disappointments in relationships, is still single while his mom is getting married for the second time and seemingly everyone else has moved on in their lives to some extent. In "Home Wreckers" (Season Five), he realizes that even if he has not fulfilled his carefully mapped out plan for the future yet—meet a nice girl, marry her, buy a house, and have two children, a boy and a girl—as long as he has not met the right woman, there is one thing he *can* do: He decides to tackle at least one part of the plan by (quite spontaneously) buying the house of his dreams in an auction. Well, at least that's what he thinks he's doing.

His friends think he has made a huge mistake by buying such a run-down shack, not knowing whether he can afford it or whether it will ruin him financially, and whether there will be a Mrs. Mosby in the foreseeable future. So, as they usually do if they do not approve of something one of their friends does, they try to talk him out of his allegedly irrational plans. Actually, it would have been the ideal situation for staging an intervention. Well, we know the result of this remarkable episode: Even though Ted is almost convinced by his friends to give up the shack, he ultimately decides to keep it, and as we learn by a glimpse into its future, this will in fact be the very house Ted will live in with his family.

Rational behavior, as many philosophers conceive of it, would not have led to this result. If Ted had acted in a purely rational manner, he would have sold the house again, making at least some good money and avoiding possible bankruptcy. The chance to lose a huge amount of money in the course of turning the shack into a cozy home was high enough to justify selling the house. However, Ted decided to take the risk because, in philosophical terms, the utility he assigned to the state of affairs that one day he will live in this house was extremely high. He ignored the chance of becoming bankrupt, although he seemed to be well aware of this risk which implies that he did not act upon false beliefs. Therefore, he cannot be blamed for acting upon false beliefs, but he can still be blamed for assigning dubious utilities to living in exactly *this* house compared to the seriously negative utility of becoming bankrupt.

What about our gut feelings here? To our mind, Ted did the right thing here, screwing philosophy, ignoring risks, chances, and utilities, trying to make his dream come true, and we even believe that there is a solid justification for these gut feelings which many of you might share with us.

A philosophical analysis of rationality and irrationality can often be of enormous assistance when the cases are as clear-cut as possible. However, as more and more factors are involved in our decisions and actions, whole situations gain complexity at a rapid pace, and philosophy and its instruments cannot always keep up with this complexity. Imagine Ted had indeed sold the run-down shack, revisited the site a couple of years later, and discovered a lovely house inhabited by a guy like him and his little family. Philosophical analysis can probably not acknowledge the remorse Ted would have felt in this moment. But when you're forced to make a decision, you have to be prepared for the feeling of later remorse when you find you've made the wrong decision. Moreover, this story tells us that there are things we can't control but that have a clear impact on our future. If Ted had kept the house but had a really serious clash with his friends, eventually losing all of them and suffering from depression, he might have lost his joy with regard to this house. If a hurricane had hit New York and destroyed the house some weeks after the purchase, this would have been a catastrophe for Ted and his dreams. But it is impossible to consider those and a myriad of other possible scenarios, not only for Ted and other ordinary people, but also for philosophy and its instruments.

Since we're unable to know the future, and since we can only rely on our beliefs and our desires to some extent, we are sometimes forced to let our gut feelings take control of our lives. In some cases, where we know exactly which factors we have to consider when making a decision and where we know that our desires are harmless and should be satisfied if this is possible, philosophy can help us to make a good or even the best decision by showing us how to act in our best interest. But in some other cases, we should be aware that philosophy does not equal clairvoyance and that the best guide becomes more and more unreliable as the number of incalculable scenarios increases.

As soon as we're overwhelmed by future developments unbeknownst to us, our gut feelings are the only remaining guides, and we *must* follow them in order to avoid doing nothing or becoming fatalists who refuse to take their lives into their own hands. We might still fail, but at least we do not have to blame ourselves for being irrational imbeciles, and this is more than hollow consolation. If we fail because of our own stupidity, we are responsible for our failure and deserve to be criticized or to criticize ourselves, but if we fail because a tornado hits our newly purchased house, we may still be desolate, but we can equally well be proud of ourselves because we actually made the brave decision to purchase it.

A Plea for Craziness

How should we, then, respond to the question of what we should do about seemingly irrational desires and actions? It depends—a truly philosophical answer.

On the one hand, irrationality can be harmful and should be avoided. On the other hand, if your calculations tell you to follow Barney to Victoria's Secret and ignore the slutty pumpkin while you *know* at the same time that you will not enjoy the models because of this hideous feeling of remorse, then let Barney have all the models to himself. There's nothing wrong with staying on the roof for one night, even if philosophy tells you that Barney's right. As long as you do not pitch a tent there, you do not harm yourself. It's the crazy little things that make life more fun, so acting irrationally on some occasions is nothing to worry about.

Irrationality is not that bad in itself, and irrational desires and actions should be taken as seriously as rational ones. In many cases, it's better to be rational than irrational, and in some of them, philosophy can guide us to our fortune. In others, however, the irrational desire is the desire that should be satisfied if no serious harm will be done. And sometimes, it's better to perform an irrational action instead of contemplating the alternatives for ever afterwards. When there's no guide left other than our gut feelings, we should listen to them, even if the world tells us that we're lunatics. It can be better to be a happy lunatic than a rational but unhappy sage. Or, as Ted tells us when reasoning about the decision to buy his future home: "Sometimes our best decisions are the ones that don't make any sense at all."

IV

Hot and Crazy

14

Barney Stinson's Theory of Truth

JOE SLATER

A lie is just a good story that someone ruined with the truth.

—BARNEY STINSON, 2010

Kids, truth is a funny thing. It's one of those topics that some philosophers are interested in that rarely strikes normal people as worrying or confusing. In this respect, though maybe not many others, Barney Stinson is completely normal. He uses the word 'true' without ever appearing to worry too much about it. Yet the way he ends a fanciful tale with the comment 'True story' seems to be an unusual use of 'true'.

If you're wondering why some philosophers are so concerned with 'truth', here are a few things to think about. Everyone accepts that knowing things is important. If Ted wants a beer, it's important that he knows the way to MacLaren's, he needs to know how to order a drink and all sorts of other things. In short, we use our knowledge all the time. Knowledge is great. A whole branch of philosophy—epistemology—is dedicated to it.

On top of that, everything you *know* has to be true. If Ted knows that MacLaren's is downstairs then it's true that MacLaren's *must* be downstairs. If it wasn't, then Ted would only believe it, and be mistaken—he couldn't *know* it. For any of your beliefs to count as knowledge, they must be true, so truth must be pretty important too.

You might also wonder about value judgments. In Season Four, Marshall raves about "the best burger in New York." What makes it true that that burger was the best? If lots of people disagreed with him, would it still be the best burger? What makes it true that the Beatles are better than the Jonas Brothers? Some people might be relativist about such questions, and say that it's all a matter of opinion. If we accept that, does it mean that *none* of your value judgments are just true, even the most obvious ones, like that the old *Star Wars* movies are better than the new ones? If we go down that route, then it seems arguments about things like whether ducks are better than rabbits (as in the episode "Rabbit or Duck") are meaningless.

Another problem about truth comes about when we talk about the future. If the future really is undecided, we might think that nothing about it is true or false—yet. If it's something isn't true, you can't know anything about it, so you can't know that in 2030 Ted has two children, what you'll have for dinner, or even whether the sun will come up tomorrow. If we get into talking about truth with fictional characters, things get even more complicated; there are lots of us who do like to say that things about characters in a TV series are 'true' in a sense, that some things about the future are true and that some value-judgments are true. Those sorts of concerns, among many others, have made philosophers struggle over the topic.

So, what does Barney have to do with all this? Here are a just a few occasions Barney mentions truth:

- **When I'm sad, I stop being sad, and be awesome instead. True story.** ("Where Were We?")

- **Whenever I start feeling sick, I just stop being sick and be awesome instead. True story.** ("How Lily Stole Christmas")

- **In my body, where the shame gland should be, there's a second awesome gland. True story.** ("Columns")

- **. . . we wait three days to call a woman, because that's how long Jesus wanted us to wait. True story.** ("The Three Days Rule")

- **Pamela Anderson is Canadian. But, more important, she was Canadian even back when she was hot. True story.** (Barney Stinson and Matt Kuhn, *The Playbook: Suit Up. Score Chicks. Be Awesome*, 2010, p. 33. Written in justifying attempting to sleep with Canadians)

As these examples testify, Barney attributes truth pretty generously. You might think that reconciling all such statements into one sensible account of truth isn't sensible or possible. Though perhaps not sensible, I'd like to compare Barney's conception of truth (the BS theory) with a view espoused by the American pragmatist William James and suggest that in some ways it is surprisingly similar! Though James was by no means the only pragmatist to talk about truth—pragmatism has developed considerably and many present-day advocates may well disagree with much of what he said—I will call James's classic pragmatist view *the* pragmatist view.

Sneaky Squirrels

Most philosophers are either rationalists (believing that reason is the source of knowledge) or empiricists (believing that the evidence of our senses is the source of knowledge). James thought that rationalists were too abstract and too far away from the real world and empiricists were too reliant on the evidence of their senses.

James saw pragmatism as an alternative, a third way. James's pragmatism looks at whether the answers to questions make any practical difference. He demonstrated his point with an example about a squirrel. Briefly summarizing what James says, it goes like this:

> Walking next to the woods, you see a tree—as you often do in the woods. In the far side of the tree, through some leaves, there is a squirrel. You walk around to the other side of the tree, but the squirrel is sneaky. While you walk around, he runs the other way around the tree. Whatever you do, he stays on the other side of the tree. You go around the tree several times, and the squirrel continues to adjust himself to the opposite side of the tree. Did you go round the squirrel? (*Pragmatism: A New Name for Some Old Ways of Thinking*, 1946, p. 43)

William James tells of friends of his having an argument about whether or not you've been round the squirrel in this case. He obviously had some weird friends, but you have to understand that they didn't have TV back then. James's answer to this problem was that it depends what you "practically mean." If you want to say you've been in a circle north, east, south, west and north again, which the squirrel is inside, then it seems you can. You could have drawn a circle around the squirrel, if you wanted to. If you wanted to go around it so you could see every side of the squirrel, perhaps because of some weird fetish—I'm not here to judge—then you'd have failed to achieve your somewhat peculiar endeavor.

James thought that the squirrel case was similar to several metaphysical disputes in philosophy, like whether God exists or whether we have free will. What James wanted was to focus on 'practical consequences'. Barney Stinson is similarly focussed upon practical goals when discussing the truth of a story.

The Monkey-Mugging

The episode of *How I Met Your Mother* in which truth is most discussed is called "Zoo or False." Here Marshall tells two contradictory stories about how he came to lose his wallet. In one version it was taken by a man at gun-point and in the other he was mugged by a monkey.

After Marshall's flip-flopping leaves Ted and Barney confused as to what happened, Barney *decides* that the mugging by a monkey did happen. He also makes it clear that he intends to tell the monkey-mugging story to his colleagues. Obviously, the monkey story is more entertaining than the alternative, so far more practical as a means for entertaining co-workers.

The other examples where Barney invokes truth can also be seen as practical. The 'true story' of his stopping being sad to be awesome instead, is both amusing to Ted and Robin and the solution he offers for Marshall's depression over Lily leaving him that summer. Noting that Pamela Anderson is both Canadian *and* hot promises to be useful in convincing the reader that sleeping with Canadian women is a respectable goal. All of the examples have some form of practical upshot.

The monkey-mugging story might seem like an odd example. We're put in a situation where, let's assume, it's impossible to know what happened. Either way, the wallet is gone and no additional evidence can be found for or against either version of events. For James, we must remember here, that without any practical effect that would result from either notion, the dispute is an idle one, just as useless as the 'round the squirrel' question is without some practical motivations. What then, would James say about what one should believe the monkey-mugging case?

Free Will, God, and More Monkey-Muggings

Let's think about how we form beliefs. What we regard as making something true may affect our belief-forming process, as we want our beliefs to be true. Holding different beliefs will result in acting differently. The gun-point mugging belief makes Lily want to buy a gun. The monkey-mugging belief leads Robin to want the news story. How then do we decide what to believe? In "Zoo or False," the characters first hear that Marshall was mugged by a man with a gun. At this point they have no evidence to doubt his testimony, so it's completely reasonable to believe him and accept, as they do, that he was robbed by an armed man. Later, this is called into question, when Marshall, fearful that Lily may purchase a gun, tells an alternative story, of his being mugged by a monkey. At this point, with embarrassment as the explanation for the first story, the group reasonably believe the monkey-mugging story.

When facing the consequences of the monkey-mugging story—the sending of Captain Bobo the monkey to a wildlife sanctuary away from his long-term mate Milly—Marshall leaves the group without confirming either story. It seems the evidence is inconclusive. This situation seems to leave us with three obvious options.

- **believe Marshall was mugged at gunpoint**
- **believe Marshall was mugged by a monkey**
- **suspend belief on what happened**

There is a fourth option of believing something else, perhaps that he was robbed by an alien, but that would seem unmotivated (and Marshall would certainly have broadcast that to the world!). Many people would think that the third option is the most rational. However, this position does not seem to be required by either pragmatism or the Barney Stinson account.

This question seems reminiscent of William James's views on the existence of God or free will. Practical utility is the guiding force for answering these questions. With regard to many questions, the possession of a true belief will guide a person to do something that relies upon the belief being true. Ted's believing that the bar is downstairs and that Barney and Marshall are at the bar allows him to go to the bar and meet them there. If, instead, he believed they were at the Lusty Leopard, he would be disappointed. The truth of the belief has a direct relevance to his acting successfully.

James compares these sorts of directly-useful truths with those which are true merely in an instrumental way. He claims that any idea that's successful in our experience in "linking things satisfactorily, working securely simplifying, saving labor; is true just so much . . . true *instrumentally*." Ideas "become true just in so far as they help us get into satisfactory relation with other parts of our experience" (p. 58). The 'satisfactory relation' James talks about seems very loose. To illustrate this, we can look at his discussion of free will.

Whether or not people have free will is an ancient debate in philosophy. If the world is deterministic, then everything that has ever happened and ever will happen has been *fixed* since time began, or God has always known exactly what you're going to do. That everything you have ever and will ever do was already known long before you were born seems to threaten your autonomy and your ability to really make decisions for yourself. If we accept that, how can we say anyone is responsible for anything they do?

James writes a considerable amount on the subject of free will, but with regard to pragmatism, he talks of free will as "novelties in the world" (p. 118). Free will would be an exception to the uniform laws of nature. He notes that knowledge of history and of the terrible pains and atrocities that have occurred, in conjunction with a deterministic outlook, can cause pessimism, as those uniform laws have caused all the horrible events of the past and that they are still in place seem destined to preclude improvement in the world. Free will, however, "holds up improvement as at least possible." James claims that there's no significance to the free will question at all, but for this practical significance (*Pragmatism*, p. 121). This practical significance, for James is enough to make free will 'become true'.

The novelty of free will doesn't seem to help in any specific practical tasks, but only with regards to a general attitude or outlook. James makes a pragmatic argument of the same sort for truth of the existence of God, arguing that "if theological ideas prove to have a value for concrete life, they will be true, for pragmatism" (p. 73). He talks about the "religious comfort" some people experience as a result of religion.

Now, back to monkeys. In deciding that the monkey-mugging story is true, Barney doesn't seem to be doing anything that James wouldn't endorse himself. How Marshall came to lose his wallet is a question which won't have any ordinary practical bearing (accepting that the mugger won't be caught, that Marshall won't get his wallet back; basically that nothing else in the lives of the group will depend upon it), this is what James would call an idle dispute, just like the squirrel question. If in the squirrel case, planting squirrel traps or satisfying some unusual fetish is the goal, the question has a different answer. Similarly, as soon as Barney's amusement comes into play, there is one reason to believe the monkey story over the alternative. This amusing story, which he can then tell in whatever way he may like, seems to provide a much more satisfactory relation to Barney's experience, thus, seemingly even for James's pragmatism, this is true.

Making Stories True and False

For both William James and Barney Stinson, an idea or story, can be *made true* by some convenience of its being true. For different people, however, this may well yield different truths. Whereas for Barney, believing the monkey-mugging story is most useful, and therefore true, it may be much more convenient for the zookeeper not to believe this, as it might mean a lot of extra paperwork. Though he doesn't state this explicitly, this must be the case for James too; if a person did not experience the "religious comfort" James mentioned, but instead lived in constant and paralyzing fear of eternal punishment, this presumably wouldn't be a satisfactory relation with her experiences, so would (without any other particular reasons) be false.

James discusses how ideas can be made true or replaced, as it becomes more practical to hold one theory over another.

James talks about this in a scientific context, explaining how one theory can replace another if it seems more useful. For Barney, I will suggest that the same is true. When Marshall first suggests that the monkey story was made up to prevent Lily buying a gun, Ted and Barney are unsure, but Barney announces that he is sticking to the monkey-mugging story. Ted is against the idea, arguing that people don't like to be lied to. Barney rejects this, instead arguing that "a lie is just a great story that someone ruined with the truth." "The truth" in question here refers to the new truth. Just as a new scientific theory replaces an old one, once a story is admitted as made up, it is replaced by a more suitable story. When you're presented with information which makes it impractical to hold your current beliefs any more, you reject them in favor of newer, more practical beliefs.

For example, also in "Zoo or False," Barney hooks up with a girl he thinks is twenty-eight, by telling her that he is Neil Armstrong. Later, she discovers he's not Neil Armstrong, and is at first angry, but then remembers that she lied to him about being twenty-eight too, as she was actually thirty-one. For Barney, her being twenty-eight ("with some sun damage") was true, until he was told that she'd lied, at which point it was replaced by a new truth, that she was thirty-one. His "great story" of having sex with a twenty-eight-year-old was "ruined by the truth."

William James claims that if any idea would help us to lead a better life "then it would be really *better for us* to believe that idea, unless, indeed, belief in it incidentally clashed with other greater vital benefits" (p. 76) and equates *this* with truth. The "greater vital benefits" here are crucial. They mainly demand that you don't form beliefs that clash with your other beliefs (as they may defeat benefits reaped by *those* beliefs). So having consistent beliefs is necessary for James. This requirement is also prevalent in Barney's belief forming; when he learns something (like a woman being thirty-one years old) he must reject whatever contradicts that.

How then, do we explain situations where Barney himself seems to have broken this rule? If making a better story was the crucial goal, why would Barney have admitted to Ted and Marshall that the woman was thirty-one, and not twenty-eight "with some sun-damage"? Barney uses this to illustrate the point that people hate to *find out* that they've been lied to. Barney would have been happier believing the girl was twenty-eight, just as the world would be better off believing that Marshall was mugged by a monkey. This example seems to meet the "greater vital benefits" requirement. Other examples where Barney doesn't tell the most entertaining story, when it seems that he could easily have done so could be explained in a variety of ways. Perhaps the most entertaining story wasn't one he thought the gang would believe, perhaps it's one that would be easily disproved, or perhaps there are other "vital benefits" being pursued.

Barney's Truth for Everyone!

When Barney tells one of his 'true stories', he doesn't do so to convince himself. He does so to convince others of the true story; to make it true *for them*. Not all of these stories that he attempts to make true for other people will even be true for himself. This is ideal for Barney's nefarious methods of seducing women.

When seducing a target, Barney often adopts a guise or a story to help him do so (many of which are detailed in *The Playbook*). When this is the case, he aims for the girl to be in the sort of position we are placed in with regard to the monkey-mugging, the squirrel question, or James's view of free will. There is no practical effect upon them of the story in question, thus no immediate way of disproving the story. The girls Barney preys on are usually the gullible or ignorant too, meaning there are a great many stories that the girl would be unable to reject by careful scrutiny, consideration, or general knowledge. As such, Barney will ideally pick a story that the girl in question cannot immediately disprove, would like to sleep with him because of it, and then give her reasons to believe it.

Therein lies the primary difference between BS and pragmatism. BS is self-serving and designed for the benefit of its practitioner, and occasionally his friends. If you didn't already know it, Barney is a master of BS. He makes others buy into truths that will satisfy his own pleasure. Pragmatism, on the other hand, would value the practical relations of an idea not only to the lives of Barney, but to everyone, and what is true would be appropriate to that.

The Barney Stinson Theory of Truth

To give a formula, then, for what counts as true for BS, we must take into account that something 'true' must be consistent with your other beliefs. Barney doesn't say this explicitly, but, it can be inferred from his backing down when contradictory information is divulged, as with his admission of the falsity of the three-way story. As in James's pragmatism, it seems permitted for different people to count different things as true, in accordance with the utility of the belief. However, in the BS account, entertainment is the primary utility. Like James, BS doesn't require that a belief's truth at one time entails its truth at another; it can change as and when it's convenient.

To prove that this chapter is a really serious piece of philosophy, we can put our conclusion more formally. An unverified (ideally, unverifiable) idea (or story), S, can be made true for person, X, at time, t if:

S is consistent with X's other beliefs, AND

Either

A. There is good reason to believe S (like seeing something that suggests S or hearing S from a reliable source), or

B. It is practically useful (often meaning entertaining) for X to believe S.

For Barney, the "practically useful" aspect of this account, means practically useful *for Barney*. This includes a great many things. It is practically useful *for Barney*, that some girls believe that he is Neil Armstrong, that he has just been mugged, or that his penis grants wishes. If other people were to adopt this theory of truth, however, it would make sense for them to play the role of Barney, telling stories that would benefit themselves, rather than merely stories that would play to the practical utility of Barney Stinson (he'll do okay without you).

I've said that the above formula accounts only for what "can be made true" for a person, because it will still require that they are put in a position where they may believe it. Also, some people may be less likely to believe some stories than others, so an appropriate amount of convincing (or guidance from *The Playbook*) may be necessary.

So, what do we make of the BS theory of truth? Compared to William James's account, it's certainly more flexible, but this seems purely because it has entrenched within it a personal value system of entertaining oneself. William James wasn't quite so hedonistic.

I should warn you, that if you follow the BS account with the stories you tell your friends, your friends may avoid you after a while. Despite all this, the show implies that even Ted comes round to the theory eventually: Barney informs Ted that when he depicts Marshall's mugging, he will tell the monkey-mugging story. Ted then challenges Barney, claiming that you "can't just tack on a new ending because you're not satisfied with how a story wraps up." Barney tells Ted that he'll change his mind. We then see a satisfying ending tacked on, in which we see the monkey steal a doll and climb the Empire State Building, echoing the imagery of *King Kong*. Future Ted then utters a convincing "True story," hinting that he has come around to Barney's way of thinking.

If even the wise Future Ted (Bob Saget) adopts the Barney Stinson Theory of Truth, who are we to question it? This completes my rigorous philosophical analysis of the Barney Stinson Theory of Truth. True story.[1]

---

[1] Special thanks to my flatmate, Elspeth Gillespie, for tolerating and joining in with the extensive amount of television-related 'research' I engaged in while writing this.

15
The Pick-Up Game

Bart van Beek

Kids, that's enough about how I met your mother, let's see if there's a game on.

JIM: Hello friends, I'm Jim Nantz. We have a full program ahead of us, so let's go to our pick-up game of the evening. Stinson is six for six and this is a tense moment. Will he complete a perfect week for the first time in his career as a player, banging seven chicks on seven consecutive nights without a single rejection? He's called his shot and is ready to run home with Christy, a blond hottie. But oh no! There's Nick Swisher, a member of the 2009 World Series Champion New York Yankees. This is going to be a rack jack for sure, unless a miracle happens. But wait for it, there's wingwoman Lily stepping up to the plate, distracting Christy and allowing Barney to score an all-hitter. The crowd roars, his team members hoist Barney up on their shoulders. What a game. What a player.

Barney's achievement is legendary. Few bros can honestly say they've done the same. This must be a proud moment for the man with a tally of two hundred random hotties without as much as a single fatty. I can't think of anyone who deserves reaching this very special milestone more than he does. As you loyal fans know, this guy is one of the most gifted and skillful players of all time. He even manages to score chicks by making them think he is a member of Secret NASA. Barney is the living embodiment of the rules and the spirit of the game as so eloquently described in the Bro Code. Nobody exercises his inalienable right to pursue tail quite like The Barnacle.

You may wonder, viewers, where this right comes from. It certainly doesn't come from God. Nor does it come from the President of the United States of America. Although Kennedy and Clinton clearly honed their skills while they were on top. With its emphasis on getting it on it appears more like a law of nature. But it's not a law of nature in the sense that the laws of gravity are, because these laws merely *describe* what happens. For example, they tell us how fast Mabel, Marshall's barrel, will fall if released from an apartment window. No, this law *prescribes* what ought to be done. Bros should score any way they can, because it's the natural thing to do. But is this really the natural thing to do, and does that mean bros ought to do it? Here's a big guy with a beard to help us answer those questions, it's my cohost and philosopher Aristotle.

Be All You Can Be

ARI: Thank you, Jim. Many of today's players lack focus. They don't know what their goal is in playing the game of life. Fortunately for them, I do. Every bro should strive to live a life informed by reason, because if he uses his rational faculty, then he does what best fits his purpose as a human being. For a bro's rationality is what distinguishes him from other animals. It's the specific difference that defines his human nature. To live in accordance with that nature is to live a good life and in living a good life a bro flourishes. Back to you Jim.

JIM: I get it Ari, we should let biology inform our ethics, but isn't all this stuff about reason defining our human nature a bit old?

ARI: Of course Jim, but then again, I've been dead for over two thousand years.

JIM: Ari, let me switch over to fellow philosophers Larry Arnhart and James Chisholm for some contemporary insight.

LARRY AND JAMES: Welcome viewers. Things today are quite different, because the theory of evolution tells us that our ultimate biological function is not to contemplate but to copulate, as the following replay shows:

Here we see Barney and Robin some weeks into their first relationship. They hate each other so much, and on top of that have become so unattractive to each other that they stop having sex. Instead they much prefer just to eat pizza and moan. Now imagine a world where everyone is like Barney and Robin during this awful phase, lacking any urge to play ball. Without the desire to do it, people would probably stop doing it altogether in favor of pursuing other passions, like laser tag. In this kind of world our fathers would never have met our mothers, because they wouldn't have hooked up. So you wouldn't be here and in fact your father and mother would never have been born either, because your grandpa and grandma would have been too busy fragging each other rather than getting it on. But we're all here, so it must be part of human nature that we like to have sex.

JIM: Ari says the game of life is all about thinking, are you saying it's about doing something else that rhymes with 'thinking' and starts with an 'f'?

LARRY AND JAMES: In a way yes, because only through having sex can we spread our genome, which is what evolution is all about. Yet enabling us to pass on our genetic material is not just the function of our desire for sex; in fact it's the ultimate function of every trait. For we may want to nail chicks, but our desire alone is not enough to score. Sheer awesomeness and a great suit help, but sometimes we need a play, a stratagem, a gambit, a bamboozle to allow us to land that plane. Say you want to pull a Lorenzo von Matterhorn, one of our favorite plays. Given the complexity of this move you need numerous skills: being able to come up with a creative fake name, knowing how to build web sites, and using the right tricks to deceive someone into believing that you're someone you're not, to name but a few. All of these skills require a certain degree of intellect, and this is where spreading our genetic material comes in. For intelligence is hereditary at least in part, and given that it's still around, it must not only be making some contribution to reproductive success in the present, but it will have made a similar contribution to copulation in the past. For if that contribution were lacking, then all the relatively intelligent cavemen probably didn't score and the "smart genes" would not have been passed on. So it's the ultimate function of all our traits, not just the desire to have sex, that they contribute to procreation. For any trait that doesn't live up to this standard fails to get passed on, and will die out.

JIM: Our natural endowment plus all the effort we put in at practice time ultimately pays off on the field. But Larry and James, what exactly has this got to do with the good life?

LARRY AND JAMES: To truly understand this complex aspect of the game, we have to look at desires. Desires motivate us to act, to live the life we lead. So if a particular kind of life is good, then the desires that lead us to live that kind of life are also good. Thus if it is good to correct everybody's pronunciation, like Ted does, and not just completely annoying, then whatever drives you to comment on their diction is also a good thing. So if living a life according to our nature is good, as Ari rightly claims, then "the good is the naturally desirable."[1] Both our desire to have sex and our intelligence are relatively universal and can therefore be seen as part of our evolutionarily constituted human nature. Therefore the desire to have sex is good, as is our intelligence as a means of getting what is desirable.

BART: Given that this view on the relation between ethics and evolution is about not overthinking things, but about accepting our natural desires as they are, I've dubbed it *Barney's evolutionary ethics style*, or 'BEES' for short. If you're into BEES, you'll define 'good' as naturally desirable.

---

[1] Larry Arnhart, *Darwinian Natural Right: The Biological Ethics of Human Nature* (State University of New York Press, 1998), p. 17.

JIM: How can we tell if a desire is natural or not? After all no caveman had any desire for an impeccably furnished loft, so not all desires can be natural desires.

LARRY AND JAMES: Well, we just have to see through all the suits, cell phones and satin sheets and look to the sort of behavior that used to contribute to reproductive success at the time our human nature was shaped. As a species we developed during the Pleistocene era (starting between one and a half and two and a half million years ago and ending at around twelve thousand years ago). So any desire that it was possible to have back then that spurned the continued spread of genetic material throughout this period will be a natural desire. Therefore by examining what sort of plays led to reproductive success over the course of our evolutionary history, we can find out about these desires.

To do this, we need to consider the fact that the process of natural selection has been going on for a long period of time. So there has been generation after generation of *Homo sapiens sapiens* and each generation has passed on its genome the next. To achieve this feat not only did each previous generation have to procreate, but they also had to ensure that their offspring would live long enough to score for themselves. Basically there are two strategies for making this happen: the *Stinson* and the *Eriksen*. Let's go to an in-depth analysis of these plays to see which one works best. If the Stinson is our winning play, then Barney is clearly acting on a natural desire and doing the right thing.

Stinson vs. Eriksen

LARRY AND JAMES: The Stinson works as follows: you go to your local cave, hut, tavern or barn after a hard day of hunting, or doing whatever it is that Barney does for a living. You chat up some random girl and every once in a while you score. If you're Barney you get down to business almost every time you play and if you're Mitch, the Naked Man, you score two out of three times. Now if you do this often enough, then you are bound to get a lot of women pregnant.

JIM: What about Article 63 of the Bro Code stipulating that your bros have to provide you with protection in your time of need?

LARRY AND JAMES: It was a very different game back then, Jim. Unless you fashioned something out of woolly mammoth gut there was no preventing pregnancy. With all the little Barneys around you would neither have had the time nor the resources to take care of them. And back in the day when you had to hunt for your own meat, if a bro didn't go out spearing bears, then his children could very well starve to death. Luckily when using the Stinson there is so much offspring that even if only a very small percentage gets to do it, at least some children will survive long enough to pass on your genetic material. Certainly nowadays we only need to look at Barney, the son of a single mother, to see how fantastic a player a son with an absentee dad can be.

Those using the Eriksen stick with one woman and have at most a couple of children with her. They may even throw the occasional elaborate birthday party for their chicks, and treat them with kindness and respect. Of course they won't get nearly as much progeny, but because they care, every Marvin has a chance of finding his own chicks. This means that children of dads using the Eriksen get to pass on their genes as well. So both strategies have something going for them.

JIM: What was the best mating strategy in the Pleistocene season? Let's turn to our mating specialist, Ed Wilson, for some in-depth insight.

ED: At the time our species developed it was the Stinson. For during the period between fertilization and actually having a baby, there's simply no way to put another bun in the oven. However a man can simply leave one oven on and poke up the fire in the next woman, and another woman, and yet another woman. As long as he beats the other guys to the women, he will have created enough offspring to feed a small town and he will have spread his genome far and wide.[2]

---

[2] Edward Osborne Wilson, *On Human Nature* (Harvard University Press, 1978), p. 125.

LARRY AND JAMES: This bodes well for grounding the right to pursue tail in evolution. For if going after a women, having sex with her, and quickly moving on to the next target used to be a bro's best bet to ensure the survival of his genetic material, then a desire to do so is likely to be part of his human nature. For this human nature was formed over the course of an evolutionary history in which that was the best strategy. So Barney is going about his life in exactly the right way. From where we're standing the Bro Code contains some sane advice on doing the right thing.

JIM: Viewers, we have a protest coming in, let's listen to what Bart has to say.

BART: But what about Barney's targets? How are the women he's playing doing? Perhaps they want to be at the receiving end of an Eriksen, perhaps they don't, but they certainly don't want to be lied to. And a play like the Lorenzo von Matterhorn is clearly a brilliantly elaborate lie, but a lie nonetheless. What's even more ethically objectionable is the fact that this lying seems sanctioned by the way Barney views women. They are, as the Bro Code describes them, "ho's" that are supposed to be hunted like wild game.[3] Is this sort of action, lying to women in an effort to score, to be tolerated on the field if you're a BEES-lover?

This is a tough nut to crack, because we really don't know whether we are natural born liars. For appearing trustworthy makes others more willing to engage in cooperative activity with you, and perhaps appearing trustworthy is best achieved through actually being honest. But in a situation of general expectancy of honesty it pays to be a liar, because people won't invest much effort in finding out whether you can in fact be trusted. So perhaps there really is no such thing as an evolutionarily determined human nature when it comes to lying, as both lying and not lying may have worked to a person's advantage over the course of our history as a species.[4]

---

[3] Barney Stinson and Matt Kuhn, *The Bro Code* (Simon and Schuster, 2008).

[4] E. Somanathan and Paul H. Rubin, "The Evolution of Honesty," *Journal of Economic Behavior and Organization* 54:1 (2004).

This means that lying is neither particularly good, nor particularly bad from the perspective of an ethical framework that judges actions by the extent to which they fit this evolutionarily constituted nature.

Given that all the lying helps to get Barney laid however, and given that getting laid is good, it does seem that in this particular case lying is a good thing. This appears to pose a dilemma for the BEES-boys: either BEES is right, we and commit ourselves to a slew of clearly morally objectionable prescripts, or BEES is wrong, but then what can evolution tell us about how we are to behave? I think that any ethical theory telling us that lying is perfectly okay is simply a bad theory. So we have to reject BEES and consider how evolutionary insights may influence our ethical views in a better way. Any form of evolutionary ethics presupposes that this kind of influence is perfectly possible, but is that really so? Back to you Jim.

The Game as It Once Was

JIM: Thanks, Bart. Now for a bit of history. In the past there has been many an outstanding player in our sport. In the eighteenth century the Scottish philosopher Dave Hume was known for hanging out at the *salons* of Paris and hooking up with one countess after the other. Of course in those days the rules were very different so you didn't just score by nailing chicks; perhaps you simply had a pleasant conversation. Still this bro had game. Dave's in our Paris studio to talk about his exploits.

DAVE: Hume here, live from Paris, the city of "love." At the height of my career playing women I always used to say that you can't derive what you ought to do from the way things are. You simply can't derive ought from is. Oddly enough there was no countess who could resist those words. Yet this isn't just a piece of history; it's a piece of bad news for all sorts of evolutionary ethics, and I mean Robin-as-a-reporter-for-Channel-22-in-Red-Deer-bad. For these ethicists argue that Barney *ought* to nail numerous women, because doing it is part of the way he *is*. So if I'm right, then they're wrong.

Notice that I'm definitely on to something. For example, from the fact that it's true that Barney and Robin cheated on Nora and Kevin, you cannot derive that it ought to be true that they cheated on Nora and Kevin. In fact they themselves feel truly guilty about their behavior. So there are certainly sentences in which we cannot replace 'is' with 'ought', and still say something true. It's essentially like substituting 'loves' for 'kicks', or 'hates' for 'paints', taking words that express completely different and unrelated concepts and replacing one with the other. That's just silly. Therefore such substitutions are never justified.

JIM: I'm going to have to stop you there Dave, because we have some recent developments; let's switch over to Bill Casebeer.

BILL: Dave's wrong, his argument's really just a piece of history. Let's suppose that statements telling us what someone ought to do simply are statements about what's the case, so that 'is' and 'ought' express intimately related concepts. Then there is really no problem of substituting 'ought' for 'is'. For it would be like substituting talk of Lily with talk of Lilypad or Justice Aldrin. And of course this is exactly what evolutionary ethicists, like me, think they're doing. As they say that someone ought to do something because it'll help fulfill a desire that's part of her human nature. So the challenge is merely to find the right definition of what we ought to do in terms of what's the case, not to stop before we've even begun.

All Talk and No Action

JIM: Bill, as you know we've got a packed show tonight. George Moore is in the studio with David and he questions your take on things.

GEORGE: Bill, you couldn't be more wrong if you tried. It's simply impossible to give a definition of what we ought to do in terms of what is the case.[5] For if we define what

---

[5] George Edward Moore, *Principia Ethica* (Cambridge University Press, 1903).

people ought to do in terms of their nature we're implicitly doing the following. We say that this person ought to do something, for example, follow the Platinum rule. Of course it seems only right to ask why this person should respect that rule. If we are a BEES-boy we will answer as follows. You have to respect the rule, because the only good way to live your life is to never, ever, ever, ever "love" thy neighbor, and this is good, because it is helps to fulfill the desires that are part of your human nature. In so doing we have provided a definition of 'good' in terms of human nature, we have judged the merits of an action on the basis of this definition and we have answered the original question.

JIM: It doesn't feel quite right to me George, I just don't know if the definition is any good. What's really so important about a desire being natural? I guess I'm just not buying into the whole BEES thing.

GEORGE: Thanks Jim, for helping my argument get underway. Basically you're asking "Is being good the same as being conducive to fulfilling our natural human desires?" This seems like a sensible question, but how could this be, if our definition of 'good' is on the money? For if that definition is correct shouldn't the question be as senseless as asking whether a cougar is an attractive, sex-crazed, middle-aged woman, usually found prowling airport bars and smoky pool halls in search of nubile flesh? Someone who knows what a word means should know whether a definition we give of the word is correct or not and there should be no further questions to ask. This applies to all terms. If you know what a term means, then you ought to know immediately whether a definition of that term is correct. As I like to put it: the question of a correct definition should not be *open*. You know what 'good' means Jim, because I remember you hooking me up with those Super Bowl tickets just to say "thanks." You're a stand-up kind of bro. So because the question about the correct definition of 'good' is still open for you, there must be something wrong with it. To my mind this will happen with any definition of 'good'. So there is simply no defining this elusive term. This is my *open question argument*, and I think Bill's going to have a hard time refuting it.

JIM: It's George and Dave versus Bill. Is he going to be the Goliath of this match, or can his logic refute this tag team of thinkers?

BILL: I can take them, Jim. George assumes that if a definition of 'good' is true, it will be true in virtue of meaning. For it is the meaning of 'good' that a competent speaker is supposed to have access to and that will allow her to identify the truth of the definition. Notice that this is a rather odd way for a sentence to be true. Take a sentence like "Ted is an architecture professor." That sentence is true as a result of the meaning of the sentence and Ted's current occupation. A couple of years ago the sentence was false, but now it's true. So sentences are generally true because of their meaning and the state of the world. When giving a definition we appear to leave out the world. And this is as it should be, because definitions are only about the relations between meanings.

However this split between meaning and the world is not that easily made. In the episode "The Possimpible," Barney and Robin concoct words like 'linkativity', 'connectitude' and 'transformitation'. These words are meaningless, simply because they get blurted out without any apparent use other than sounding confident. This is in sharp contrast to words like 'architect', 'bro', or 'undercarriage'. They are meaningful words and their meaning derives from the way we use them, for example, to refer to Ted's private parts. But the way we use words is a matter of fact. So, even the truth of a definition, like the definition that we have provided of 'good' is in part a matter of fact, a matter of the world being a certain way. For we have to consider the way that 'good' is used in order to answer the question whether 'good' means what we think it does. No wonder that it may not be evident, even to someone who is comfortable speaking of 'good', whether a proposed definition of it is correct.

JIM: So if I think 'good' means 'being yellow', somehow anything not yellow, like friendship, won't count as good anymore?

BILL: You keep asking some sensible questions, Jim. There is of course significant disagreement about what's good.

So we cannot just make an inventory of the different ways in which people use good. We need some sort of theory of the good, to separate the sensible from the stupid uses of 'good'. A proper evolutionary ethics is just this kind of theory; aimed precisely at telling us what is good in a way that meshes with part of what we previously thought of as good, and probably your views will not be part of those it meshes with Jim. This gives us what we are after when seeking a proper perspective on 'good'. However we have already seen that BEES cannot do justice to all the important things we think are good. So it's time we consider a different kind of ethics, mine.

Taking the Game to a New Level

BILL: Barney's plays seem right to the BEES-bro's because they help fulfill a desire that is part of our universal human nature. To ascertain whether such a desire existed we considered the time at which this nature was formed, but of course much has changed since twelve thousand years ago. This difference explains why many of the things we desire aren't really all that good for us. Replay how fat Barney got during his first relationship with Robin, because he was now his own "wingman", eating wings by the bucket-loads. Devouring this much meat makes a lot of sense if your chances of finding food are relatively small and if you burn a lot of calories as you go out hunting cougars (of the non-human variety). Yet it just makes you fat if all you do is sit around the office shredding paper or calling Korean companies to close obscure deals.

JIM: So what if we don't judge what is good with reference to the desires that are part of human nature as formed during the Pleistocene? What if we consider what is good by determining whether it ultimately contributes to reproductive success in our present-day environment?

BILL: That's a great suggestion, Jim. As this alternative demands that we think about what is really good for us, let's call this way of thinking about evolutionary ethics *Behavior is reflectively determined stupid* or BIRDS for short. If you're into BIRDS, then it is good to follow your human nature only insofar as it contributes *in the present* to the reproduction of your genome. Of course Barney's habitat is urban New York. In this sort of environment you're never going to reproduce if you don't commit. Women may be willing to sleep with you, but they will use all manners of contraceptive devices unless there is some long-term prospect. Barney's behavior therefore contributes to a lot of copulation, but it does not contribute to procreation. So it makes sense for Barney to ultimately commit to one woman if he is to do the right thing according to BIRDS. And this is exactly what we have seen him do recently. It's almost like he knows my work. I am one proud Bill.

JIM: Perhaps Barney would have to commit someday, but what's wrong with trying out a couple of teams, before you sign that life-long deal? In fact won't it have made him a better player, because he knows how to please a woman and because he's now certain that commitment is what he wants?

BILL: This may very well be, but we still have to consider the lying and bamboozling, which I think is wrong. Cooperative activity has been tremendously important to our development as a species and lying sucks the fun out of working together. We need a degree of mutual trust to sustain a functioning government, if only because the costs of checking that everybody pays there taxes would otherwise be too high. There would be no businesses if we could not trust each other because no business owner could rely on people to pay their bills or to deliver ordered goods. In short we would have none of the modern conveniences, like suits, fine scotch, or artisanal porn. But more importantly, from the perspective of evolutionary ethics, our future would be very insecure and the ability of our children to procreate would be flushed down the drain. As these conveniences are what allows us to live in relative prosperity and peace, which in turn give us the opportunity to raise our children, to feed them, to allow them to develop, and to create healthy babies for themselves. Therefore in a world in which everybody lied our reproductive success as a species, and thereby the success of each individual member of our species, would be significantly diminished. So it's wrong to lie.

JIM: And this night's fair play award goes to Bill Casebeer. Friends, I hear we have another objection from Bart coming in.

BART: Bill talks as if lying is an all or nothing matter, but of course we may sometimes choose to lie, while refraining from lying on other occasions. Doing so may be conducive in many ways to present reproductive success. Through lying it may be possible for you to get two wives to have children with. Talk about playing the spread. Hence lying may be good on the face of it, even in today's environment. In no way does this isolated bit of behavior have to lead to a breakdown of the sort of mutual trust that is necessary for a well-organized and complex modern society.

Furthermore even though through procreation this two-wived man will get more offspring, and his children may be more likely to lie, there is no reason to suppose that lying will spread through society in the long run, which would be bad for genome reproduction given the societal effects described by Bill. For it's likely that in a society in which trust is less prevalent, more time will be spent on weeding out those who can't be trusted, which will lead to fewer opportunities for liars to take advantage of their dishonesty. To the extent that dishonesty plays a role in their strategies for achieving reproductive success, liars will thereby loose much of the advantages they previously had and honest humans will get a bigger chance of putting more people like them on this planet. So, there doesn't seem to be a general prohibition of lying inherent in evolutionary ethics. In fact lying may well be justified on occasion, and the lies perpetrated by Barney are a case in point.

If you're into the BIRDS and the BEES, you're bound to agree with Barney's behavior. Evolutionary ethics supports the Bro code. Whether it's worth supporting? That's a whole different ball-game.

16
Telling Your Life Story

ELIZE DE MUL

Kids, at some point in our lives we're all confronted with the expansive question "So, what's your story?" Giving an answer can prove troublesome. Where would you begin your life story? Where should it end? Which people should be included in the plot? What situations matter enough to recount? What fragments of experiences shape and define who you are? What anecdotes would you never even consider sharing?

Telling stories is an important part of our lives. We may find ourselves sitting with people in an apartment or bar, just like Ted and his friends, telling each other about our days. In doing so, we present ourselves to them and we put together our own life story. The things that we do, the way we look at things, the people we meet, the friends we love, as well as the stories we tell about each other are all part of this story-telling.

How we tell the stories of our lives is the theme of *How I Met Your Mother*. Season after season the mother of Ted's children fails to make an appearance, yet we learn, together with Ted's children, a whole lot about the lives of Ted and his friends. A voice-over of an older Ted, leads the way through stories of his past, from his own perspective as well as those of his friends. As these characters tell their tales, their identities take shape.

How I Met Your Mother can be a cultural fun-house mirror, not only telling us a story about some young New York architect and his friends, but also telling us a story about our own modern identities and how they are constructed. Sit down and let me tell you a story.

How I Met Myself

For a long time not only famous philosophers like René Descartes (1596–1650), but also less philosophically trained people assumed that human identity is hidden within the depths of ourselves, as sort of a pre-given fact. Everybody was assumed to have a 'core self' that could probably even exist without their body, according to religion.

When modernity kicked in, due to the scientific revolution, the marble towers of religion showed their first cracks and some thinkers started to doubt the traditional view of human identity too. The assumption of a fixed essence of the 'self' was questioned. Thinkers began to see human identity not as fixed but as something always under construction.

Telling Stories

The French philosopher Paul Ricoeur (1913–2005) represents this new view of human identity. Ricoeur sees identity as constructed by narratives. He distinguishes three aspects of human identity: spatial continuity, temporal continuity, and a reflective dimension. Spatial continuity refers to the fact that all of our body parts and our mind form a whole together. The temporal continuity of identity lies in the fact that our minds and bodies persist through time. The reflective aspect of identity consists in our perception of our own identity. We are aware of the fact that we exist and we constantly form an idea of who we are.

According to Ricoeur, storytelling is a very important part, or even precondition of, reflectivity, because in this self-presentation we both express and recognize ourselves. Without expressing ourselves in a narrative, we have no real understanding of who we are. In his view the act of storytelling is a medium enabling us to know who we are, while without it we have no immediate access to our 'self'.

Although Ricoeur mainly focusses on classic narratives like books, other media also tell stories. A play, movie, game, or television series also narrate in its own way. The characters in *How I Met Your Mother* are portrayed as highly narrative beings. The whole series revolves around the stories they tell about themselves and their friends, presenting and constructing their identity in this process.

In our daily lives, we also tell stories. We seek to present ourselves and understand ourselves using different media such as the clothes we wear, the music we listen to, the house we live in, or the videos and photos we make. In *How I Met Your Mother,* Ted and his friends are keenly aware of this, as they carefully hide taped evidence of teenage mistakes ("Slap Bet," "Sandcastles in the Sand," "Glitter"), construct outrageous audiovisual resumes ("The Possimpible") or try to shut 'that bitch' one of them is dating out of the photos of important group events ("Say Cheese"). This attempt at hiding or presenting aspects of the self is an ongoing process, since our expressions alter in time, just like we do. It's like reading the same book over and over from a different perspective. Even Ted asks himself about his altering conception of James Joyce's *Ulysses*: "Has the book changed, or have I?" It proves that talking to your friends at a bar or in an apartment is very important, for this is how you meet yourself (again and again).

Damn You, Past Self

Not really feeling like having an argument, Ted and Marshall settle the question of who will get their apartment when they part their ways by stating that "future Ted and Marshall" will be very capable of dealing with this matter ("The Duel"). When a real conflict occurs and they have to decide what will happen with the apartment, nothing has yet been settled. Ted curses himself for this, or to be precise he curses a *past* version of himself, exclaiming "damn you, past Ted!"

Another philosopher who tries to break with pre-modern beliefs on human identity is Martin Heidegger (1889–1976). One of his most important theoretical findings is his emphasis on our being as existing in time. While it's true that all beings on this Earth exist in time, Heidegger points out that besides existing in time, the being of humans itself has a fundamentally temporal character. This means that, in comparison with plants or animals, we do not only exist in the 'now', we are also living in the past because of our memories and are always aimed at our future as well. Everyone has baggage, as is literally shown in *How I Met Your Mother* when Ted's dates are carrying around luggage labeled with their past inadequacies. Hopes and dreams are also a part of this, as Ted himself shows by buying a house for his nonexistent family ("Home Wreckers").

The time we find ourselves in goes by in a linear fashion. The arrow of time points in one direction only. Because of this, Ricoeur follows Heidegger's notion of the temporal character of human beings, but distinguishes between a cosmological and phenomenological experience of time. The cosmological time is the one with the arrow, which we experience as linear: the passing by of minutes, weeks, or years. This time is measurable and irreversible and can be seen as objective. Our experience of phenomenological time by contrast—time as we actually experience it—is typified by fragmentation and non-linearity. Experiences are met differently by every individual human being.

Because of these two experiences of time, we not only experience our being as something happening in the now (the cosmological time), but also as something that has happened and has to yet happen. Our phenomenological experience of time can affect the way we act in the present, because we take past accomplishments and actions into account to determine who we are and what we do. Future possibilities may also influence decisions we make in the present.

Sometimes the tension between the cosmological 'arrow of time' and our phenomenological experience of time causes collisions of different 'selves'. Some may be quite innocent, like Marshall cursing his thirteen-year-old self for picking up smoking. While Robin, at one point, states that "You can't kick a story in the nuts" ("Natural History"), we see present Marshall in a fantasy walking back to the moment where he picked up his first cigarette to do exactly this to his past self. This is the kind of fantasy we might all have had when thinking about our past mistakes.

Sometimes collisions between selves are more severe. Marshall and Lily seem to be the perfect couple and they feel the same about this most of the time. At one point 'past Lily' has big plans for making it in the arts and is really getting in the way of 'present Lily', who is a kindergarten teacher and about to settle down. The conflict between the two Lilys, Lily's two selves, even results in her leaving Marshall to take an art fellowship in San Francisco and pursue old dreams, though present Lily is quite happy in her relationship with Marshall ("Come On").

In Robin's case, it's not her past selves that hold back her relationship with Ted, but her possible future selves. She could become a famous news anchor, or move to Argentina or Japan. Because of these possibilities she feels she can't be in a relationship as her present self. It's future Ted who tells present Ted that breaking up is for the best, because his future self wants to have kids and Robin doesn't ("Something Blue").

Telling a story about yourself and constructing your identity can be seen as an ongoing conversation and debate between different selves. Because we and our relationships with others change with the passing of time, our views change with us, altering the story we tell about ourselves. While still young, and without a wife or kids, Ted looks ahead to the time when he will become a dad and sarcastically jokes: "Yeah, I'm really going to sit my kids down one day and tell them about the time uncle Barney scored seven chicks in a row." As it turns out this is exactly what he does, and future Ted can't help but turn to his kids and wonder: "Am I a bad dad?" ("The Perfect Week"). While these kinds of conversations with yourself usually take place in your head, Ted finds a way to have a very literal conversation between past and present selves. After a bad break up, Ted writes to his future self, telling him to not make the mistake of trying to get back together. His past self presents his future self all the reasons not to ("Twin Beds"), afraid his present mind might be blurred in a moment of nostalgia.

I Had the Story Wrong

Because living is quite a chaotic affair and our experience of our time on Earth shares this quality, Ricoeur sees storytelling as an important way of bringing some unity to this disorder. Thinking about a classic narrative, with a beginning, a middle, and an end, we have to agree that this structure organizes experiences in quite a neat manner. Being introduced to such orderly stories can teach us to deal with our experiences of the world and ourselves. They help to give us a coherent sense of self, an identity that is seemingly continuous in time.

When understanding a television show as a mirror of our contemporary state of mind we have to wonder what has become of us. The classic narrative structure is barely found in modern books, movies, or TV shows. Puzzle-plots with mingled layers of time, lack of causality, and unclear boundaries between real life and fantsy are in fashion. Storytelling has shifted from representing cosmological time to representing phenomenological time, the way we as human beings actually experience the time we spend on our planet.

How I Met Your Mother doesn't try to imitate real life, which is inextricably connected to linear time. Instead it tries to represent the human experience—that of Ted and his friends—of phenomenological time. This means a mix of the past, present, and future, where real life and fiction sometimes happen to intertwine and memories get mixed up. So, a goat makes an appearance in Ted's story about his thirtieth birthday ("The Goat"), while by the end of this anecdote it turns out the animal has nothing to do with this particular occasion. In *How I Met Your Mother,* the past, present and future co-exist and time moves in loops rather than in one direction.

Why are today's TV shows, movies, and novels increasingly marked by fragmented and flexible experiences of time? By looking at the society in which these cultural expressions are formed we might find an answer. Our Western culture is increasingly dominated by technologies and new media. This alters our experience of our world and ourselves. Nowadays we experience the world through different channels: smartphones, televisions, laptops, radios, iPods, and social media invade and widen our spaces of experience.

The notion of a fragmented self already existed in literature before the occurrence of these new media. We always have had multiple identities. We are someone's child, as well as an employer or employee, brother or sister or father or mother simultaneously. According to sociologist Sherry Turkle, normally only one identity manifests itself at a time, while new media offer a way of showing them all at once in a parallel manner. Multiple windows of the self can be opened at the same time, according to Turkle. She sees new media as a concretization of and appliance for cultural trends that encourage us to think about identity in terms of flexibility and multiplicity. It doesn't seem that strange that our attempts of representing our fragmented and flexible experiences of ourselves and the world in a cultural fashion have become rather complex as well.

New media not only split our experience of the world into fragments, but bring about a fragmented presentation of ourselves as well, since we can tell different stories in many ways and even at the same time. We can experiment with different identities online, as Ted demonstrates by having a female avatar in the online game *World of Warcraft* ("How I Met Everyone Else"). While this provides us with a virtual playground for identity experimentation, media don't easily forget. We're haunted by past expressions of the self that swing around in cyberspace, like Marshall's 'Beercules' video ("The Naked Truth").

Due to new media and globalization our life story is not pre-ordained anymore. In the old days, being born the son of a farmer, you would most likely become a farmer too. It was not strange to live in the same village all your life, or to practice only one job your whole life long. Our present culture offers more room for mobility and flexibility in the development of our life stories. Witness Ted's contorted quest for "the One" and a perfect family, Lily's doubts about past decisions, or Robin's sacrifices in the name of future possibilities.

The main new characteristic of the way we assemble our identities is that we have more flexibility and we reflect more on the process. Following Barney's advice on how to boost our career ("The Possimpible") we might call this modern phenomenon of human identity construction "Reflexibility."

Reflexibility

The sociologist Anthony Giddens states that identity construction in our modern times has become a strongly reflexive project, which he sees as something inevitable. When the idea of a pre-given core self was given up and some people started to question the influence of God in their life, the task of the designing of self was put in our own hands.

Giddens sees the reflexive project of the self as a way to resolve the uncertainty about our self and our place in the world stemming from the rather fragmented and chaotic experience of being. By constantly constructing a consistent life story in which the past, present, and future come together we get a coherent sense of ourselves. This story is continually under revision with the progressing of our lives, until our death. In the last few decades our society has undergone rapid and radical changes due to technological developments. Because of that we should add something to Giddens's theory.

While Giddens sees the reflexive project of the self as a way to diminish uncertainties that we experience as temporal beings, our new social structures seem to only increase them, *because* of reflexivity. Our possibilities are endless and we are fully accountable for past accomplishments, since we are the only ones that give form to our identities. Reflexivity refers to self-awareness and the having of a self-image. Adding to this, 'reflexibility' is about having a self-image and being highly aware of the fact we can construct, alter and design ourselves. More than ever we are conscious about the 'construction' of ourselves that comes about with the stories we tell about who we are, what we do, what we like, what we want and acting upon them (or not as may be the case).

Our narrative identity is a fiction, but can't be understood as only being an abstract idea. It affects the choices we make or the way we act. Our narrative identity can be described as 'virtual', because it exists outside of reality, but can have an effect on this reality nonetheless. It is, as philosopher Michael Heims (1944) aptly expresses, not real in fact, but in effect.

Eating a Sandwich

Past Ted and Marshall enjoyed some casual weed from time to time when attending college, but future Ted (now being a dad and wanting to be a good one) replaces these parts of the story of his life by telling his children he was eating a sandwich. As a viewer you see the visual presentation of Ted's narrative, in which the joint indeed has been replaced by a sandwich. Leaving the rest of the memory unaltered, this leads to some funny scenes.

The viewer knows, as does future Ted, what is being censored, and because of this everybody is experiencing past (college) and future (father) Ted simultaneously. Self-censoring or polishing while telling a story is a recurring theme in *How I Met Your Mother*, varying from saying another person cried while it was actually you ("Slapsgiving 2"), to making the plot of *Dirty Dancing* seem to be your first sexual experience ("First Time in New York"). Sometimes this 'polishing' is a group activity. This happens when Lily and Marshall go to Atlantic City for an unplanned wedding and Ted hesitates to go with them. They tell him that they "are all going to tell this story for the rest of our lives. Don't you want to be a part of that?" Ted decides to join them, but asks: "When we tell the story, can we leave the part out where I hesitate?" ("Atlantic City").

While this is a rather innocent form of reflexibility, we already saw that memories and future possibilities get in the way of Ted and his friends from time to time. Doubts about the self-formation reflect on the way they act in the present. An example of this is the reflexibility Ted experiences during his first day as an architect professor. He has major problems deciding what kind of professor he will be—formal, funny, or laid-back. As a result he ends up being all of these versions of Professor Ted at the same time ("Definitions").

The previous examples of Lily leaving Marshall or Robin breaking up with Ted can be seen as an ongoing conversation and debate with different versions of their selves; a reflexibility concerning the way they want to see themselves. But the two examples above show that the 'other' can play an important role in the reflexibility of the self as well.

You Are *Not* Pulling Them Off

While the narrative model of identity as introduced by Ricoeur gives us an interesting insight into the way we construct our own identities, it can also shed some light on the social dimension of human identities. After all it is not only the stories we tell about ourselves that give form to who we are, but also the way in which these stories are received by others. And others will always play an important role in our own life story, as the story of Ted's life evidently illustrates, and we will play an important role in theirs. Just as you might act differently among different people and have various relationships with various people, they might as well. This results in a multiplicity of stories being told about yourself and others. All these narrative relationships form a web of stories in which our identities take shape. Our self is always a 'multiple self', consisting of many stories about how we see ourselves and others see us.

The sociologist Erving Goffman (1922–1982) tries to explain the way social constructions and the presentation of the self in everyday life work by comparing them with theater. In Goffman's view our lives are like the production of *How I Met*

Your Mother, including scenes, scripts, front stages, back stages, and performances. While the script (given form in rituals in our daily interactions, like greeting people on the street, interacting with co-workers or family members, or paying for groceries) is important in the way we present ourselves, Goffman emphasizes that a great deal of improvisation is involved.

When you throw yourself on stage while wearing, let's say, red cowboy boots and with your own pre-imagined subtext saying that you are "totally pulling them off," this presentation of the self (because it indirectly states that you have a bold and original identity) will stand or fail with the opinion of those around you. When your best friends laugh in your face, telling you that you are most definitely *not* pulling them off, they redefine your identity regardless of your own ideas. Just like your actions, your stories can be doubted as well. Many times Ted will recount stories told by his friends in the course of his narration, but he can be quite cynical about them. We see for example Marshall and Lily jump out of their apartment from a ridiculous height ("Okay Awesome") and see Robin make a double flip over traffic on a little girl's bike ("I Heart NJ"). They told Ted it happened exactly like that, but Ted expresses his doubts about it in the act of recounting.

Who Are You?

Goffman's use of theatrical terms when analyzing self-presentation is more than just metaphor. We rely on the appearance and presentation of other persons when getting to know them, just as we represent ourselves to others. It doesn't really matter if these self-presentations are intentional or unintentional, honest or dishonest; they are a form of performance nonetheless.

According to Goffman, we will try to get to know the people that surround us not only out of interest, but also, because we want to know what we can expect of them, and how to act around them. This is why Barney is such a conundrum for his friends (as well as female strangers). He won't admit much about his daily activities, like his job, or about his past. The others see these parts of Barney's story as fundamental to understanding who he is. At one point Ted even blurts out: "I actually don't know where you went to college. Who *are* you?" ("The Drunk Train").

Eventually Barney's highly imaginative personality become part of his identity. That's why, when he suddenly presents himself differently, he receives an equally confused reaction from his friends. When Barney takes Robin on a date, for example, and treats her like a gentleman while she keeps trying to provoke him without success, she too, yells out "Who *are* you?" ("Do I Know You?"). Robin has a rather closed personality as well, especially when it comes to expressing her feelings. It's because of this that her friends have no clue she is devastated about her breakup with Barney and they act pretty rude in her proximity without realizing it. They make up a song about Barney "banging" other girls, dancing around Robin singing "Bang, bang, bangity, bang!" ("Of Course"). When they find out that she's heartbroken, they all feel really bad about their behavior.

All participants in a daily 'scene' contribute together to a definition of a given situation. This definition has, just like our narrative identities, a 'virtual' character to it, because it does not exactly concern what really exists, but rather concerns agreements as to whose claims will be temporarily accepted. Take for example the debate whether Marshall is Ted's best friend. Settling this discussion normally (that is to say when you're not Barney) would generally be a simple matter, because human beings are usually concerned with avoiding possible conflicts.

Games and Masquerades

In the social life of a group of friends, however, disruption can play an important role in relationships and humor. You can think of retelling embarrassing anecdotes of the time your friend got mugged by a monkey ("Zoo or False"), or forgot to bring his pants to work ("Sorry, Bro"). Or you can ridicule long lost footage of a friend performing in an embarrassing video clip or sobbingly singing love songs to a lost girlfriend ("Game Night"). Or you can play social games based on embarrassment and fear, like Slap Bet ("Slap Bet"). Disruption can also take place by undermining the self-presentation of the other person, as we saw with the case of Ted's red cowboy boots. Here the performer (Ted) is fully taken in by his own act, he *believes* that he can pull the boots off. In other words, he thinks the scene he's staging (which is part of his 'virtual identity') is part of reality.

If the others had agreed with him it could have become part of reality, but instead they ridicule him. With that Ted's performance comes to an end (or should come to an end; Ted is not easily convinced). In another case, as Ted illustrates at his first day of teaching, the performer might not be all that convinced about his acting himself. In this case Ted is still sincere in his acting though, because all he wants to be is a good professor for his students, he just doesn't know how to act upon it.

Someone may also present himself insincerely. Goffman gives the example of a doctor who prescribes a placebo. Although the doctor might not believe in what he's doing, it can have real results for a patient believing in the doctor's sincerity and the power of medicine. Goffman calls this sort of performance a masquerade, a term that fits Barney's daily activities. In his performances towards women he is not in the least sincere with respect to the personas he represents or the things he promises them. On the other hand Barney does very much believe in his acts, since he knows they work to get women into bed. He even writes a book about it ("The Playbook").

From time to time a performance will crumble because of the actions and reaction of others. Barney's belief in his performance as a womanizer is fundamentally shaped by the first sexual experience of past Barney. The story he built around his identity stems from his assumption that the woman who took his virginity had the best sex of her life while doing so. When he encounters her later and she tells him this is not true at all, suddenly all his stories about his life as a womanizer lose their meaning. He loses faith in his performance as a lover. His memories become altered and they affect the way he acts in the present; he has a bad case of the yips and suddenly doesn't know how to approach women at all ("The Yips").

Barney's mother shows the same characteristics as her son by lying to her children all the time. She doesn't do this out of self-interest, but because she wants to protect her sons. She tells a young Barney that no kids have shown up for his birthday because the Postmaster General lost his invitations ("Cleaning House"), and that Bob Barker is his dad. While Barney at times seems really naive and retells his mother's stories as though they were real, he's not always sincere when recounting them as being part of his life story. He admits to his friends that (despite his efforts to get on *The Price Is*

Right) he's well aware of the fact that Bob Barker is not his father. He just thought this made him more interesting ("Cleaning House").

Umbrella, Fungus, *Crocodile Dundee 3*

We started with the question of how to tell your life story. When looking at *How I Met Your Mother*, a series formed in a modern society of which reflexibility is an important feature, we could say it doesn't really matter where you begin and where you end. Our identities have a very fragmented, flexible, and temporal character, with various 'selves' existing next to each other simultaneously.

While we still might strive for a linear narrative to sum up our own identify or life, or that of our loved ones, we can ask ourselves if this is necessary or even fruitful. When Marshall's father dies, Marshall feverishly tries to recall the last words his father ever spoke to him. Retracing his last conversations with his father, his last words vary from a remark about an umbrella, to an observation about foot fungus or *Crocodile Dundee 3* ("Last Words"). This makes Marshall extremely sad, because he really wants the last words to mean something. He feels like his dad's life story (at least the version including him) did not end in a perfect manner. Rethinking this, he finally concludes that he has many beautiful memories of his father, and in a way he will always be present in Marshall's own life story. While life itself is a linear affair, a life story proves to be missing a clear beginning, middle, or end.

How I Met Your Mother presents us with a fun-house mirror reflection of our contemporary identity construction. We exist in our own changing stories as well in those of others. We can maintain several different identities at once (a possibility Barney demonstrates perfectly) and we have many possible roads to walk. *How I Met Your Mother* playfully elucidates our fragmented, self-aware, narrative identities and by playing with different types of storytelling—voice-overs, different perspectives, and visuals—the show not only makes clear that self-construction is a never-ending and self-reflecting process, but also that identity has multiple and paradoxical features all existing next to each other simultaneously.

Oh, and do rent *Crocodile Dundee 3*. I saw it on cable last night and it totally holds up.

17
Awesome Logic for the Possimpible World

MICHELA BORDIGNON

Kids, what is the possimpible? At a first sight, the possimpible seems to be just a nonsense word made up to impress chicks, employers, and people watching TV shows. Nothing could be more wrong. Let's look carefully at Barney's words in his video resume in the fourteenth episode of Season Four:

> **BARNEY:** All my life, I have dared to go past what is possible.
>
> **FAKE INTERVIEWER:** To the impossible?
>
> **BARNEY:** Actually, past that . . . to the place where the possible and the impossible meet to become . . . the possimpible. If I can leave you with one thought, it's this: Nothing . . . and everything . . . is possimpible. ("The Possimpible")

In the possimpible two opposites—the possible and the impossible—become one. The possible is what can normally happen the way things are. The impossible is what can't happen the way things are. Saying that there's something such as the possimpible means that something that cannot happen actually can happen. The possimpible basically turns something into something that it is not. Therefore, the possimpible apparently is nonsense and this is why Lily derides Barney's resume, and more specifically the passage on the possimpible, as ridiculous and insane.

Lily's skepticism towards the possimpible can be traced back to the traditional skepticism of classical logic towards contradictions. Logic studies the relations between different forms of sentences and the implications of these relations. Contradiction is a particular kind of relation between sentences that has been widely discussed in logic.

More precisely, contradiction is the conjunction of two sentences, each one being the negation of the other. So, a contradiction could be a statement such as 'Barney is awesome and Barney is not awesome'. Contradiction can also be defined as the conjunction of two sentences, where if one is true, the other is necessarily false (If 'Barney is awesome' is true then 'Barney is not awesome' is necessarily false, and vice versa).

Barney's discourse on the possimpible perfectly embodies what a contradiction is. In the possimpible the possible and the impossible meet and become one: the impossible becomes possible and therefore it can be said to be both *something that cannot happen* and *something that can happen*. How can this be possible? Can someone assert a sentence and its own negation at the same time and in the same sense? Things seems to get difficult for Barney. To make things clearer we could picture the following situation in our mind.

Strange Encounters in a Bar

Barney's sitting in MacLaren's drinking a beer and looking around for the next chick to make a move on. A handsome Greek guy dressed in a toga suit, small beard and a self-confident look, comes and sits on Barney's right.

With a surprised look in his eyes, Barney says: "What's up, dude? Nice suit, by the way. Is it a toga party suit, like in the *Animal House* movie?" The Greek guy impatiently answers: "No, Barney. I come from the past. I'm Aristotle. I've been reading your blog lately. The crap you wrote about the possimpible really pissed me off. Have you ever read my *Metaphysics*? Or have you at least heard of the law of non-contradiction? And Barney answers: "Hey dude! Calm down! What is it with this law of non-contradiction?"

Aristotle says: "Okay, blondie, I'll be your wing-man. I'll help you out here with this nonsensical talk about the possimpible. There were no blogs for my fans in ancient Greece, but I used to make notes of the awesome things I was teaching them. These notes have been published in a book titled *Metaphysics*.

That was done after I died and some people made a whole shipload of money from it, but—whatever, that's off-topic.

"The important thing is that if you read this book, you'll get rid of your crazy, contradictory talk about the possimpible. My *Metaphysics* is a kind of philosophical Bro Code, where the most important philosophical questions are addressed. Rule number one of the philosophical Bro Code is the law of non-contradiction. Article number one is the logical formulation of this law: it says that contradictory propositions can never be true at the same time and in the same sense: you just can't say that the chick down there is hot and that she is not hot, the two sentences cannot both be true.[1]

"Article number two is the psychological formulation of this law; it says that contradictions are not even thinkable: you cannot even think that the chick down there is hot and that she is not hot, because you can think only one of the two at a time.[2] Article number three is the ontological formulation of the law, that says that contradictions cannot exist: the chick down there cannot be both hot and not hot, because she necessarily is only one of the two (being hot and not being hot are incompatible properties).[3]

"So, listen up Barney, everyone would agree with me about the law of non-contradiction: it's intuitively true and no way magic tricks will get rid of it. So, please stop this crazy talk of the possimpible. The possible and the impossible cannot be one and the same thing. Every reasonable person would reject this. Surely you can see that this must be right!"

Aristotle has just finished talking and a creepy guy in a monk suit strolls into MacLaren's and sits on Barney's left. With an admiring look in his eyes Barney says: "What's up, dude? Nice suit, by the way. Is it the Obi-Wan Kenobi suit?" The creepy medieval guy, with a super-mean look in his eyes, whispers: "No Barney, I too come from the past, but I am not as old as Toga Guy. I'm Duns Scotus, and I'm not here to teach you

---

[1] "The most certain of all basic principles is that contradictory propositions are not true simultaneously" (*Metaphysics*, lines 1011b13–14).

[2] "No one can believe that the same thing can (at the same time) be and not be" (1005b23–24).

[3] "It is impossible that the same thing belong and not belong to the same thing at the same time and in the same respect" (1005b19–20).

how to live, I'm here to teach you how to talk and think properly. Of course, this will change your life too, because you will stop all this senseless blabbering about the possimpible."

Barney's a bit put out. He replies: "Okay bro, Toga Guy told me that trying to think the possimpible is crazy, and I get that, even if I think there can be a kind of sense in being crazy. But why do you call it 'senseless blabbering'?"

Scoto takes a long breath, and then he answers: "Barney, this is not going to be easy, but I will try to explain. The problem with what you say about the possimpible is not just the law of non-contradiction. There's another law you should be aware of when you try to say that contradictory things such as the possimpible actually exist. I didn't discover this law, even though lot of people think I did, but I am fond of it. The name of this law is *ex falso quodlibet*, but I prefer to call it in a more playful way, the principle of explosion. This law makes your whole discourse about the possimpible explode.

"Let's consider the example given by Toga Guy. Let's assume that 1. 'The chick down there is hot *and* the chick down there is not hot'. If we take this contradictory statement to be true, we have to conclude that *both* parts of it are true, which means that 2. 'The chick down there is hot' is true and 3. 'The chick down there is not hot' is also true'."

So Barney goes: "Okay, that's obvious. You don't need to be monk-suited-up to say that." And Creepy Monk Guy smiles creepily and goes: "Wait for it, Barney, wait . . . for it . . . there's more to come. You got that both 'the chick down there is hot' and 'the chick down there is not hot' are true. From this you can infer that 4. 'The chick down there is hot or bimbos love studying formal logic'."

At this point Barney's a little skeptical: "Oooookay, tell me how!" Creepy Monk Guy starts sniggering: "You see, my dear bro, it's quite easy . . . I hope you can follow me. Think of a sentence of the form 'p or q' where p is the first sentence 'The chick down there is hot' and q is the second sentence 'The chick down there is not hot'. The truth of one of the two sentences, that is, the truth of either p or q, is sufficient for the whole statement to be true. Therefore, in the statement 4. 'The chick down there is hot or bimbos love studying formal logic' the truth of either 'the chick down there is hot' or 'bimbos love studying formal logics' is sufficient for the whole pair of statements to be true, and we know this is the case since we know from point 2. that 'the chick down there is hot' is true."

Barney's a tad confused and so he orders another beer, then he says: "Okay bro, how do bimbos studying whatever deal with the chick down there? And, by the way, if formal logic is something like what you're doing with me now, believe me, bimbos don't like this. They would get lost at point 1. The sentence 'Bimbos love studying formal logic' is crap." Creepy Monk Guy jumps up, kisses Barney on the forehead (yup, creepy) and shouts: "Bang! Got it! That's the point!"

Barney starts to feel a little scared here. "You see, you remember point 2., 'The chick down there is hot'. But now look at point 3. 'The chick down there is not hot'. If this sentence is true, its negation, or we could also say its opposite, that is, 5. 'The chick down there is hot', is false." Barney can feel the approaching danger; he's on his knees begging the monk weirdo to stop. But Creepy Monk Guy has no pity and goes: "Oh Barney, my best bro Barney, if 5. 'The chick down there is hot' is false and 4. 'The chick down there is hot or bimbos love studying formal logic' is true, this can only be because 'bimbos love studying formal logic' is true. That's logical, that follows. True story!"

Barney is lying twisted on the floor. He can't really explain what's just happened. Tears come to his eyes and he goes on moaning like a dead man walking, waiting for the end to come: "Bimbos can't love formal logic! Bimbos can't love formal logic!" Then he raises his hands, looks up at the ceiling, he cries out: "Noooooooooooooooooooooo!" And pitiless Creepy Monk Guy pours further salt into Barney's wound: "Muahahahahahaha! Yes Barney, they can and they do love formal logic! This is what must become true if you admit true contradictions. Everything can be true as well as false if you allow that even one contradiction exists!

"Read my lips. I could have replaced the sentence 'Bimbos love studying formal logic' with any other sentence. Things would have worked out just the same. You see where we're going with this? Assuming the truth of a contradiction in any system, and thus also in your crazy possimpible state of mind, means to say that in this system everything is true. But if everything is true there is no longer *any* difference between truth and falsity, and every sentence or thought, even the most absurd one, like 'Bimbos love studying formal logic', turns out to be true. Contradiction is something that makes any system that allows it explode."

Now Barney seems to be definitely beaten. He's sadly staring at the floor thinking of bimbos loving formal logic or doing other preposterous things, like wearing a nun's habit and spending the night praying at the church, instead of trying to get over their daddy issues by drinking beer at the bar. Aristotle and Duns Scotus are both grinning, waiting for Barney to concede that it's senseless to talk about the possimpible.

But Barney's not beaten. He slowly raises his head, smiles and says: "Challenge accepted! Guys, see you tomorrow here, same place, same suits. I promise you I will turn your dreary, normal, boring world into a contradictory, possimpible, and legen . . . wait-for-it . . . dary world!"

Aristotle and Duns Scotus look at each other, puzzled. They weren't actually thinking of what they'd said as a challenge, but as the *coup de grâce*. And as for Barney's confident promise, well . . .

Challenge Accepted!

Barney's a pragmatic person. First thing he does is to call his bet guy. But Barney knows that he cannot win this challenge by himself. Everyone knows that Barney has a suit guy, a whip guy, and so on. What few people know is that Barney also has two philosophy guys.

The first of Barney's philosophy guys is a Kraut. He calls himself Georg Wilhelm Friedrich Hegel. Barney doesn't have time to waste, so he just calls him Georgy. He seems a little lame, not really good looking and he sometimes has the 'crazy eyes'. The other guy's a Brit and always wears a Karate Kid suit. He has the mysterious and wise look of David Carradine in *Kill Bill*, the jaunty stride of Bruce Willis in *Pulp Fiction*, and the childlike crazy smile of Juliette Lewis in *Natural Born Killers*. His name is Graham Priest. Barney calls him Gramey. Now, it so happens that Barney knows something most philosophers don't: that Georgy and Gramey are really terrific friends.

Barney gives them a call. Actually, he calls Gramey because Georgy is super old (about 250) and asks them both to be his wingmen in the fight against Toga Guy and Creepy Monk Guy. What they have to do is show Barney a way of proving the existence of the possimpible.

So Gramey and Georgy rush over to MacLaren's. They find Barney all alone, lost in his thoughts. They tell him: "Let's take another look at your video resume, bro. Maybe we can fix this possimpible thing."

Barney shows them the video resume. Everyone knows that the video starts with an explosion from which Barney's name comes out. When Georgy and Gramey see this explosion, they look at each other, and Georgy says: "Are you thinking what I'm thinking, Herr Doktor Professor Priest?" Gramey goes "Yup, I think I am thinking what you're thinking, I mean, the explosion . . ." And Georgy says: "Yes, my friend, the explosion, we're both thinking the same thing."

And he continues: "You see, the explosion at the beginning of your video resume is not accidental. More precisely, this explosion is triggered by your conception of the possimpible. As Creepy Monk Guy surely explained to you, a true contradiction in a system—such as the one taking place in the possimpible where the possible and the impossible become one—is like a bomb in the system itself. Now Barney, listen, faced with that bomb, you need to choose. You can stay with Toga Guy and Creepy Monk Guy and leave this bomb under the ground, just ignore it. That way you'd remain faithful to rule number one of Toga-Guy philosophy bro code—the law of non-contradiction. You'd have most bros—all the normal bros—on your side. But then you'd have to give up the the possimpible and gracefully concede defeat.

"Yet there is a way to win the bet against Toga Guy and Creepy Monk Guy. You need to learn to handle the fire of the explosion triggered by the contradiction of the possimpible. This would mean going *beyond the limits of thought* of normal bros and trying to join the band of legendary philosophy bros."

Barney's a bit nervous. He says: "Okay guys, I'm with you. No bro leaves a bro behind. But how can I break rule number one of the philosophy bro-code? As far as I understood it, this Toga Guy bro-code is for normal bros. Are there any other philosophy bro-codes? I mean, are there bro-codes for *legendary* philosophy bros? Toga Guy said that the possimpible is impossible in principle and Creepy Monk Guy proved that a contradiction can send me and my crazy talk about the possimpible straight to hell."

Gramey pats Barney on the back and says: "Don't worry, bro, we're here to help you. First of all, if someone says that the possimpible is impossible because the impossible cannot be possible he's simply begging the question. He's simply saying that the possimpible is impossible because it's impossible. He's not really proving anything to you. He needs something more to destroy your possimpible world. But you also need something more to change his world and to prove that the possimpible does exist. They say they want to teach you how to think and live, but actually, you can change their way of thinking and living if you find a good argument for proving the existence of the possimpible."

And Georgy goes on (finally slipping into the twenty-first-century way of talking): "Yeah Barney, Gramey's right, and you don't need to be afraid of breaking rule number one of Toga Guy's philosophy bro code. That philosophy bro code is great, but it mostly teaches you how to handle only standard-bros' philosophical situations. There are situations which are not common and dynamics which are not standard—such as the possimpible—that aren't covered by the Toga Guy bro code.

"But you're lucky, dude! Look at me and Gramey. We both wrote legendary philosophy bro codes to handle things that can't be captured by standard philosophy bro codes. We'll teach you how to handle the explosive fire of the contradiction involved in the possimpible. To do that, you'll need to go beyond the limits of standard thought and to come up with thoughts capable of grasping uncommon, non-standard things. We can call the world of these uncommon, non-standard things the *world of the awesome*. So, we have to go from standard thinking to awesome thinking, and then we can handle the explosive power of contradictions.

Barney looks at Gramey and Georgy. He takes a long breath and shouts: "I knew it! I knew it! I knew I was right even if I still don't know why! Okay guys—he gives them a victory fist bump——you've gotta bump this!" But Gramey says: "Calm down, Barney. The victory fist bump needs to wait. First, pay attention. The legendary contradiction path taking us into the dimension of awesomeness is not an easy path to walk. Are you ready to follow us and meet the dark side of philosophy?"

Barney's becoming more and more curious and excited: "Okay guys! This is not going to be easy, but nothing easy is awesome, and I want to be not only awesome in a manly way, but awesome from every possible point of view, which means absolutely awesomely awesome, and so, my dear bros, also philosophically awesome. Come on! Show me exactly why I've been right all along!"

Georgy takes out of his bag a big book, titled *Science of Logic*. He puts the book in Barney's hands and solemnly says: "Barney, this is my philosophy bro code and it's meant to capture the essence of the dimension that we have named awesomeness. In the very core of the book there is a statement which will help you to understand how to win the challenge of thinking the contradiction of a possimpible world.

"In this book I write that everything is inherently contradictory, which could be translated by saying that everything in our world is possimpible. This is not a nonsensical statement. Quite the contrary, what I want to say is exactly that the true nature of everything involves a kind of contradictory structure. For instance, everything has limits, right? Everything begins and ends somewhere. So let's look at the structure of the limit itself. A limit doesn't have to be seen merely as the place in which something stops being what it is. It's also the place within which something begins to be what it is.

"Look at the beer you're drinking. The limit of the beer is not simply the place in which the beer is not the beer anymore. It's also the place within which the beer starts to be the beer. In this sense, the limit of the beer is both the beer and not the beer. You see, Barney, this is a contradiction, and if you think that everything is limited, and that the limit of everything, and of the beer as well, is what tells us what something is, we can really say that everything has a contradictory structure."

Georgy looks at Gramey, he raises his hand and says: "Contradiction high five!" Obviously, Gramey high-fives him back and says: "Okay bro, you really get the point and actually, when I was writing my philosophy bro code I was thinking about you, because I wanted to show that you are absolutely right in claiming that there are true contradictions in reality and I do think that Barney is right in the way he talks about the possimpible. I named the thesis that there are true contradictions 'dialethism' and the title of my philosophy bro code actually is *In Contradiction*. In this bro code I try to teach people how to think and live a world that contains true contradictions, or, to put it in Barney's terms, how to think and live in a possimpible world.

"Okay Barney, I don't have this philosophy bro code with me now, but I can give you a few pages I wrote on the same topic, where you will find something really interesting for your challenge. The title of this bunch of pages is "What Is So Bad about Contradiction?" but I could just as easily have called it "What's So Bad about the Possimpible?" In this article I also talk about limits, and I spell out the structure of the limit in the same way that Georgy did in his *Science of Logic*.

"Let's consider the limit of MacLaren's. My dear Barney, we could ask: What's the limit of MacLaren's? Suppose you're walking into MacLaren's and so you are at the very limit (at the very edge) of the pub. Are you in or not in MacLaren's? You can't say that you simply are in MacLaren's because there are an infinite number of points in MacLaren's that are MacLaren's without being the limit of MacLaren's. But you can't say that you're not in MacLaren's either because there are an infinite number of points that are not MacLaren's without being the limit of MacLaren's. In order to say the limit of MacLaren's, or in order to say where you are when you are getting into MacLaren's, you need to say that you are both in and not in MacLaren's. Only the unity of these two opposite sentences, only this contradiction, can say what the limit is by saying where you are when you are exactly in this limit."

Then Georgy chimes in: "Well put, Gramey! You see, Barney, my conception of the limit and Gramey's conception actually mirrors your conception of the possimpible. We do not think of the limit as a fixed place where something simply ends, nor do we think of what is limited as a kind of fixed entity which is kept in prison by its limits. Quite the contrary, we have a dynamical conception of reality where the limit is the place where something overcomes itself and meets its not-being. We could think of the relationship between the possible and the impossible along the same terms. Let's say that the possible is like what is limited and the impossible is its not-being, that is, what the possible cannot be, or, the place where the possible stops. We have two choices.

"On the one hand, we can think of the relationship between the possible and the impossible in Toga Guy's terms and see the possible and the impossible as fixed entities each one in front of the other, none of them affecting the field of the other or tending to mix up with it. There is no contradiction there, but there is no movement either. Each one of the two opposites stands on its side, there is nothing possible turning into the impossible and, above all, there is nothing impossible becoming something possible. The possible remains possible and the impossible remains impossible. There is no point of connection between the two.

On the other hand, we can think of the relationship between the possible and the impossible in non-classical terms, or, we could say, in awesome terms, that is to say, such as a dynamical relationship where the two opposite terms turn one into another. And so something that happens, and therefore something which is actually possible, once it has happened, it becomes impossible because it belongs to a past dimension that can never come back. Or, something that is impossible, that is, something belonging to a future dimension that can never become present, actually does happen since the conditions which prevent it from happening change, and make it happen. Therefore, there is something possible that turns into something impossible, and something impossible that turns into something possible. In the very turning point of one opposite into the other, the two opposites touch one another, or, to quote you, Barney, this point is the place where the possible and the impossible meet to become . . . the possimpible."

Gramey enthusiastically says: "But there's another important thing to remember. None of the two points of views at stake—neither the fixed coherent nor the dynamical here contradictory—is simply wrong. They just provide a different view on reality. The first one is like a fixed picture of a process. It gives you a precise and coherent but surely not-complete view of what happens within the process itself. The second one is like seeing a movie and having the chance to get a glance at how the whole process develops. It provides a more complete understanding of what's going on; but it also tries to handle the more complex logic underlying the process.

"Let's suppose, Barney, that you're in a strip club. The view on reality number one would be like having a series of pictures of the strippers' stripping process. This would be a perfectly coherent and pleasant view of the strip club reality. But consider the view on reality number two. It would be like looking at the live stripping dynamical process and developing an all-encompassing knowledge of the process itself. Nevertheless, the logic of the live stripping process would be more complex than the pictures-in-series one. Take the instant in which a stripper is removing the last article of clothing. Is she or is she not naked? She is at the limit of being naked and thus, if we want to describe what's going on, we seem to be forced to accept the contradictory statement according to which in the very moment in which the stripper is getting completely undressed, she is both naked and not naked. The logic underlying the undressing process would be more difficult to handle, but wouldn't this way of looking at the strip club reality be happier?

"Barney, as you said, 'Nothing and everything, is possimpiple'. And now we can really get this straight: nothing is possimpible if you take the first non-contradictory Toga-Guy path; everything is possimpible if you take the path I took with Georgy, that is, the path of contradiction."

Then Barney asks: "Yes, bros, I'm starting to understand what you mean. But what do I actually need to do in order to embrace this awesome contradictory path?"

Georgy says: "You just need to do what you always do without thinking every time you say: 'Challenge accepted!' You only need to take your own limits not as something that prevents you from doing what you want to do and that everyone says is impossible. Your limits are not like a prison that separates you from the outer world and hold you back from actually acting in it. Quite the contrary, your own limits are something there to be overcome, they are the very place where you meet the outer world and that thus allow you to actually live the world not as something fixed in front of you, but as something that can be changed and improved by changing and improving yourself.

"This is exactly what I was trying to explain in my bro-code when I analyzed what the finite is. I claim that the finite is not something fixed, as against infinity, because the finite is itself only insofar as it ends and it is not itself anymore, namely it is itself only insofar as it passes over into its not-being. At the same time, in the very place where the finite ends and it is not itself anymore, that is, in the place where the finite passes over into its not-being, the finite is this not-being, or, it is not itself anymore. Therefore, in order to be truly itself, the finite has to overcome its own limit, and in this very limit a contradiction is involved, because in this limit the finite is itself, and it is not itself in the same time and in the same sense. The process in which the finite overcomes itself in order to be truly itself is what I call infinity, which is nothing but what you, Barney, call the possimpible. In fact, whereas infinity is the process through which the finite overcomes its limits in order to meet and be one with its not-being, that is the infinite itself, the possimpible is the process through which the possible overcomes its limit in order to meet and be one with its not-being, that is the impossible."

Gramey claps his hands: "Very well put, Georgy! I just wish you'd been that clear in your bro code! Trying to understand what is going on there is like playing laser tag in a labyrinth! But I tried to do that and I tried to make things clear in another book I wrote, titled *Beyond the Limits of Thought*. Don't worry, Barney, this is not a commercial. I just wanted to say that in that book I show what happens when thought overcomes what are supposed to be its standard limits. Surprisingly, thought does not get lost, but as shown by Georgy's example of the finite, thought ends up discovering new dimensions of itself, new horizons to look at, and a new path to walk through.

"So, every time you say "Challenge accepted!" you focus on a limit you face in the way you are. This limit traces a line between what is possible and what is impossible. If you endorse a classical conception of the limit and you refuse to think and live in a world containing true contradictions, the limit turns out to be something which definitely separates you from the impossible, and the impossible itself remains something that you will never reach. If instead you endorse an "awesome" dynamical conception of the limit and accept the challenge of thinking and living in a world containing true contradictions, the limit becomes something that connects you and the impossible, which turns into a task to be accomplished, or, a goal to be reached, or, a challenge to be won. The limit is the place where the possible and the impossible meet to precisely become the possimpible. The limit is the possimpible itself. True story!"

How to Be Really Awesome

Barney grabs Gramey's and Georgy's hands and says: "Thank you guys, you really are my philosophy wingmen and I really think I get you now. Now I have all I need to show Toga Guy and Creepy Monk Guy why what I said about the possimpible was not nonsensical, but something that everyone should take as a mantra—or maybe even as the new rule number one for legendary philosophy bros.

Living in a possimpible world is like living on an edge that always needs to be overcome in order for everyone to reach the dimension of awesomeness. When Barney asks people and himself to be awesome, he is not asking to be something which is completely out of our hands. He is just encouraging people to live life as if it was not set inside certain limits which cannot be crossed, that is to say, we should not take life as something that has already been planned by someone else, or, we should not feel like we have to wear a suit which someone else chose for us. Life needs to be taken as an ever changing life where every single moment is a chance to overcome ourselves, our limits and all the fears and prejudices that prevent us from becoming what we would like to be, that is what we inherently are. And the overcoming of a limit, as we have seen in our story, always involves the challenge to think and live a contradiction, which is the challenge to think and live the possimpible.

This is exactly what Barney did when he was a lame hippie crying his eyes out because of abandonment by his girlfriend Shannon. When he realized how lame he was, a complete change occurred in him and Barney became an awesome suited-up guy. Are the lame hippie guy and the awesome suited up guy the same guy? Actually, they are, since they both are Barney Stinson. And if we pay attention to the passage between the two, we can see the possimpible taking place. We can see the lame hippie guy becoming someone that he was not, we can see the dimension of lameness turning into the dimension of awesomeness, we can see the possible meeting the impossible, we can see the possimpible: the two opposites becoming one.

How did it happen? How can the impossible turn into the possible? The lame hippie guy managed to focus on his limits and had the courage to overcome them, by trying to realize himself, that is, his identity, by completely changing this very identity and by becoming someone else.

To fully accomplish his true nature and make him become the awesome person he is, Barney lives his identity as an identity that necessarily involves difference in itself. Barney's barneytude[4] is always the same, but it can be the barneytude it is only by being an ever-changing barneytude, by becoming always something new and making him touch new dimensions of awesomeness.

Nevertheless, by being built on a process of self-differentiation, this identity, that is to say, Barney's barneytude, is an inherently contradictory identity. Thus, the only way for Barney—but also for us—to be really what he is, that is, to express and realize his own nature, his awesomeness, is to be able to make room for the possimpible and for the contradictions it will imply in both his and our thought, world, and life. Only if we learn to think and live the contradiction of the possimpible, will we follow the same path that Barney is walking—the legendary path that will lead us to be like him: awesome![5]

---

[4] The essence, or, the true nature of Barney.

[5] I thank Elena Tripaldi for her suggestions and helpful remarks. A special thank to Luca Illetterati. I owe him everything I know about limits and their overcoming.

About the Authors

THOMAS AINSWORTH read Classics at Magdalen College, Oxford, where he also completed the BPhil in philosophy. He then jumped ship to Corpus Christi College, and is about to be examined for his doctorate, which is entitled "The Grounds of Unity: Substantial and Sub-substantial Being in Aristotle." Adopting a peripatetic attitude to Oxford colleges, he has held lectureships at St. Anne's College, and Lady Margaret Hall. His philosophical interests are not confined to ancient metaphysics, and he has taught courses on logic, epistemology, ethics, and the philosophy of language, as well as diverse periods from the history of philosophy. When he isn't serenely contemplating the nature of being, in a tailor-made Italian suit of course, he enjoys playing laser tag and performing magic tricks.

MARYAM BABUR received her Hon. BSc with a Major in Biochemistry and Major in Philosophy from the University of Western Ontario and in 2012, graduated *cum laude* from the University of Amsterdam with a Research Master's in Philosophy. Because she's a Muslim, politically correct folks feel obliged to tolerate her dirty jokes and otherwise ridiculous sense of humor. This form of affirmative action doesn't seem to bother her, as she knows there's no shame in being bro-tastic. (As the eldest and only daughter, it's always been her four bro-some bros before hoes, so she's always had her priorities straight.) Like most self-styled intellectuals, she always lists 'reading' as a hobby— 'cause c'mon let's face it, sometimes you just wanna lay there . . . and read philosophy. She loves street hockey, field hockey, publicly humiliating others in a friendly way (slap bet anyone?), tea, coffee, really all forms of caffeine, cake, foam, Tetris, humming Super Mario tunes on repeat, and kung fu.

BART VAN BEEK is a Lecturer in Philosophy of Language and Logic at the Radboud University Nijmegen. He's interested in the semantics of proper names, the role of beliefs and desires in theories of language, and vagueness, but is unlikely to publish in any of these areas as he is currently setting up shop as a philosophical counselor and all-round wise guy.

MICHELA BORDIGNON got her PhD in Philosophy at Padua University. She was reading Hegel's *Science of Logic* for six years and then fortunately her friends pushed her into a rehab center. Now she works at Punky Reggae Pub (San Zenone degli Ezzelini) and at Fattoria Sociale La Conca d'Oro (Bassano del Grappa). She is highly qualified in washing dishes and in making a special kind of panini called *panino onto*. Nevertheless, she continues to collaborate with the Padua Research Group on German Idealism.

KRIS GOFFIN is a young Belgian philosopher of emotion. He has studied philosophy at the University of Antwerp and at the University of Leuven. He's now completing a PhD on music and emotion at Ghent University. In his search for emotional meaning Kris is breaking down the boundaries between psychology and philosophy, which is awesome. He also teaches two awesome seminars: one on contemporary philosophy and one on contemporary art. Barney Stinson is his personal hero and intellectual father.

TOBIAS HAINZ is a philosopher specializing in applied ethics, with a focus on future technologies in general and human enhancement in particular. He has recently completed a PhD thesis on the ethical evaluation of life extension technologies. Although he loathed math in high school, he frequently uses pseudo-mathematical methods in order to support his philosophical reasoning. When he is not engaging in philosophizing, he tries to convince his friends and colleagues that he is not a mixture of Marshall Eriksen and Sheldon Cooper (from *The Big Bang Theory*), but his arguments are usually regarded as unsound.

CARTER HARDY is a philosophy graduate student, working towards his PhD, and specializing in phenomenology of mind and emotion. You can think of him as a philosopher version of Marshall. Just replace Lily with his significant other, whom he has also been with his entire adult life. Replace Marshall's son Marvin with two destructive ferrets. And replace being a kind-hearted giant with being a pretty nice, normal-sized guy, and there you have him. To sum him up in a word, it would have to be "philososome." Part philosopher, part awesome. Barney would be proud.

FRANK G. KARIORIS is a latecomer to *How I Met Your Mother*, but has been known to suit up from time to time—though more of a blazer guy really. He lived in England for two years, doing a master's, where he also learned about the Bro Code from his bros Dan and Ron. He's currently working on a PhD at Central European University in Budapest. From Milwaukee, and having gone to university at Marquette, he's a big fan of beer and is thoroughly intrigued to try Randy's prize-winning Hazelnut Pilsner.

MANOLO MARTÍNEZ worked putting ice cream in boxes and selling yogurt for more years than he cares to remember. Then he started doing philosophy, which he's been at for quite some time too (but he's fine with that). He was a lecturer at the University of Barcelona and is now enjoying a Beatriu de Pinós post-doctoral research grant at The Graduate Center of CUNY, New York. He spends an inordinate amount of time chasing his three-year-old son through some Brooklyn playground or other.

LORENZO VON MATTERHORN has been, under a pseudonym, serving as Professor of Philosophy and BOF Research Professor at the University of Antwerp and Senior Research Associate at Peterhouse, Cambridge University. He's the author, still under a pseudonym, of *Between Perception and Action* and *Aesthetics as Philosophy of Perception*.

ELIZE DE MUL gets violently competitive when playing Zitch Dog. She holds a BA in Film and Television studies, an MA in New Media and Digital Culture, and another one in Philosophy. Surprisingly, this combination resulted in her current position as a PhD candidate at the Leiden Law Faculty in the Netherlands. She once spent an adventurous night with Abraham Lincoln when visiting New York (it was really him, he showed her his Facebook page), and he assured her he would call her. Sadly, he never did.

BENCE NANAY normally watches 'angsty, existentialist Italian black and white movies', like the one we see in "Romeward Bound" (Season Eight). So *How I Met Your Mother* is a bit of a change of pace. He also likes to publish and edit books, under pseudonyms of a certain "reclusive billionaire who likes to take balloon flights to the North Pole as a feat of pure daring and imagination."

JORDAN PASCOE is a philosopher and retired Canadian pop star who has almost certainly never been in Zamboni-themed porn. She lives in Brooklyn with her husband, two awesome step-kids, and a very well-behaved goat. She was seen at the Stone Road Mall Tim Horton's eating a double chocolate glazed.

M. Chris Sardo is a PhD student at Northwestern University, studying political theory. When not fantasizing about leaving academia to buy a bar, his research focuses on post-Kantian philosophy and pluralist democratic theory. His current project is a political reading of Kant's theory of the sublime, but he often finds that he really needs a scotch and soda and a cigar.

Miguel Ángel Sebastián, like Marshall, managed to convince a jury, not to become a judge but to get his PhD at the University of Barcelona. Like Ted, he had decided to move into academic life, not from architecture but from engineering, to do research in Philosophy. Miguel specializes in Philosophy of Mind and Cognitive Sciences, more precisely in the study of consciousness, perception, and the first-person perspective, but is also interested in Philosophy of Language and Metaphysics. Like Robin, Miguel moved away to work, not to the States but to Mexico where he has worked as a postdoc at the Universidad Nacional Autónoma de México (UNMA) since Summer 2012. Like Barney, . . . well you know, nothing can be compared to Uncle Barney.

Joe Slater is a philosophy student, mostly concerned with the demands of morality. He has been looking for the mother of his future children under the tables in various bars in St. Andrews for the past seven years. He prefers rabbits to ducks and he likes olives.

Tina Talsma received her PhD from Florida State University in 2012 and works in Philosophy of Religion. Like Robin, she's Canadian and will defend her homeland to the death. She is married to a Ted Mosby—well, a structural engineer, so close enough. And she feels inspired by Marshall and Lily to break out the old saxophone and make up a ridiculous bedtime lullaby for her two-year-old son, Owen.

Radu Uszkai and Emanuel Socaciu are philosophical bros at the University of Bucharest. Radu is a PhD candidate, while Emanuel is a lecturer in the Department of Philosophy. Their common research agenda revolves around the study of the emergence and evolution of norms (such as the Bro Code) in interactions. Radu has also published papers on classical liberalism, the norms of file-sharing, and intellectual property. Emanuel's main publications address topics in moral philosophy, applied ethics, and the epistemology of the social sciences.

YVONNE WÜRZ is a biologist with a focus on ethology. Her favorite animals—besides cats, of course—are zebra finches which is why she is conducting research on their personality and writing a PhD thesis about her findings. In general, she believes that there's not much of a difference between the personality of finches and humans, so that she regards herself as qualified to discuss phenomena like human rationality with professional philosophers. When you replace Robin Scherbatzky's dogs with cats, you get a good impression of Yvonne's apartment at an unknown point in the future.

AMANDA YPMA holds a BA degree in History and Political Science from Grand Valley State University. She has a passion for television and film studies and has been analyzing television shows to a Ted-ish degree for the better part of her life. In her free time you can find her suiting up, being awesome instead, and tirelessly debating all things *How I Met Your Mother* at various online discussion forums.

Index